A Dog's Guide To Making It In America

Volume 2

Rodolfo G Ledesma

Published in the U.S.A. by the author.

Ledesma, Rodolfo G.

A Dog's Guide to Making It in America, Volume 2

ISBN-10: 0984887415

ISBN-13: 978-0-9848874-1-5

Printed in the U.S.A.

Cover design and illustrations by the author.

First Edition

For my mom, Emma

And in loving memomery of my dad, Enrique

Acknowledgment

My son, Ian, helped by drawing many of the outlines of the figures in the illustrations. All three children, Ian, Steven and Maia, were a source of inspiration for this project. Many of my students in the U.S. and South Korea, both local and foreign, failing and unfailing in their faith in higher education and beyond, were, too.

Contents

Play-Acting and the Scourge of Cheap Imports

MY MASTER'S SON, JOE-MAHRI . . .
WHAT'S WRONG?
I WANTED TO BE A CHINESE PIRATE, THE JACK SPARROW OF THE SOUTH CHINA SEA. MY OWN VERSION.
THAT'S GOOD. DERIVATIVE BUT ORIGINAL.
BUT MY FRIENDS DON'T KNOW WHERE SOUTH CHINA SEA IS. THEY SAID THERE'S NO SUCH PLACE.
I TRIED SHOWING IT ON THE MAP. BUT THEY WON'T HEAR ME OUT. THEY WON'T TAKE MY CALLS ANYMORE.
SO THEY WON'T PLAY WITH YOU AT ALL. NEVER?
THEY SAID MAYBE NEXT YEAR. JUST MAYBE, AFTER THEY PASS GEOGRAPHY.

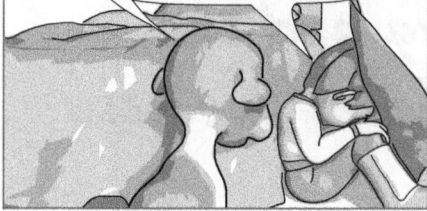

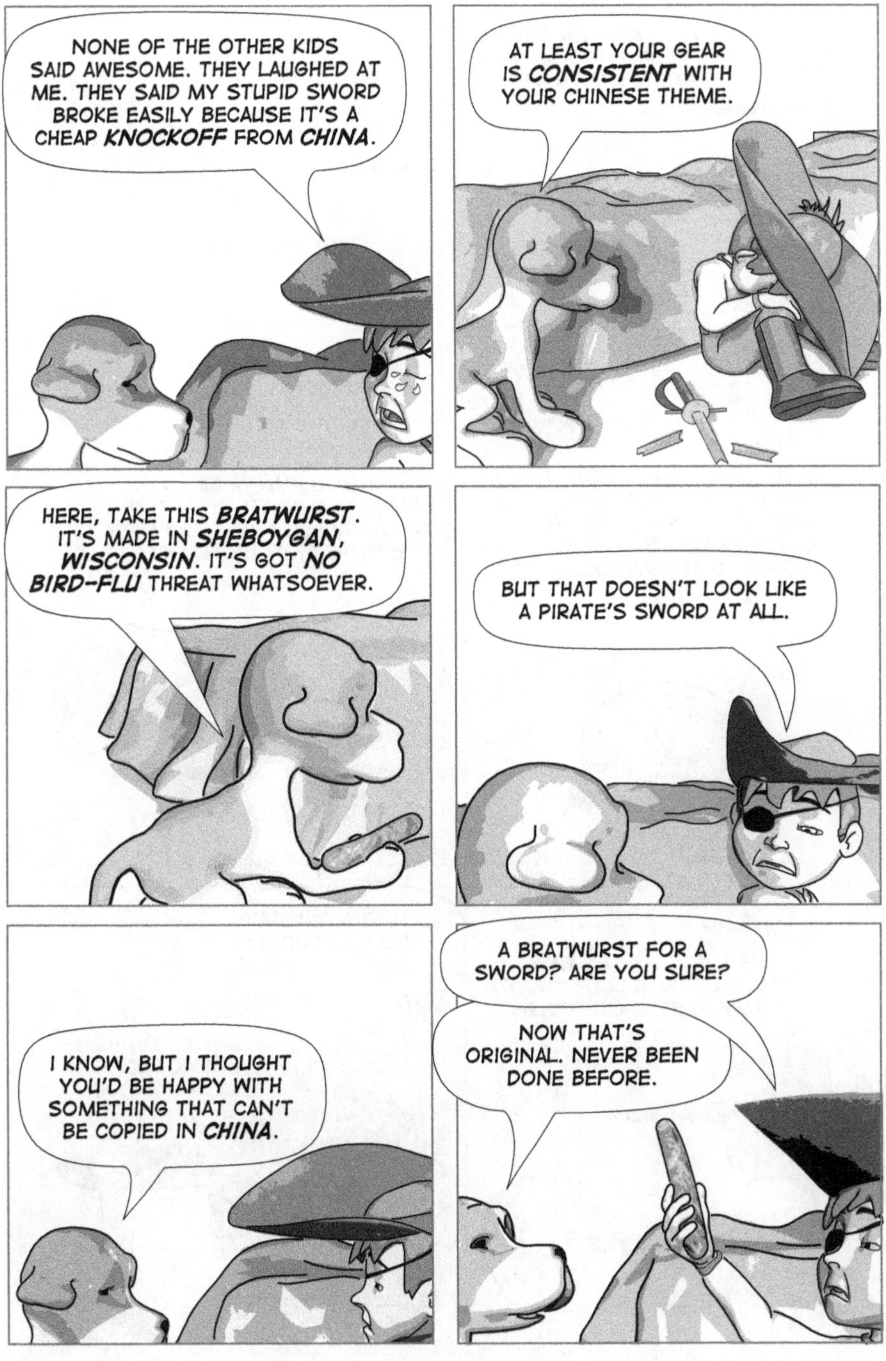
NONE OF THE OTHER KIDS SAID AWESOME. THEY LAUGHED AT ME. THEY SAID MY STUPID SWORD BROKE EASILY BECAUSE IT'S A CHEAP ***KNOCKOFF*** FROM ***CHINA***.
AT LEAST YOUR GEAR IS ***CONSISTENT*** WITH YOUR CHINESE THEME.
HERE, TAKE THIS ***BRATWURST***. IT'S MADE IN ***SHEBOYGAN, WISCONSIN***. IT'S GOT ***NO BIRD-FLU*** THREAT WHATSOEVER.
BUT THAT DOESN'T LOOK LIKE A PIRATE'S SWORD AT ALL.
I KNOW, BUT I THOUGHT YOU'D BE HAPPY WITH SOMETHING THAT CAN'T BE COPIED IN ***CHINA***.
A BRATWURST FOR A SWORD? ARE YOU SURE?
NOW THAT'S ORIGINAL. NEVER BEEN DONE BEFORE.

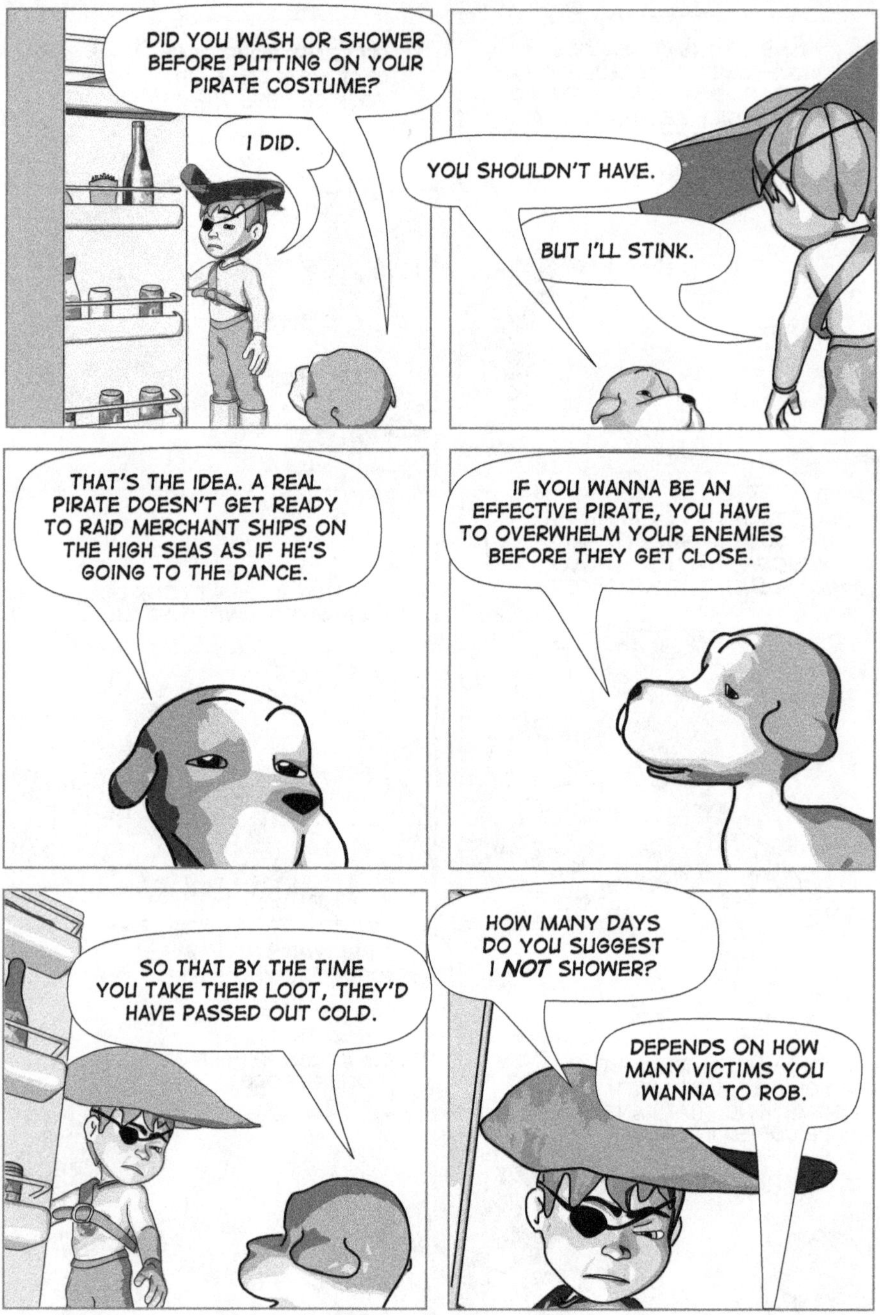
DID YOU WASH OR SHOWER BEFORE PUTTING ON YOUR PIRATE COSTUME?
I DID.
YOU SHOULDN'T HAVE.
BUT I'LL STINK.
THAT'S THE IDEA. A REAL PIRATE DOESN'T GET READY TO RAID MERCHANT SHIPS ON THE HIGH SEAS AS IF HE'S GOING TO THE DANCE.
IF YOU WANNA BE AN EFFECTIVE PIRATE, YOU HAVE TO OVERWHELM YOUR ENEMIES BEFORE THEY GET CLOSE.
SO THAT BY THE TIME YOU TAKE THEIR LOOT, THEY'D HAVE PASSED OUT COLD.
HOW MANY DAYS DO YOU SUGGEST I ***NOT*** SHOWER?
DEPENDS ON HOW MANY VICTIMS YOU WANNA TO ROB.

WHAT ARE YOU LOOKING FOR IN THE FRIDGE?
CAN'T YOU SEE? I'M STARVED AFTER LISTENING TO YOU.
BE CAREFUL NOW. I HOPE YOU DON'T FIND IN THERE TAINTED FOOD FROM *CHINA*.
GIVE ME A BREAK.
ARE YOU GONNA BRUSH YOUR TEETH LATER?
WHAT NOW?
YOU MIGHT WANT TO SKIP THAT ONE, TOO.
JEEZ. WHAT IS IT WITH YOU?

REAL PIRATES DON'T BRUSH. BESIDES, IF YOUR TOOTHPASTE IS IMPORTED FROM *CHINA*, IT MIGHT BE LACED WITH AN *ANTI-FREEZE* INGREDIENT.

YOU MAKE IT HARD FOR ME TO PLAY *PIRATE*. NOT ONLY DO I HAVE TO SMELL, I ALSO HAVE TO HAVE BAD BREATH *LIKE YOU*. WHY CAN'T YOU LEAVE ME ALONE?

MAYBE I'LL JUST PLAY *VAMPIRE* INSTEAD.

SURE. I HAVE NO PROBLEM WITH THAT

BUT IF I PLAY VAMPIRE, WILL YOU LET ME SLEEP AT NIGHT — IN MY BED?

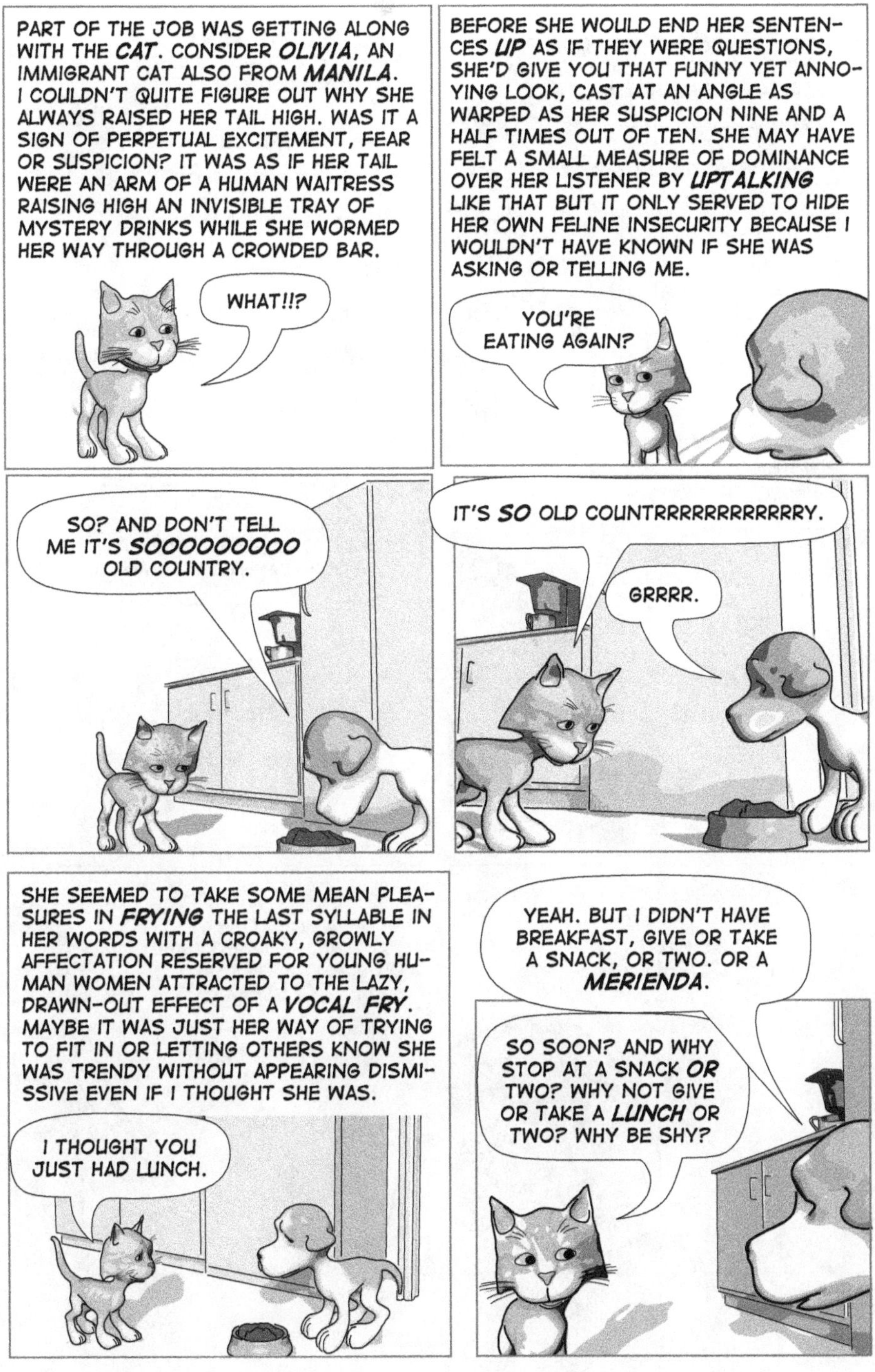
PART OF THE JOB WAS GETTING ALONG WITH THE CAT. CONSIDER OLIVIA, AN IMMIGRANT CAT ALSO FROM MANILA. I COULDN'T QUITE FIGURE OUT WHY SHE ALWAYS RAISED HER TAIL HIGH. WAS IT A SIGN OF PERPETUAL EXCITEMENT, FEAR OR SUSPICION? IT WAS AS IF HER TAIL WERE AN ARM OF A HUMAN WAITRESS RAISING HIGH AN INVISIBLE TRAY OF MYSTERY DRINKS WHILE SHE WORMED HER WAY THROUGH A CROWDED BAR.
WHAT!!?
BEFORE SHE WOULD END HER SENTENCES UP AS IF THEY WERE QUESTIONS, SHE'D GIVE YOU THAT FUNNY YET ANNOYING LOOK, CAST AT AN ANGLE AS WARPED AS HER SUSPICION NINE AND A HALF TIMES OUT OF TEN. SHE MAY HAVE FELT A SMALL MEASURE OF DOMINANCE OVER HER LISTENER BY UPTALKING LIKE THAT BUT IT ONLY SERVED TO HIDE HER OWN FELINE INSECURITY BECAUSE I WOULDN'T HAVE KNOWN IF SHE WAS ASKING OR TELLING ME.
YOU'RE EATING AGAIN?
SO? AND DON'T TELL ME IT'S SOOOOOOOOO OLD COUNTRY.
IT'S SO OLD COUNTRRRRRRRRRRRY.
GRRRR.
SHE SEEMED TO TAKE SOME MEAN PLEASURES IN FRYING THE LAST SYLLABLE IN HER WORDS WITH A CROAKY, GROWLY AFFECTATION RESERVED FOR YOUNG HUMAN WOMEN ATTRACTED TO THE LAZY, DRAWN-OUT EFFECT OF A VOCAL FRY. MAYBE IT WAS JUST HER WAY OF TRYING TO FIT IN OR LETTING OTHERS KNOW SHE WAS TRENDY WITHOUT APPEARING DISMISSIVE EVEN IF I THOUGHT SHE WAS.
I THOUGHT YOU JUST HAD LUNCH.
YEAH. BUT I DIDN'T HAVE BREAKFAST, GIVE OR TAKE A SNACK, OR TWO. OR A MERIENDA.
SO SOON? AND WHY STOP AT A SNACK OR TWO? WHY NOT GIVE OR TAKE A LUNCH OR TWO? WHY BE SHY?

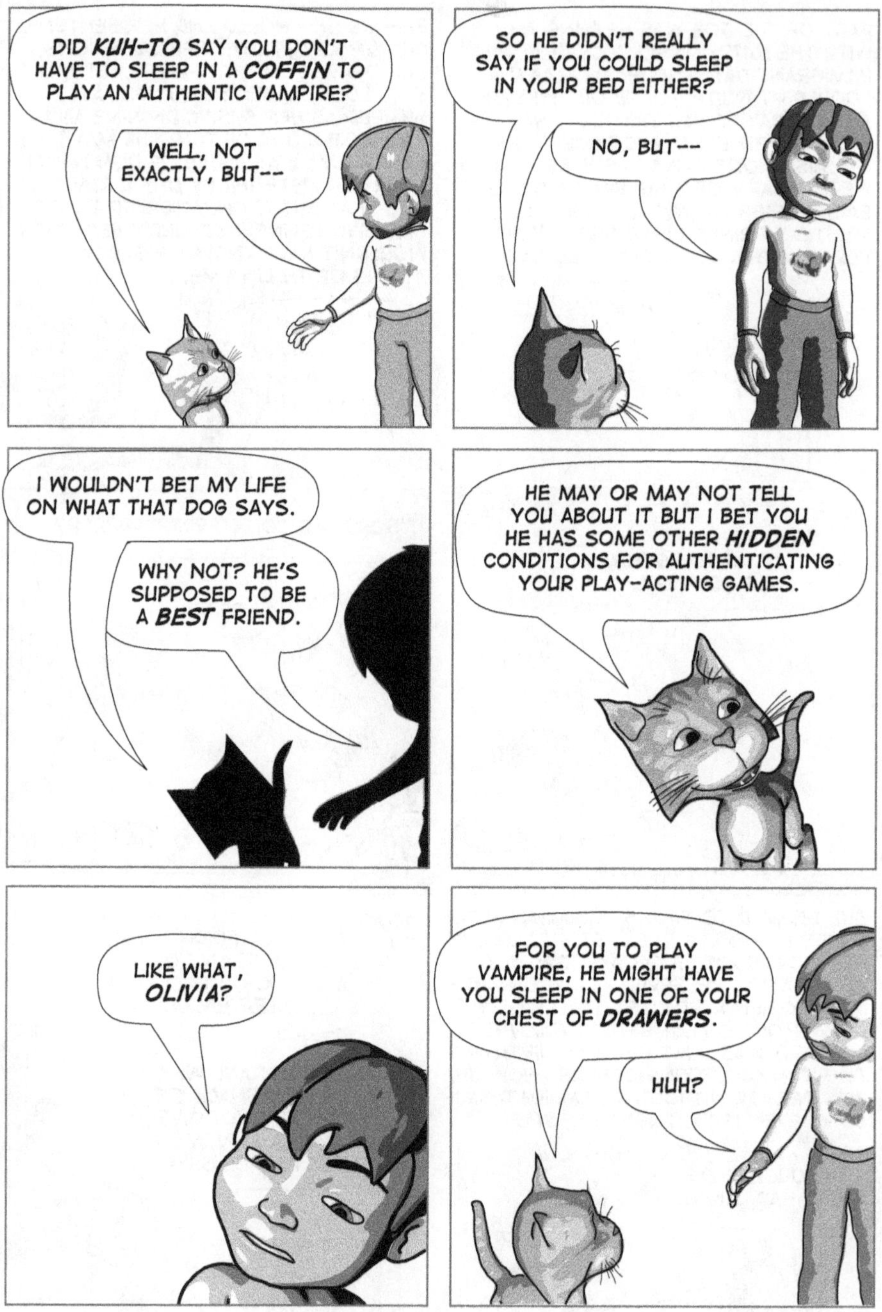
DID KUH-TO SAY YOU DON'T HAVE TO SLEEP IN A COFFIN TO PLAY AN AUTHENTIC VAMPIRE?
WELL, NOT EXACTLY, BUT--
SO HE DIDN'T REALLY SAY IF YOU COULD SLEEP IN YOUR BED EITHER?
NO, BUT--
I WOULDN'T BET MY LIFE ON WHAT THAT DOG SAYS.
WHY NOT? HE'S SUPPOSED TO BE A BEST FRIEND.
HE MAY OR MAY NOT TELL YOU ABOUT IT BUT I BET YOU HE HAS SOME OTHER HIDDEN CONDITIONS FOR AUTHENTICATING YOUR PLAY-ACTING GAMES.
LIKE WHAT, OLIVIA?
FOR YOU TO PLAY VAMPIRE, HE MIGHT HAVE YOU SLEEP IN ONE OF YOUR CHEST OF DRAWERS.
HUH?

INSIDE ONE OF THESE? BUT HOW WILL I BREATHE?
YOU KEEP THE DRAWER OPEN.
WHICH ONE OF THESE —— THE UPPER OR LOWER DRAWER?
WHICH ONE HAS THE SOFT, CUSHY CLOTHES THAT ARE COMFY ON YOUR BACK?
THE *UPPER* DRAWER HAS SOCKS THAT ARE BALLED UP. IT'S ALSO GOT TENNIS BALLS AND SOME BASEBALLS.
THE *LOWER* ONE HAS FOLDED T-SHIRTS AND PAJAMAS. SO, MAYBE YOU WANNA PLAY ALONG WITH ME?
SURE. *YOU* TAKE THE *UPPER* DRAWER, I'LL TAKE THE LOWER ONE.

BUT I'M AFRAID OF HEIGHTS.
JOE-MAHRI, REAL VAMPIRES AREN'T AFRAID OF HEIGHTS.
WHY DON'T YOU TAKE THE UPPER DRAWER? IF YOU FALL, YOU'LL ALWAYS LAND ON YOUR FEET. ME, I CAN'T DO THAT.
I'M AFRAID OF GETTING BALL MARKS ON MY BACK. BESIDES I DON'T HAVE NINE LIVES.
JOE-MAHRI HAD NO IDEA BUT OLIVIA WAS ONCE A STOWAWAY ON AN OCEAN FREIGHTER FROM HONG KONG TO MANILA.
HAVE YOU EVER SLEPT ON A SACK OF POTATOES? I HAVE.
HAVE YOU EVER SLEPT ON A BAG OF ONIONS? I HAVE.
YOU CATS ARE PICKY. WHAT'S THE MATTER? DON'T YOU LIKE ONION RINGS?

Dinner by the Dumpster

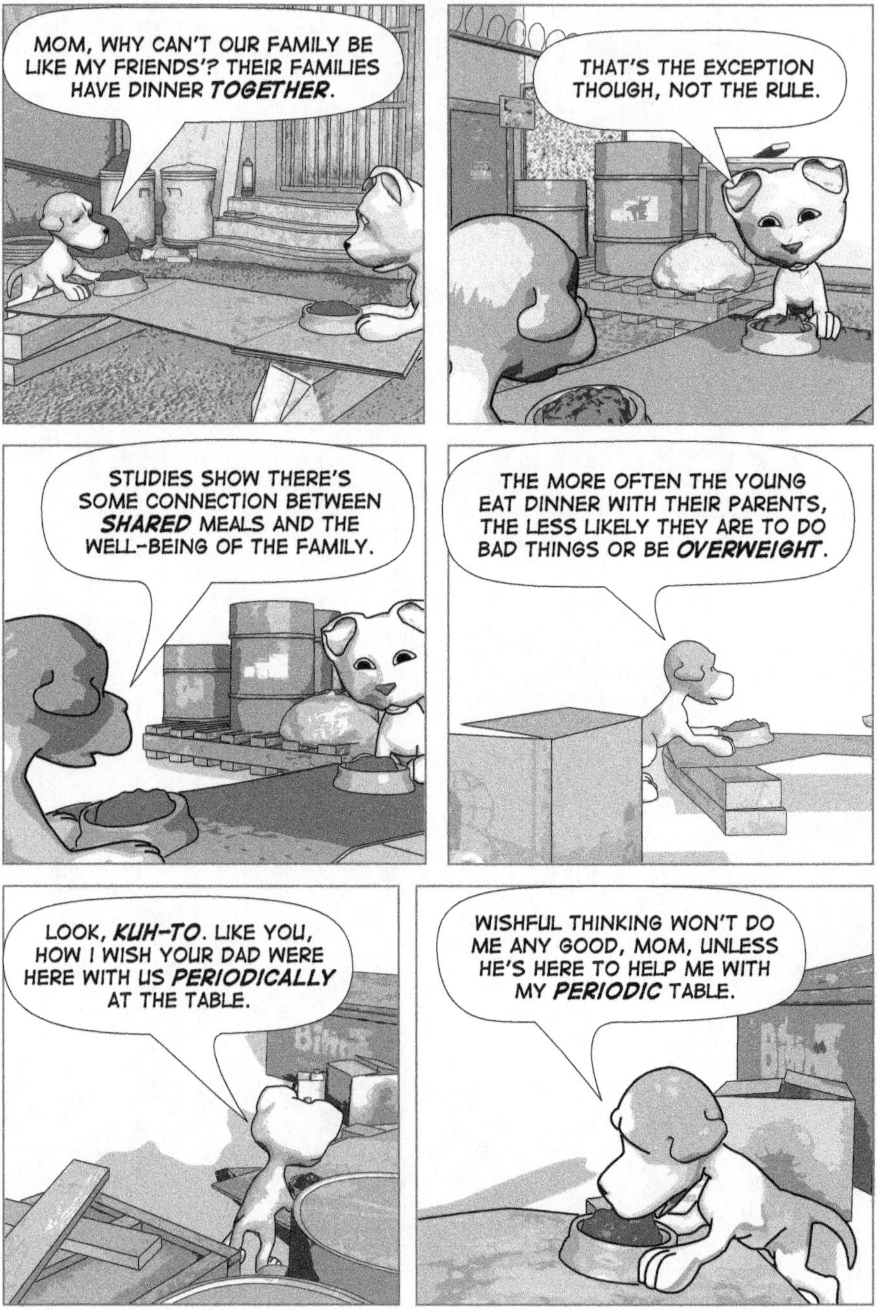
MOM, WHY CAN'T OUR FAMILY BE LIKE MY FRIENDS'? THEIR FAMILIES HAVE DINNER *TOGETHER*.
THAT'S THE EXCEPTION THOUGH, NOT THE RULE.
STUDIES SHOW THERE'S SOME CONNECTION BETWEEN *SHARED* MEALS AND THE WELL-BEING OF THE FAMILY.
THE MORE OFTEN THE YOUNG EAT DINNER WITH THEIR PARENTS, THE LESS LIKELY THEY ARE TO DO BAD THINGS OR BE *OVERWEIGHT*.
LOOK, *KUH-TO*. LIKE YOU, HOW I WISH YOUR DAD WERE HERE WITH US *PERIODICALLY* AT THE TABLE.
WISHFUL THINKING WON'T DO ME ANY GOOD, MOM, UNLESS HE'S HERE TO HELP ME WITH MY *PERIODIC* TABLE.

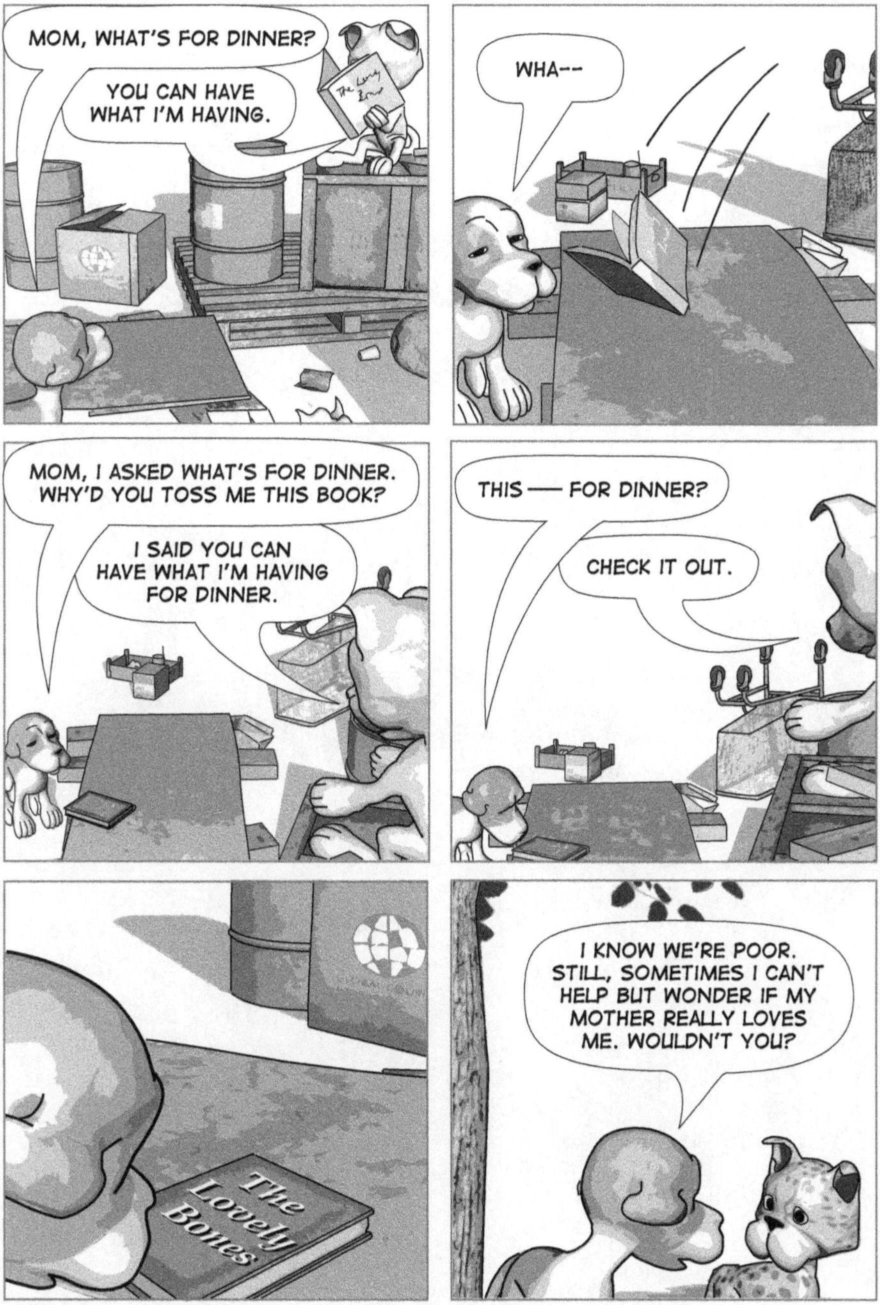
MOM, WHAT'S FOR DINNER?
YOU CAN HAVE WHAT I'M HAVING.
WHA--
MOM, I ASKED WHAT'S FOR DINNER. WHY'D YOU TOSS ME THIS BOOK?
I SAID YOU CAN HAVE WHAT I'M HAVING FOR DINNER.
THIS — FOR DINNER?
CHECK IT OUT.
The Lovely Bones
I KNOW WE'RE POOR. STILL, SOMETIMES I CAN'T HELP BUT WONDER IF MY MOTHER REALLY LOVES ME. WOULDN'T YOU?

Schooling and Political Campaigns

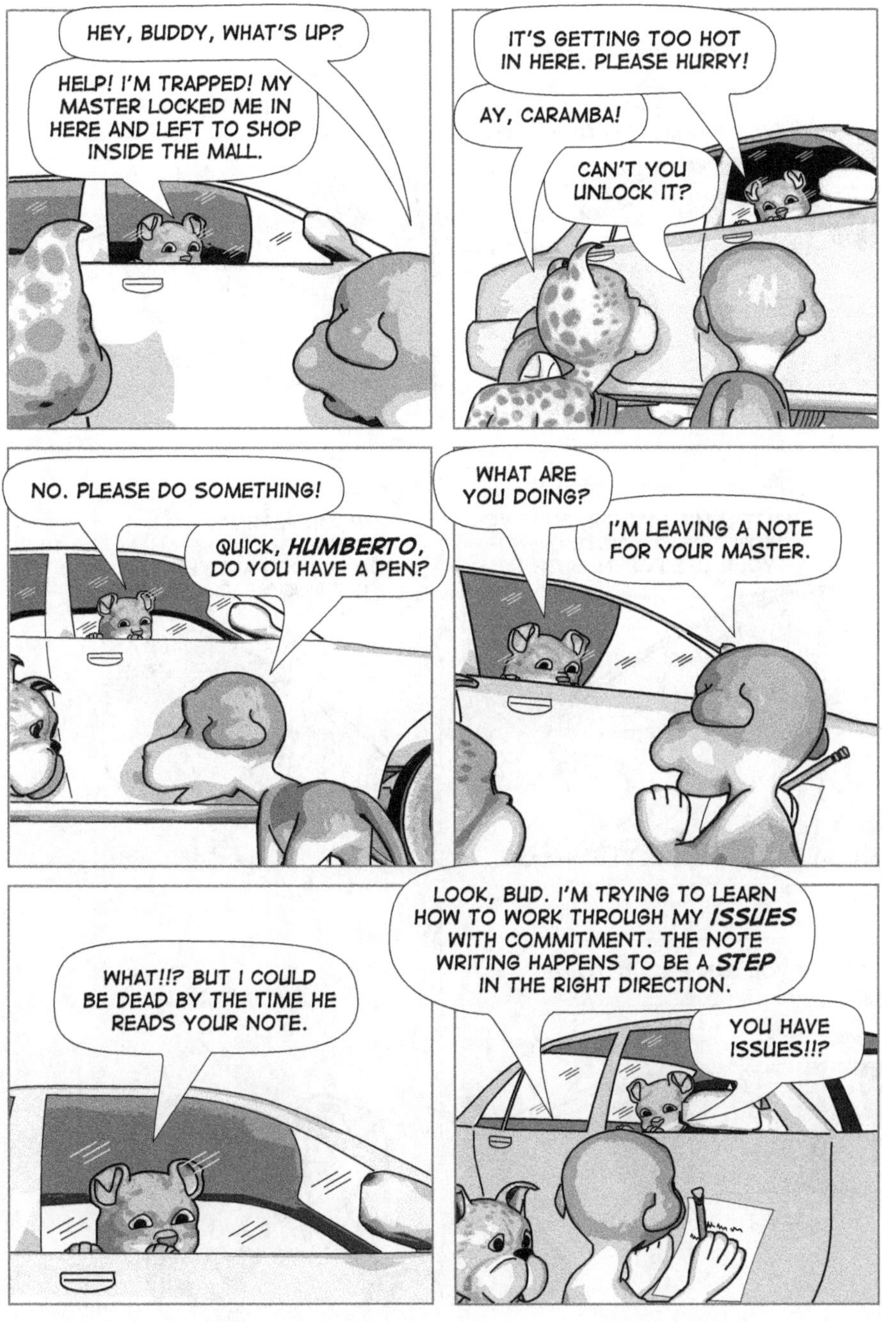
HEY, BUDDY, WHAT'S UP?
HELP! I'M TRAPPED! MY MASTER LOCKED ME IN HERE AND LEFT TO SHOP INSIDE THE MALL.
IT'S GETTING TOO HOT IN HERE. PLEASE HURRY!
AY, CARAMBA!
CAN'T YOU UNLOCK IT?
NO. PLEASE DO SOMETHING!
QUICK, *HUMBERTO*, DO YOU HAVE A PEN?
WHAT ARE YOU DOING?
I'M LEAVING A NOTE FOR YOUR MASTER.
WHAT!!? BUT I COULD BE DEAD BY THE TIME HE READS YOUR NOTE.
LOOK, BUD. I'M TRYING TO LEARN HOW TO WORK THROUGH MY *ISSUES* WITH COMMITMENT. THE NOTE WRITING HAPPENS TO BE A *STEP* IN THE RIGHT DIRECTION.
YOU HAVE ISSUES!!?

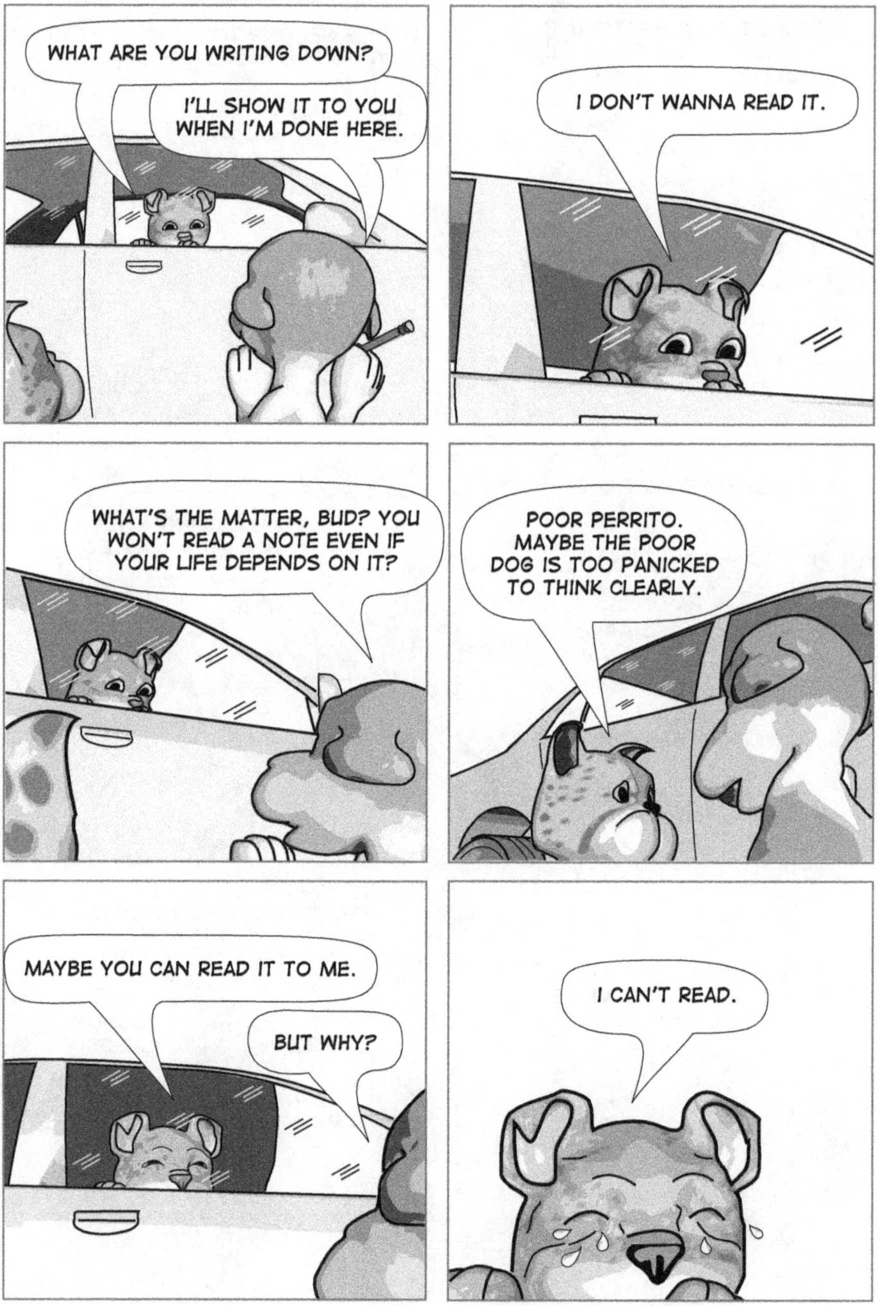
WHAT ARE YOU WRITING DOWN?
I'LL SHOW IT TO YOU WHEN I'M DONE HERE.
I DON'T WANNA READ IT.
WHAT'S THE MATTER, BUD? YOU WON'T READ A NOTE EVEN IF YOUR LIFE DEPENDS ON IT?
POOR PERRITO. MAYBE THE POOR DOG IS TOO PANICKED TO THINK CLEARLY.
MAYBE YOU CAN READ IT TO ME.
BUT WHY?
I CAN'T READ.

INSTEAD OF LEAVING A NOTE, WHY DON'T WE GO LOOK FOR HIS MASTER INSIDE THE MALL? PRONTO!
GOOD IDEA.
HEY, BUD, WE'RE GONNA GO LOOK FOR YOUR MASTER INSIDE THE MALL. SO HANG IN THERE.
WAIT. IF YOU JUST TELL HIM ABOUT ME WHEN YOU FIND HIM, IT WON'T WORK. HE WON'T BELIEVE YOU.
WHY NOT?
IT'S COMPLICATED. BUT IF YOU HAVE A NOTE THAT COMES FROM ME, IT MIGHT WORK.
SO I'LL COMPOSE AN URGENT NOTE FOR HELP COMING FROM YOU.
BUT NOT JUST ANY NOTE. HOW DO I SAY THIS? IT ALMOST HAS TO SOUND LIKE A POLITICAL CAMPAIGN MESSAGE. KNOW WHAT I MEAN?
WHAT!!?
HE'S A STRANGE BREW, MY MASTER. HE FINDS IT BELIEVABLE IF AT THE END OF THE NOTE YOU ADD RIGHT AFTER MY NAME THE STATE-MENT: "I APPROVE THIS MESSAGE."

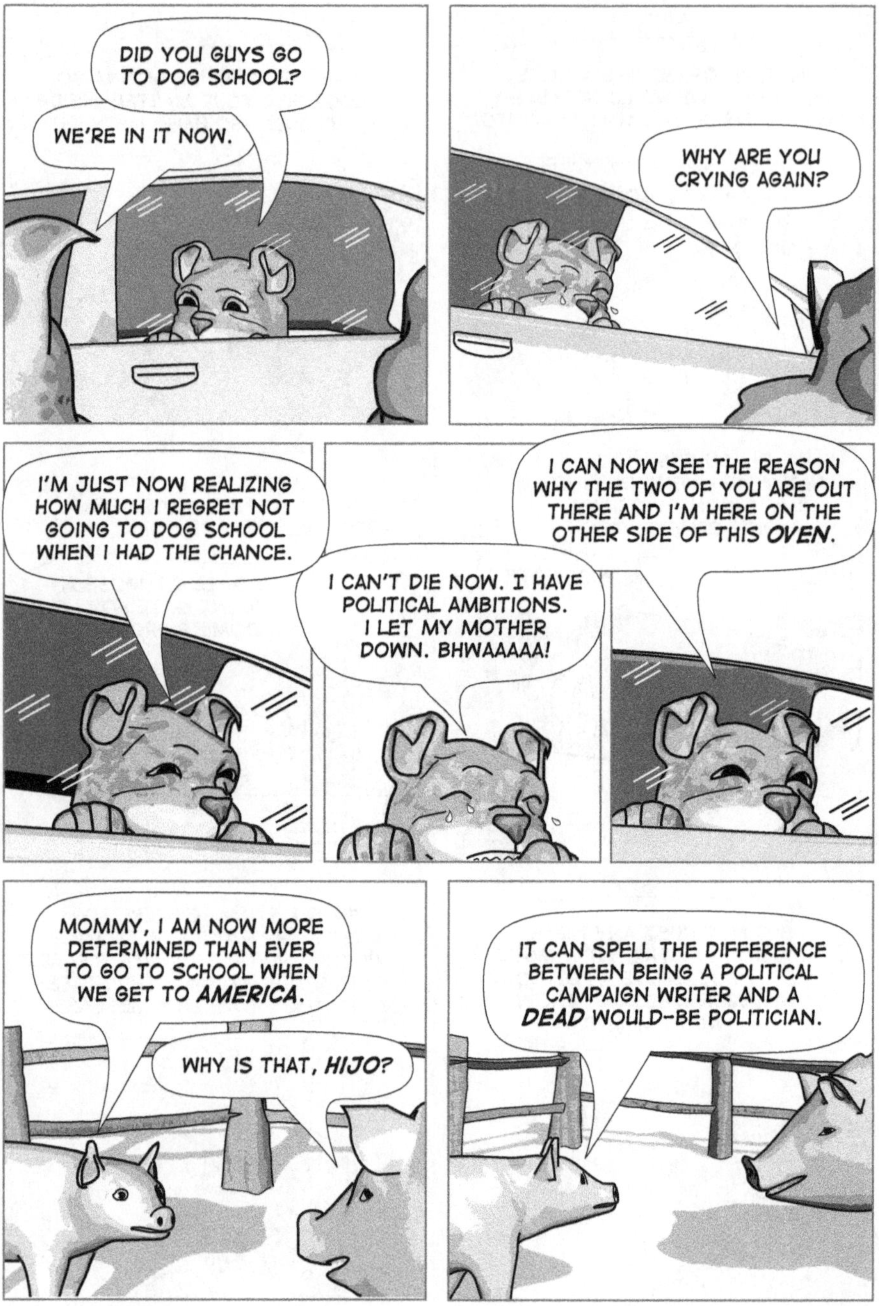
DID YOU GUYS GO TO DOG SCHOOL?
WE'RE IN IT NOW.
WHY ARE YOU CRYING AGAIN?
I'M JUST NOW REALIZING HOW MUCH I REGRET NOT GOING TO DOG SCHOOL WHEN I HAD THE CHANCE.
I CAN'T DIE NOW. I HAVE POLITICAL AMBITIONS. I LET MY MOTHER DOWN. BHWAAAAA!
I CAN NOW SEE THE REASON WHY THE TWO OF YOU ARE OUT THERE AND I'M HERE ON THE OTHER SIDE OF THIS *OVEN*.
MOMMY, I AM NOW MORE DETERMINED THAN EVER TO GO TO SCHOOL WHEN WE GET TO *AMERICA*.
WHY IS THAT, *HIJO*?
IT CAN SPELL THE DIFFERENCE BETWEEN BEING A POLITICAL CAMPAIGN WRITER AND A *DEAD* WOULD-BE POLITICIAN.

The Art of the Interview

JOB INTERVIEWS CAN BE NERVE-WRACKING. I GET SWEATY PAWS.
THIS INTERVIEW IS MAKING ME THIRSTY. CAN I GET A DRINK OF WATER?
THE TOILET IS NEXT DOOR ON YOUR RIGHT.
DOES IT FLUSH?
I'M SURE IT DOES. BUT WHY DO YOU ASK?
I DON'T KNOW IF YOU'VE TRIED IT BUT I GET A RUSH FROM *SWIRLING* WATER. IT'S MORE REFRESHING AND BETTER ON MY NERVES.
AND YOU DON'T GET BAD BREATH?

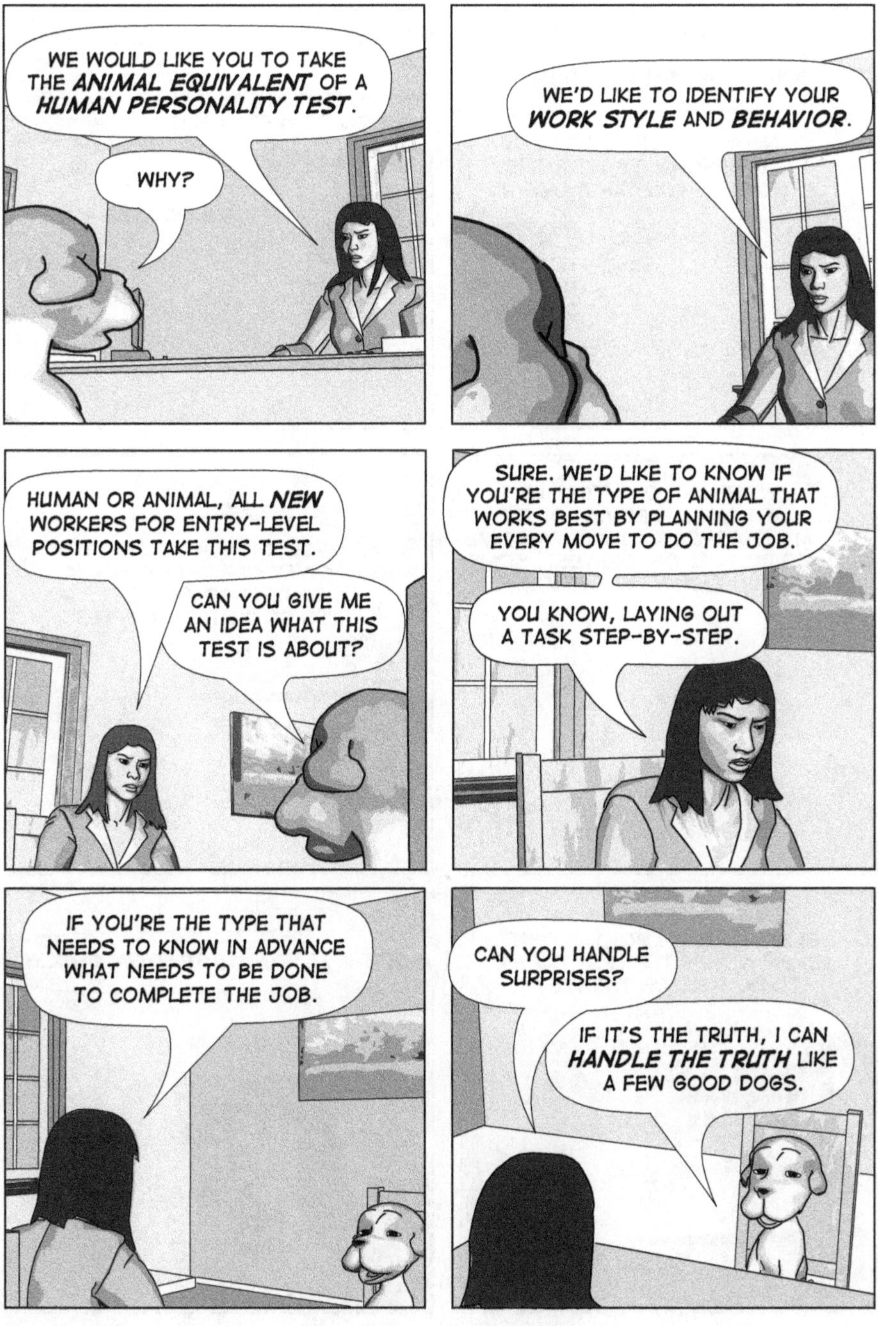
WE WOULD LIKE YOU TO TAKE THE ANIMAL EQUIVALENT OF A HUMAN PERSONALITY TEST.
WHY?
WE'D LIKE TO IDENTIFY YOUR WORK STYLE AND BEHAVIOR.
HUMAN OR ANIMAL, ALL NEW WORKERS FOR ENTRY-LEVEL POSITIONS TAKE THIS TEST.
CAN YOU GIVE ME AN IDEA WHAT THIS TEST IS ABOUT?
SURE. WE'D LIKE TO KNOW IF YOU'RE THE TYPE OF ANIMAL THAT WORKS BEST BY PLANNING YOUR EVERY MOVE TO DO THE JOB.
YOU KNOW, LAYING OUT A TASK STEP-BY-STEP.
IF YOU'RE THE TYPE THAT NEEDS TO KNOW IN ADVANCE WHAT NEEDS TO BE DONE TO COMPLETE THE JOB.
CAN YOU HANDLE SURPRISES?
IF IT'S THE TRUTH, I CAN HANDLE THE TRUTH LIKE A FEW GOOD DOGS.

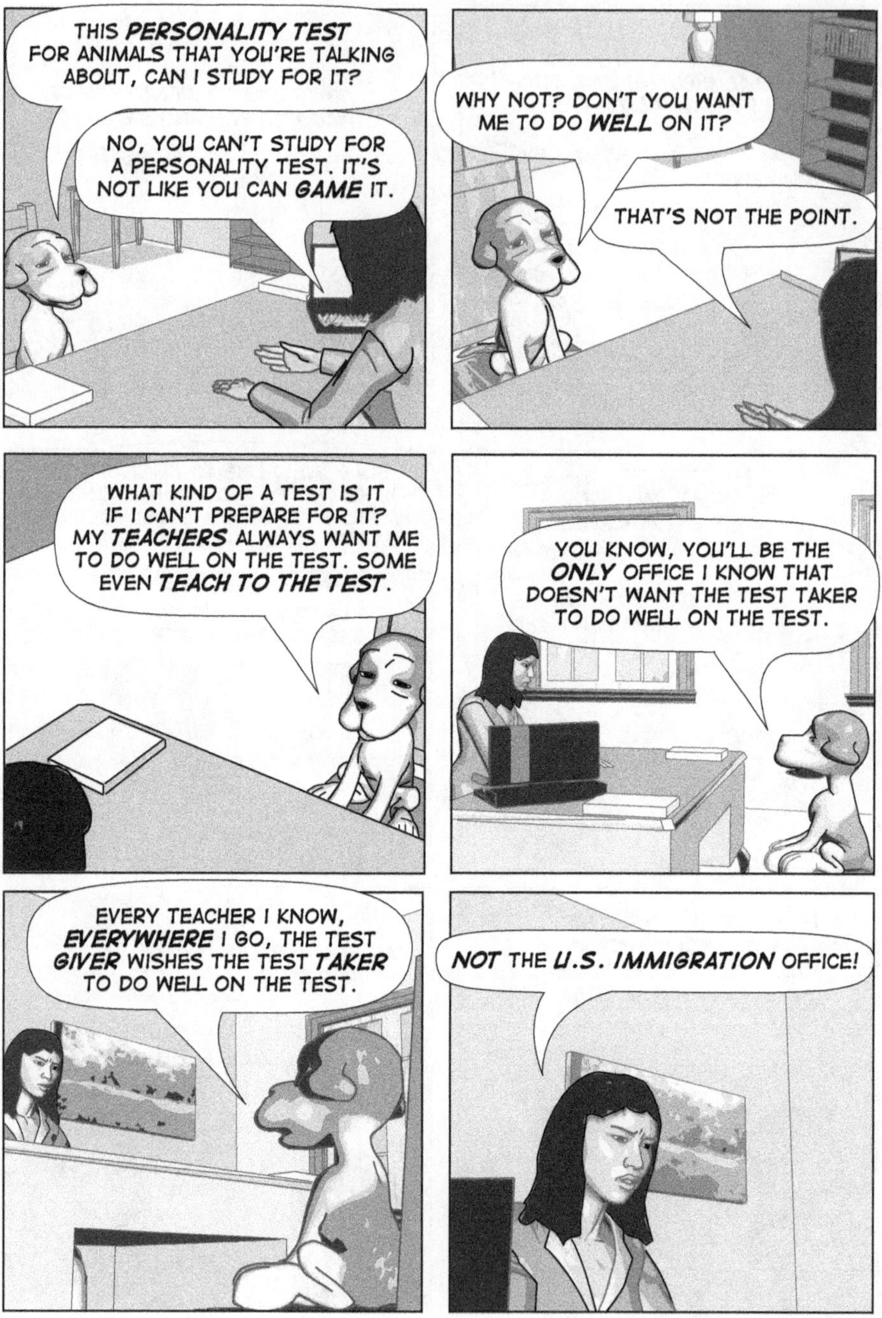
THIS PERSONALITY TEST FOR ANIMALS THAT YOU'RE TALKING ABOUT, CAN I STUDY FOR IT?
NO, YOU CAN'T STUDY FOR A PERSONALITY TEST. IT'S NOT LIKE YOU CAN GAME IT.
WHY NOT? DON'T YOU WANT ME TO DO WELL ON IT?
THAT'S NOT THE POINT.
WHAT KIND OF A TEST IS IT IF I CAN'T PREPARE FOR IT? MY TEACHERS ALWAYS WANT ME TO DO WELL ON THE TEST. SOME EVEN TEACH TO THE TEST.
YOU KNOW, YOU'LL BE THE ONLY OFFICE I KNOW THAT DOESN'T WANT THE TEST TAKER TO DO WELL ON THE TEST.
EVERY TEACHER I KNOW, EVERYWHERE I GO, THE TEST GIVER WISHES THE TEST TAKER TO DO WELL ON THE TEST.
NOT THE U.S. IMMIGRATION OFFICE!

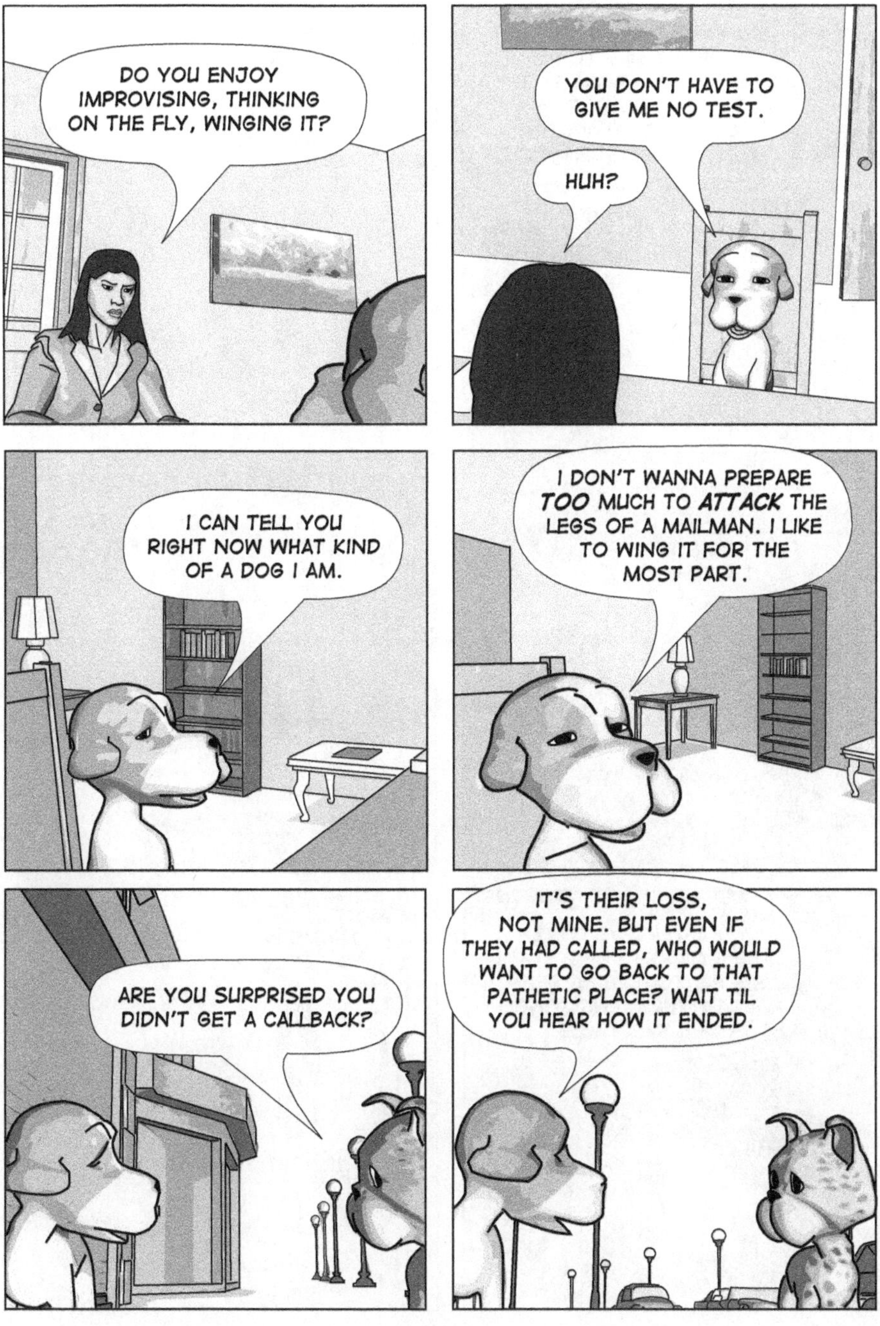
DO YOU ENJOY IMPROVISING, THINKING ON THE FLY, WINGING IT?
YOU DON'T HAVE TO GIVE ME NO TEST.
HUH?
I CAN TELL YOU RIGHT NOW WHAT KIND OF A DOG I AM.
I DON'T WANNA PREPARE *TOO* MUCH TO *ATTACK* THE LEGS OF A MAILMAN. I LIKE TO WING IT FOR THE MOST PART.
ARE YOU SURPRISED YOU DIDN'T GET A CALLBACK?
IT'S THEIR LOSS, NOT MINE. BUT EVEN IF THEY HAD CALLED, WHO WOULD WANT TO GO BACK TO THAT PATHETIC PLACE? WAIT TIL YOU HEAR HOW IT ENDED.

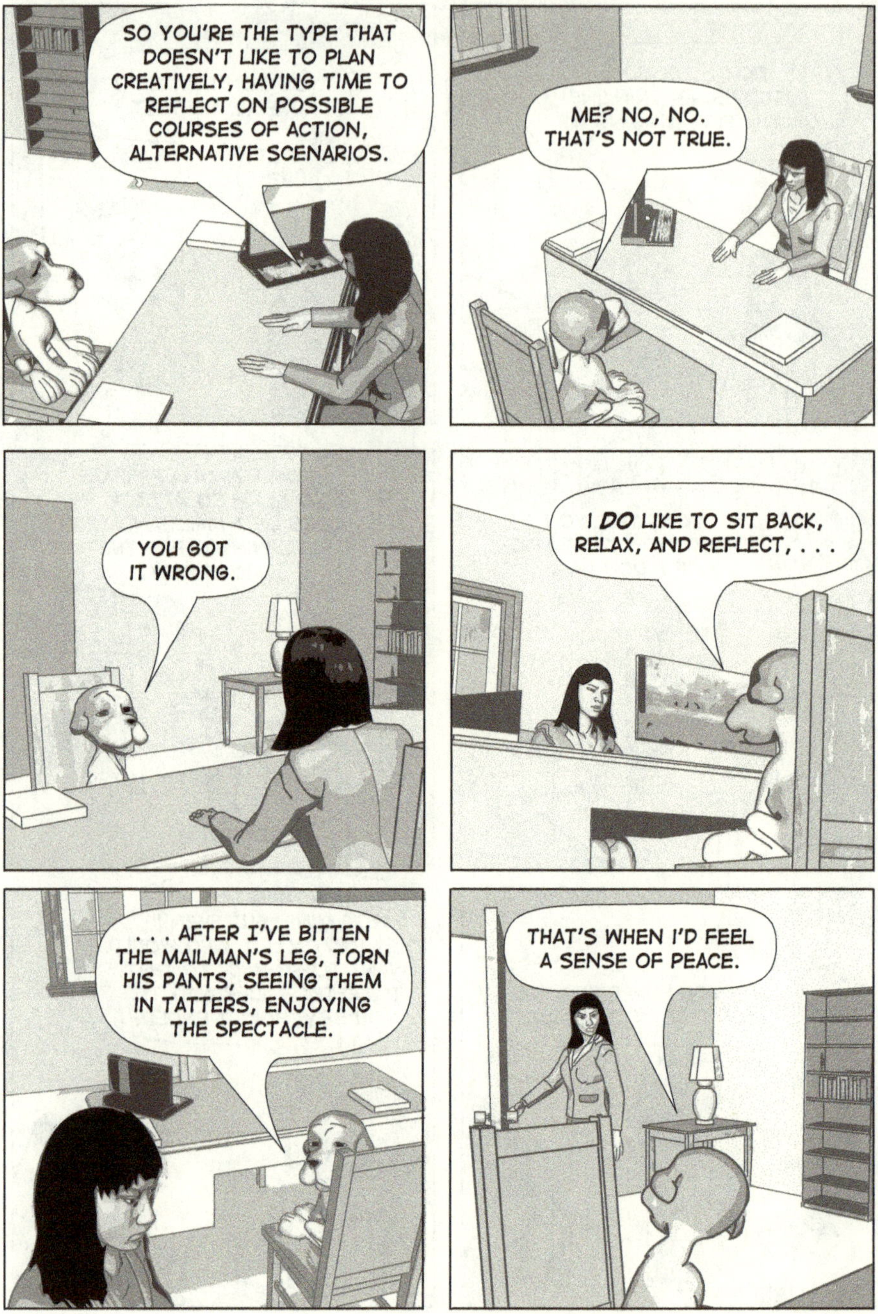
SO YOU'RE THE TYPE THAT DOESN'T LIKE TO PLAN CREATIVELY, HAVING TIME TO REFLECT ON POSSIBLE COURSES OF ACTION, ALTERNATIVE SCENARIOS.
ME? NO, NO. THAT'S NOT TRUE.
YOU GOT IT WRONG.
I *DO* LIKE TO SIT BACK, RELAX, AND REFLECT, . . .
. . . AFTER I'VE BITTEN THE MAILMAN'S LEG, TORN HIS PANTS, SEEING THEM IN TATTERS, ENJOYING THE SPECTACLE.
THAT'S WHEN I'D FEEL A SENSE OF PEACE.

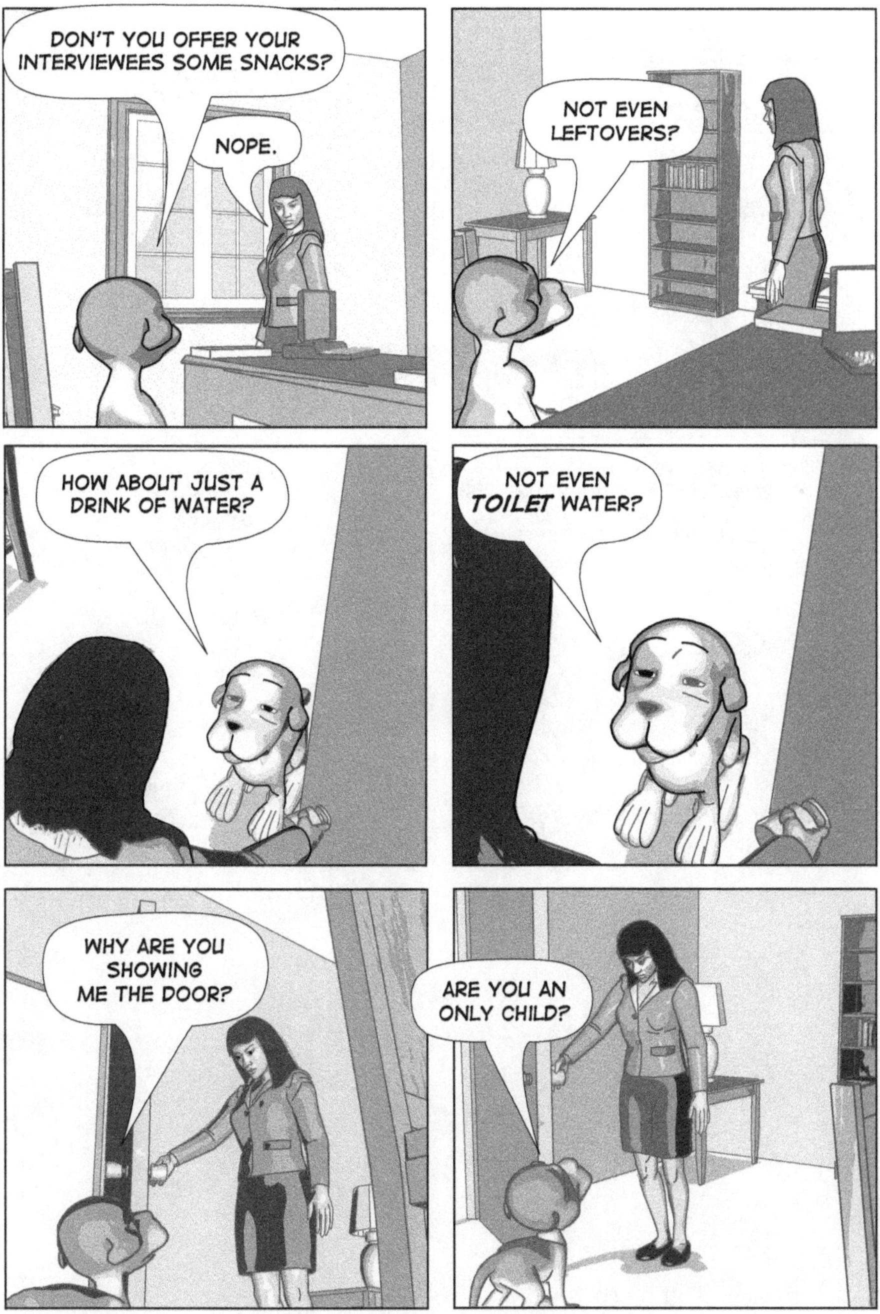
DON'T YOU OFFER YOUR INTERVIEWEES SOME SNACKS?
NOPE.
NOT EVEN LEFTOVERS?
HOW ABOUT JUST A DRINK OF WATER?
NOT EVEN *TOILET* WATER?
WHY ARE YOU SHOWING ME THE DOOR?
ARE YOU AN ONLY CHILD?

AMIGO, WHY DON'T YOU TRY *FAITH-BASED* NETWORKING? IT MIGHT HELP YOU IN YOUR SEARCH FOR A JOB OR AN INTERNSHIP.
HOW'S THAT WORK?
PRIVATE
YOU REACH OUT TO MEMBERS OF YOUR CONGRE-GATION AND OTHERS IN YOUR *RELIGIOUS CIRCLE*.
I CAN'T BELIEVE YOU TOLD HIM THAT, *HUMBERTO*. WHAT RELIGIOUS CIRCLE? YOU'RE KIDDING. NO, NOT YOUR FRIEND *KUH-TO*.
HIS *RELIGION* IS WARMED UP *LEFTOVERS*. HE WORSHIPS INSIDE THE *MICROWAVE OVEN*.

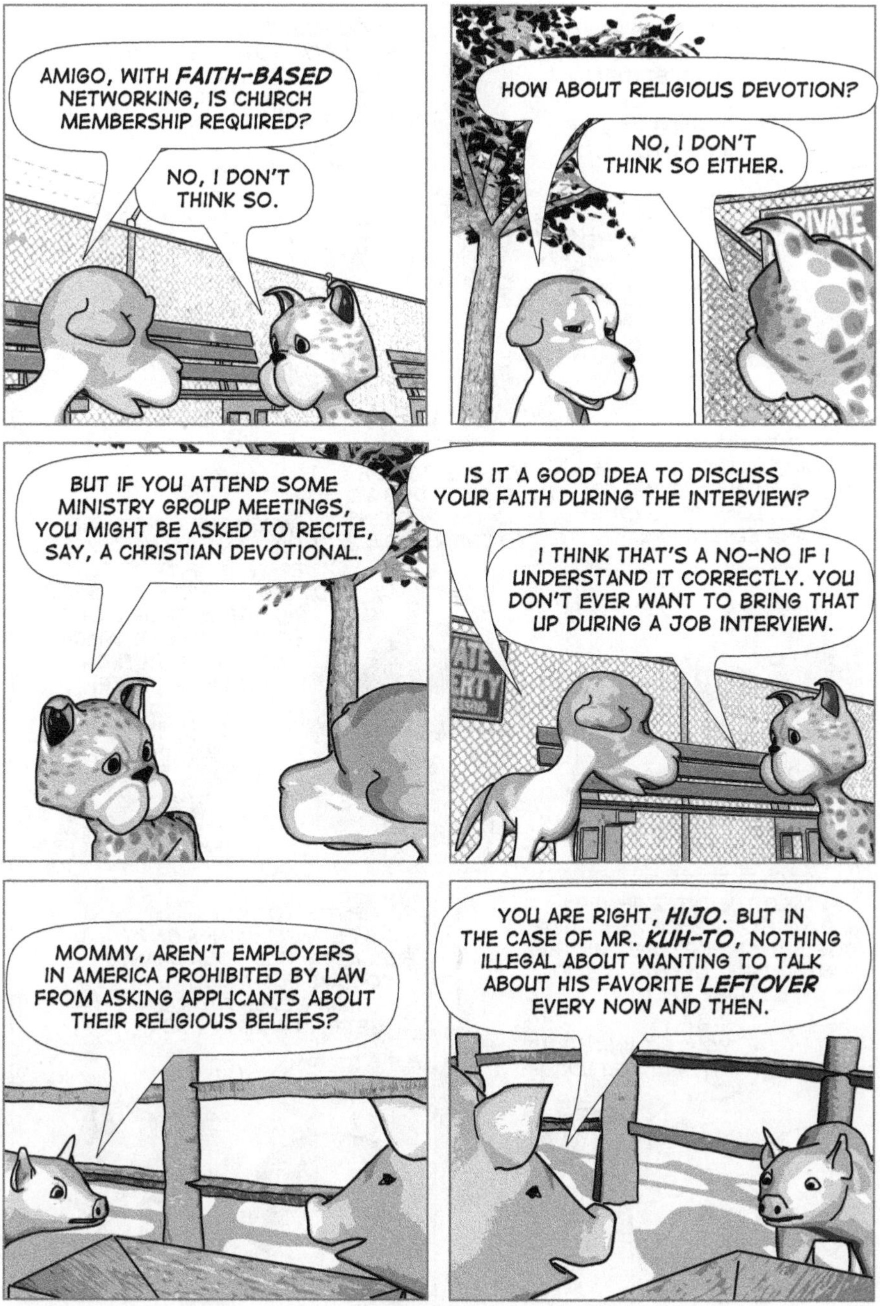
AMIGO, WITH FAITH-BASED NETWORKING, IS CHURCH MEMBERSHIP REQUIRED?
NO, I DON'T THINK SO.
HOW ABOUT RELIGIOUS DEVOTION?
NO, I DON'T THINK SO EITHER.
PRIVATE
BUT IF YOU ATTEND SOME MINISTRY GROUP MEETINGS, YOU MIGHT BE ASKED TO RECITE, SAY, A CHRISTIAN DEVOTIONAL.
IS IT A GOOD IDEA TO DISCUSS YOUR FAITH DURING THE INTERVIEW?
I THINK THAT'S A NO-NO IF I UNDERSTAND IT CORRECTLY. YOU DON'T EVER WANT TO BRING THAT UP DURING A JOB INTERVIEW.
MOMMY, AREN'T EMPLOYERS IN AMERICA PROHIBITED BY LAW FROM ASKING APPLICANTS ABOUT THEIR RELIGIOUS BELIEFS?
YOU ARE RIGHT, HIJO. BUT IN THE CASE OF MR. KUH-TO, NOTHING ILLEGAL ABOUT WANTING TO TALK ABOUT HIS FAVORITE LEFTOVER EVERY NOW AND THEN.

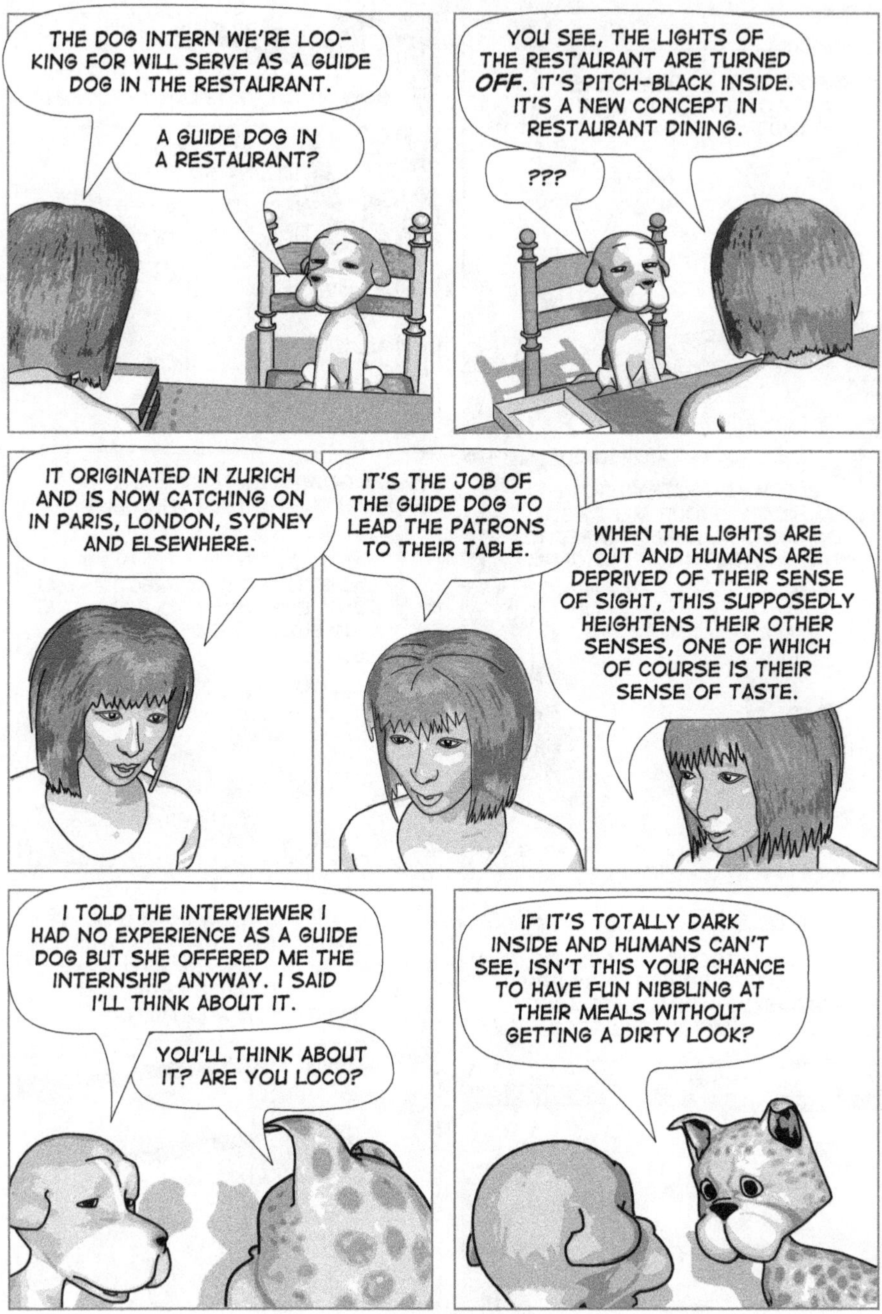
THE DOG INTERN WE'RE LOO-KING FOR WILL SERVE AS A GUIDE DOG IN THE RESTAURANT.
A GUIDE DOG IN A RESTAURANT?
YOU SEE, THE LIGHTS OF THE RESTAURANT ARE TURNED OFF. IT'S PITCH-BLACK INSIDE. IT'S A NEW CONCEPT IN RESTAURANT DINING.
???
IT ORIGINATED IN ZURICH AND IS NOW CATCHING ON IN PARIS, LONDON, SYDNEY AND ELSEWHERE.
IT'S THE JOB OF THE GUIDE DOG TO LEAD THE PATRONS TO THEIR TABLE.
WHEN THE LIGHTS ARE OUT AND HUMANS ARE DEPRIVED OF THEIR SENSE OF SIGHT, THIS SUPPOSEDLY HEIGHTENS THEIR OTHER SENSES, ONE OF WHICH OF COURSE IS THEIR SENSE OF TASTE.
I TOLD THE INTERVIEWER I HAD NO EXPERIENCE AS A GUIDE DOG BUT SHE OFFERED ME THE INTERNSHIP ANYWAY. I SAID I'LL THINK ABOUT IT.
YOU'LL THINK ABOUT IT? ARE YOU LOCO?
IF IT'S TOTALLY DARK INSIDE AND HUMANS CAN'T SEE, ISN'T THIS YOUR CHANCE TO HAVE FUN NIBBLING AT THEIR MEALS WITHOUT GETTING A DIRTY LOOK?

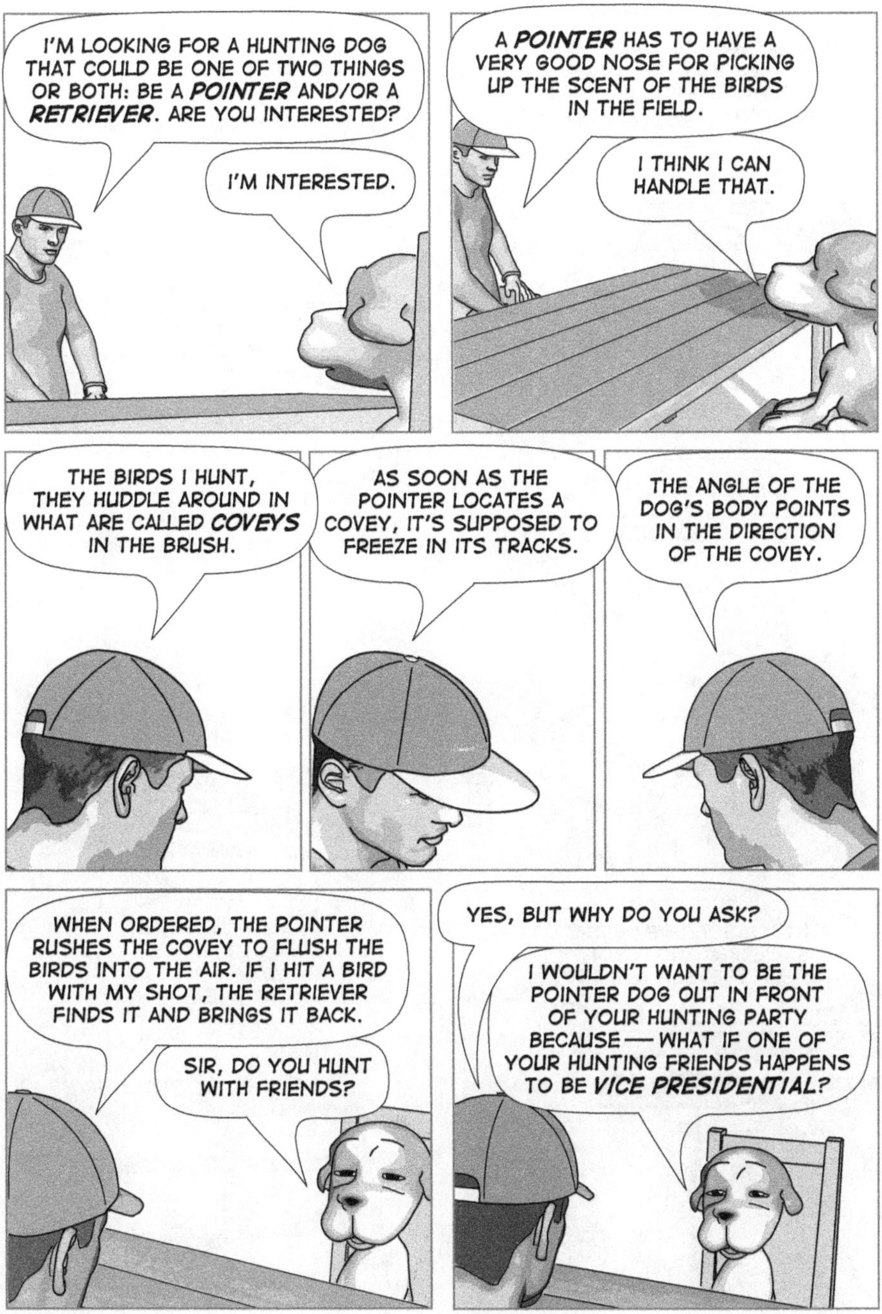
I'M LOOKING FOR A HUNTING DOG THAT COULD BE ONE OF TWO THINGS OR BOTH: BE A *POINTER* AND/OR A *RETRIEVER*. ARE YOU INTERESTED?
I'M INTERESTED.
A *POINTER* HAS TO HAVE A VERY GOOD NOSE FOR PICKING UP THE SCENT OF THE BIRDS IN THE FIELD.
I THINK I CAN HANDLE THAT.
THE BIRDS I HUNT, THEY HUDDLE AROUND IN WHAT ARE CALLED *COVEYS* IN THE BRUSH.
AS SOON AS THE POINTER LOCATES A COVEY, IT'S SUPPOSED TO FREEZE IN ITS TRACKS.
THE ANGLE OF THE DOG'S BODY POINTS IN THE DIRECTION OF THE COVEY.
WHEN ORDERED, THE POINTER RUSHES THE COVEY TO FLUSH THE BIRDS INTO THE AIR. IF I HIT A BIRD WITH MY SHOT, THE RETRIEVER FINDS IT AND BRINGS IT BACK.
SIR, DO YOU HUNT WITH FRIENDS?
YES, BUT WHY DO YOU ASK?
I WOULDN'T WANT TO BE THE POINTER DOG OUT IN FRONT OF YOUR HUNTING PARTY BECAUSE — WHAT IF ONE OF YOUR HUNTING FRIENDS HAPPENS TO BE *VICE PRESIDENTIAL*?

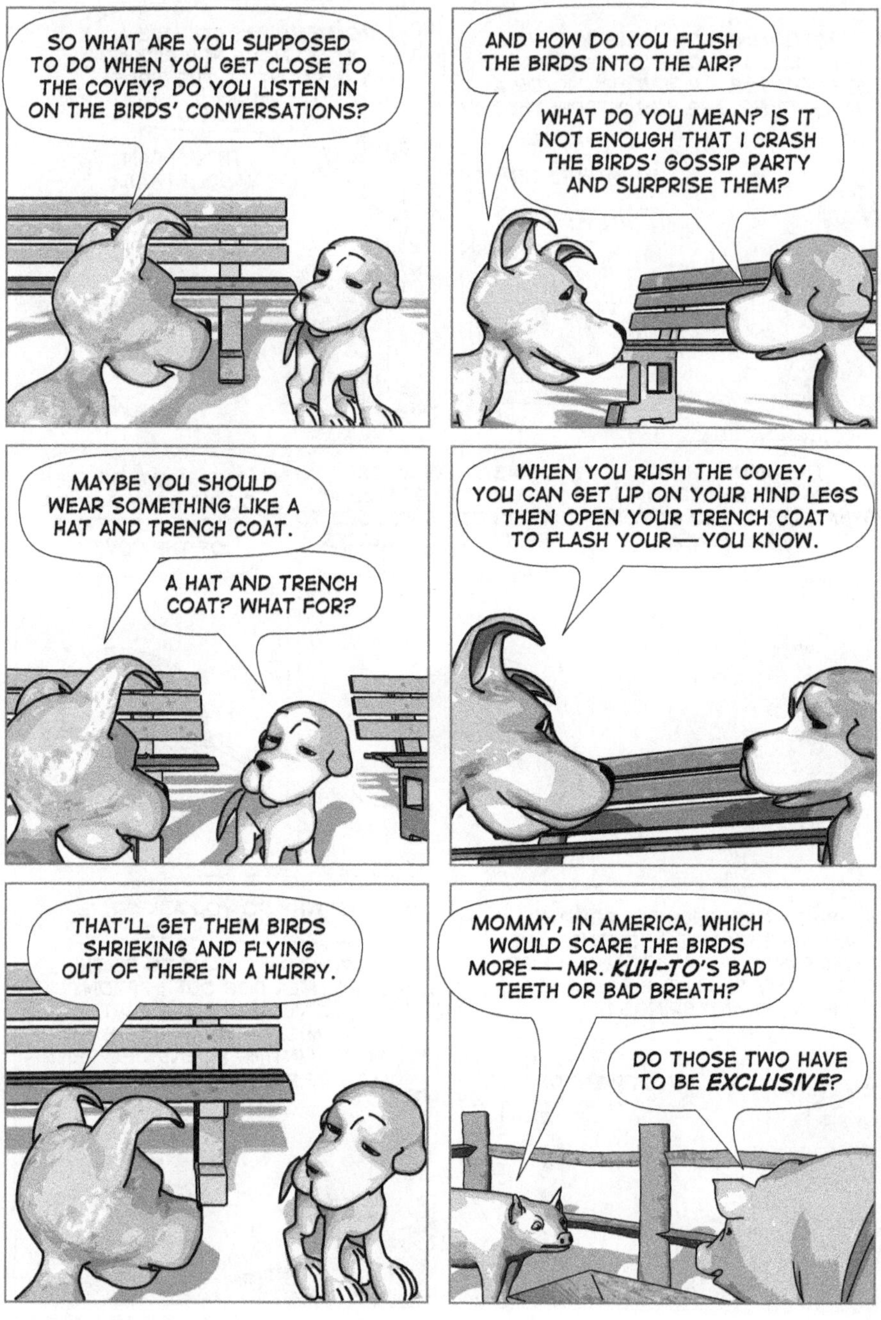
SO WHAT ARE YOU SUPPOSED TO DO WHEN YOU GET CLOSE TO THE COVEY? DO YOU LISTEN IN ON THE BIRDS' CONVERSATIONS?
AND HOW DO YOU FLUSH THE BIRDS INTO THE AIR?
WHAT DO YOU MEAN? IS IT NOT ENOUGH THAT I CRASH THE BIRDS' GOSSIP PARTY AND SURPRISE THEM?
MAYBE YOU SHOULD WEAR SOMETHING LIKE A HAT AND TRENCH COAT.
A HAT AND TRENCH COAT? WHAT FOR?
WHEN YOU RUSH THE COVEY, YOU CAN GET UP ON YOUR HIND LEGS THEN OPEN YOUR TRENCH COAT TO FLASH YOUR—YOU KNOW.
THAT'LL GET THEM BIRDS SHRIEKING AND FLYING OUT OF THERE IN A HURRY.
MOMMY, IN AMERICA, WHICH WOULD SCARE THE BIRDS MORE—MR. *KUH-TO*'S BAD TEETH OR BAD BREATH?
DO THOSE TWO HAVE TO BE ***EXCLUSIVE***?

WHY DID YOU LEAVE YOUR LAST JOB?

MY MASTER WANTED TO MAKE A CHANGE AND MOVE IN A DIFFERENT DIRECTION. THAT'S WHY I'M AVAILABLE.

I'M CURIOUS ABOUT YOUR FORMER MASTER. WHAT WAS HE, OR SHE, BY PROFESSION?

A PROFESSIONAL *RACE CAR* DRIVER.

AND THAT'S WHAT THREW ME FOR A LOOP.

I KEPT ASKING MYSELF AFTER I LEFT: WAS HE REALLY SERIOUS ABOUT LOOKING TO *CHANGE* DIRECTIONS, YOU KNOW, TAKING THE ROAD LESS TRAVELED?

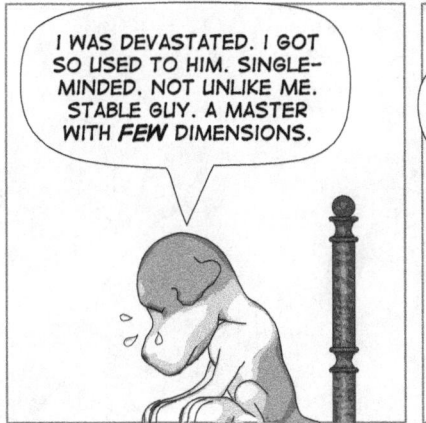

I WAS DEVASTATED. I GOT SO USED TO HIM. SINGLE-MINDED. NOT UNLIKE ME. STABLE GUY. A MASTER WITH *FEW* DIMENSIONS.

FEWER STILL WHEN IT CAME TO RACING.

WHY CHANGE NOW? IT'S ALWAYS BEEN *LEFT*, *LEFT*, GO *LEFT*.

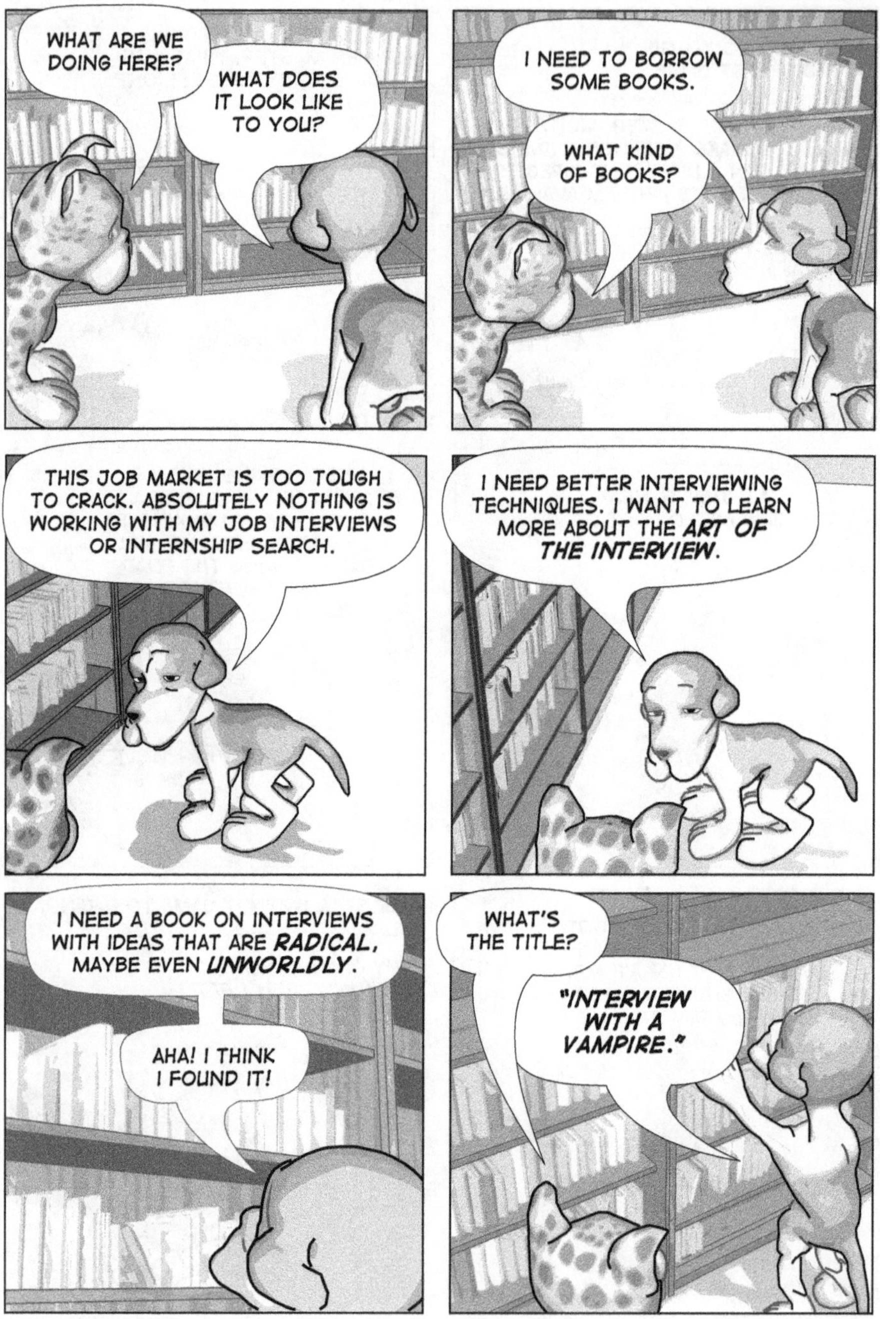
WHAT ARE WE DOING HERE?
WHAT DOES IT LOOK LIKE TO YOU?
I NEED TO BORROW SOME BOOKS.
WHAT KIND OF BOOKS?
THIS JOB MARKET IS TOO TOUGH TO CRACK. ABSOLUTELY NOTHING IS WORKING WITH MY JOB INTERVIEWS OR INTERNSHIP SEARCH.
I NEED BETTER INTERVIEWING TECHNIQUES. I WANT TO LEARN MORE ABOUT THE ***ART OF THE INTERVIEW***.
I NEED A BOOK ON INTERVIEWS WITH IDEAS THAT ARE ***RADICAL***, MAYBE EVEN ***UNWORLDLY***.
AHA! I THINK I FOUND IT!
WHAT'S THE TITLE?
"INTERVIEW WITH A VAMPIRE."

Soft Skills

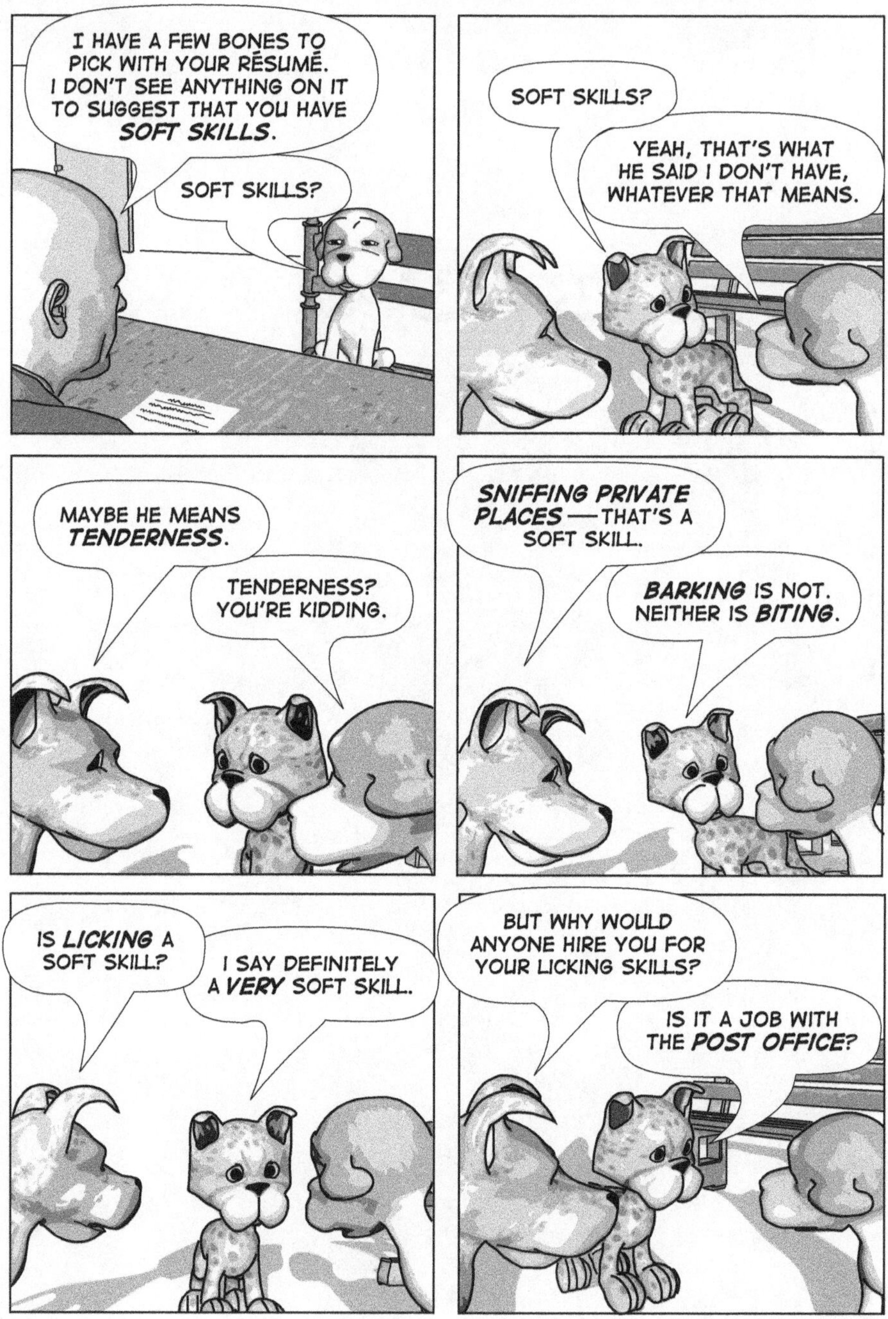
I HAVE A FEW BONES TO PICK WITH YOUR RÉSUMÉ. I DON'T SEE ANYTHING ON IT TO SUGGEST THAT YOU HAVE *SOFT SKILLS*.
SOFT SKILLS?
SOFT SKILLS?
YEAH, THAT'S WHAT HE SAID I DON'T HAVE, WHATEVER THAT MEANS.
MAYBE HE MEANS *TENDERNESS*.
TENDERNESS? YOU'RE KIDDING.
SNIFFING PRIVATE PLACES—THAT'S A SOFT SKILL.
BARKING IS NOT. NEITHER IS *BITING*.
IS *LICKING* A SOFT SKILL?
I SAY DEFINITELY A *VERY* SOFT SKILL.
BUT WHY WOULD ANYONE HIRE YOU FOR YOUR LICKING SKILLS?
IS IT A JOB WITH THE *POST OFFICE*?

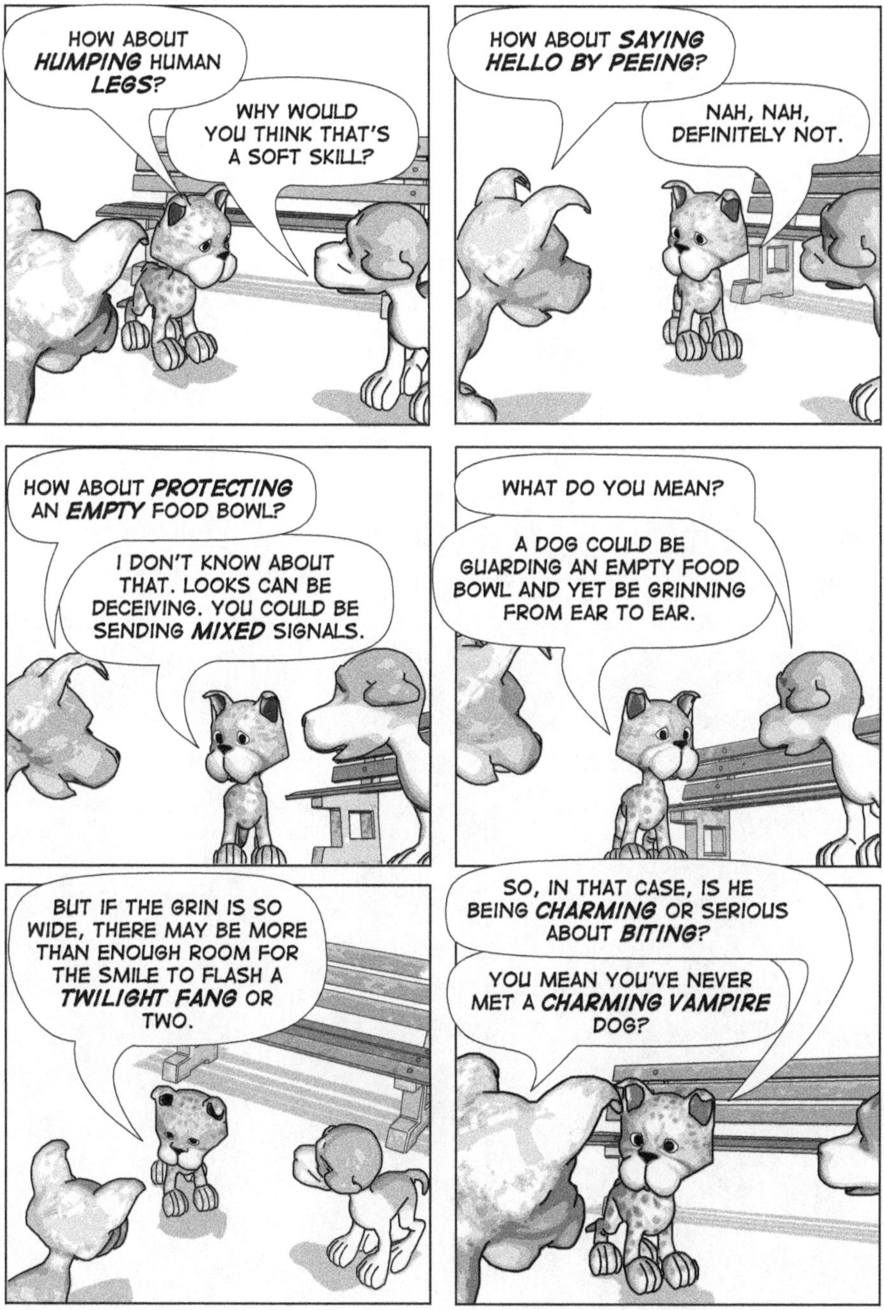
HOW ABOUT *HUMPING* HUMAN *LEGS?*
WHY WOULD YOU THINK THAT'S A SOFT SKILL?
HOW ABOUT *SAYING HELLO BY PEEING?*
NAH, NAH, DEFINITELY NOT.
HOW ABOUT *PROTECTING* AN *EMPTY* FOOD BOWL?
I DON'T KNOW ABOUT THAT. LOOKS CAN BE DECEIVING. YOU COULD BE SENDING *MIXED* SIGNALS.
WHAT DO YOU MEAN?
A DOG COULD BE GUARDING AN EMPTY FOOD BOWL AND YET BE GRINNING FROM EAR TO EAR.
BUT IF THE GRIN IS SO WIDE, THERE MAY BE MORE THAN ENOUGH ROOM FOR THE SMILE TO FLASH A *TWILIGHT FANG* OR TWO.
SO, IN THAT CASE, IS HE BEING *CHARMING* OR SERIOUS ABOUT *BITING?*
YOU MEAN YOU'VE NEVER MET A *CHARMING VAMPIRE* DOG?

The Rise of Dead Résumés

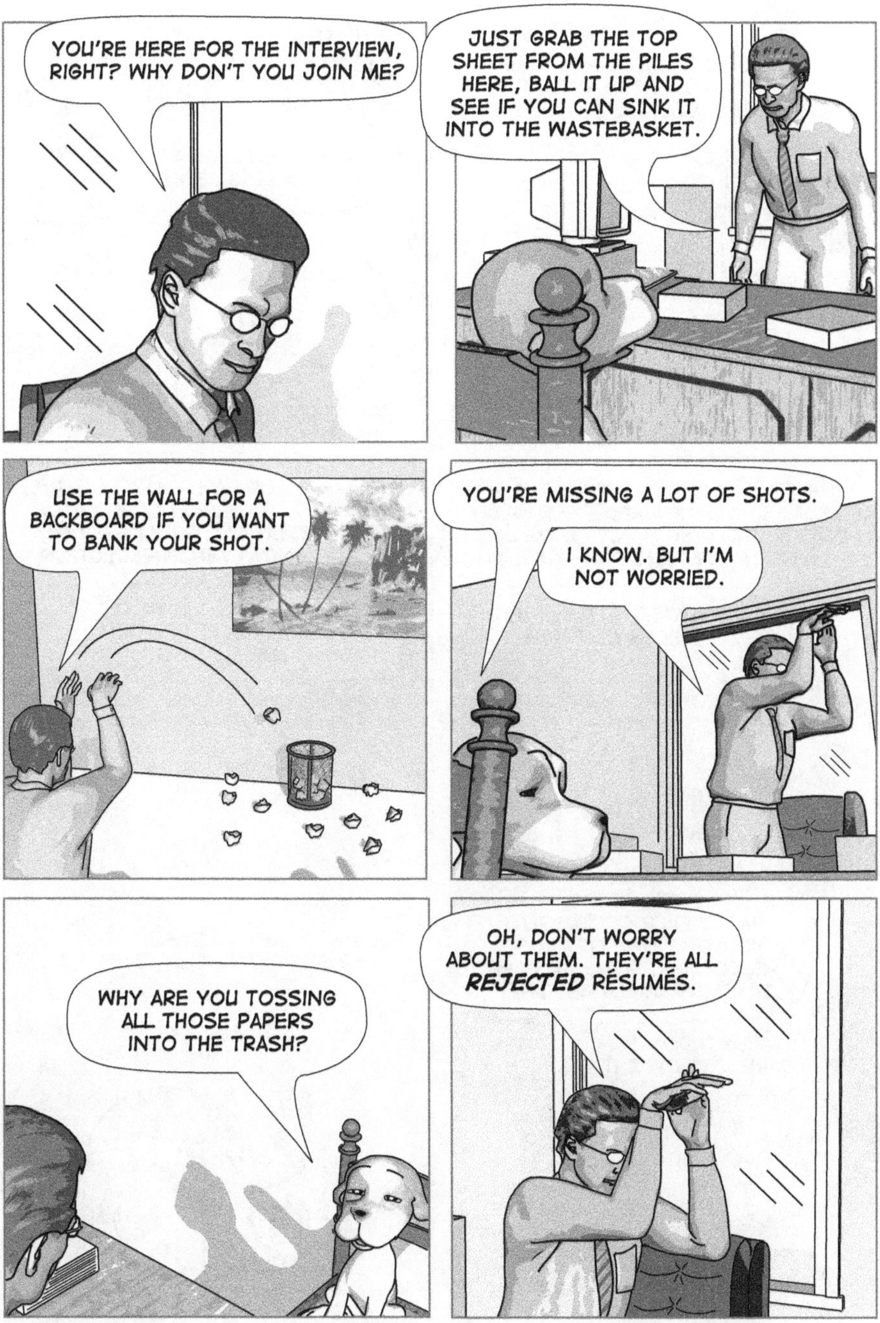
YOU'RE HERE FOR THE INTERVIEW, RIGHT? WHY DON'T YOU JOIN ME?
JUST GRAB THE TOP SHEET FROM THE PILES HERE, BALL IT UP AND SEE IF YOU CAN SINK IT INTO THE WASTEBASKET.
USE THE WALL FOR A BACKBOARD IF YOU WANT TO BANK YOUR SHOT.
YOU'RE MISSING A LOT OF SHOTS.
I KNOW. BUT I'M NOT WORRIED.
WHY ARE YOU TOSSING ALL THOSE PAPERS INTO THE TRASH?
OH, DON'T WORRY ABOUT THEM. THEY'RE ALL *REJECTED* RÉSUMÉS.

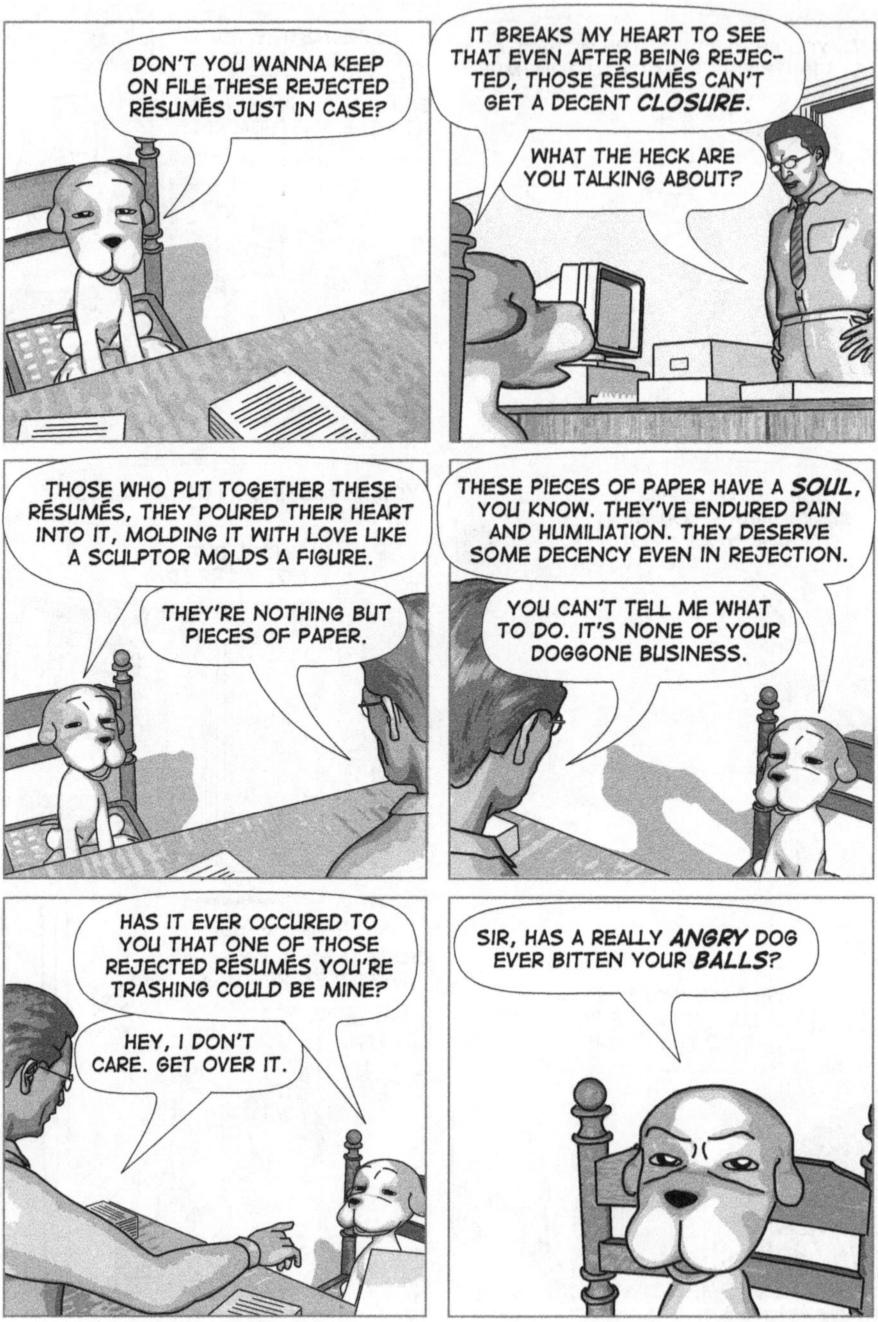
DON'T YOU WANNA KEEP ON FILE THESE REJECTED RÉSUMÉS JUST IN CASE?
IT BREAKS MY HEART TO SEE THAT EVEN AFTER BEING REJEC-TED, THOSE RÉSUMÉS CAN'T GET A DECENT CLOSURE.
WHAT THE HECK ARE YOU TALKING ABOUT?
THOSE WHO PUT TOGETHER THESE RÉSUMÉS, THEY POURED THEIR HEART INTO IT, MOLDING IT WITH LOVE LIKE A SCULPTOR MOLDS A FIGURE.
THEY'RE NOTHING BUT PIECES OF PAPER.
THESE PIECES OF PAPER HAVE A SOUL, YOU KNOW. THEY'VE ENDURED PAIN AND HUMILIATION. THEY DESERVE SOME DECENCY EVEN IN REJECTION.
YOU CAN'T TELL ME WHAT TO DO. IT'S NONE OF YOUR DOGGONE BUSINESS.
HAS IT EVER OCCURED TO YOU THAT ONE OF THOSE REJECTED RÉSUMÉS YOU'RE TRASHING COULD BE MINE?
HEY, I DON'T CARE. GET OVER IT.
SIR, HAS A REALLY ANGRY DOG EVER BITTEN YOUR BALLS?

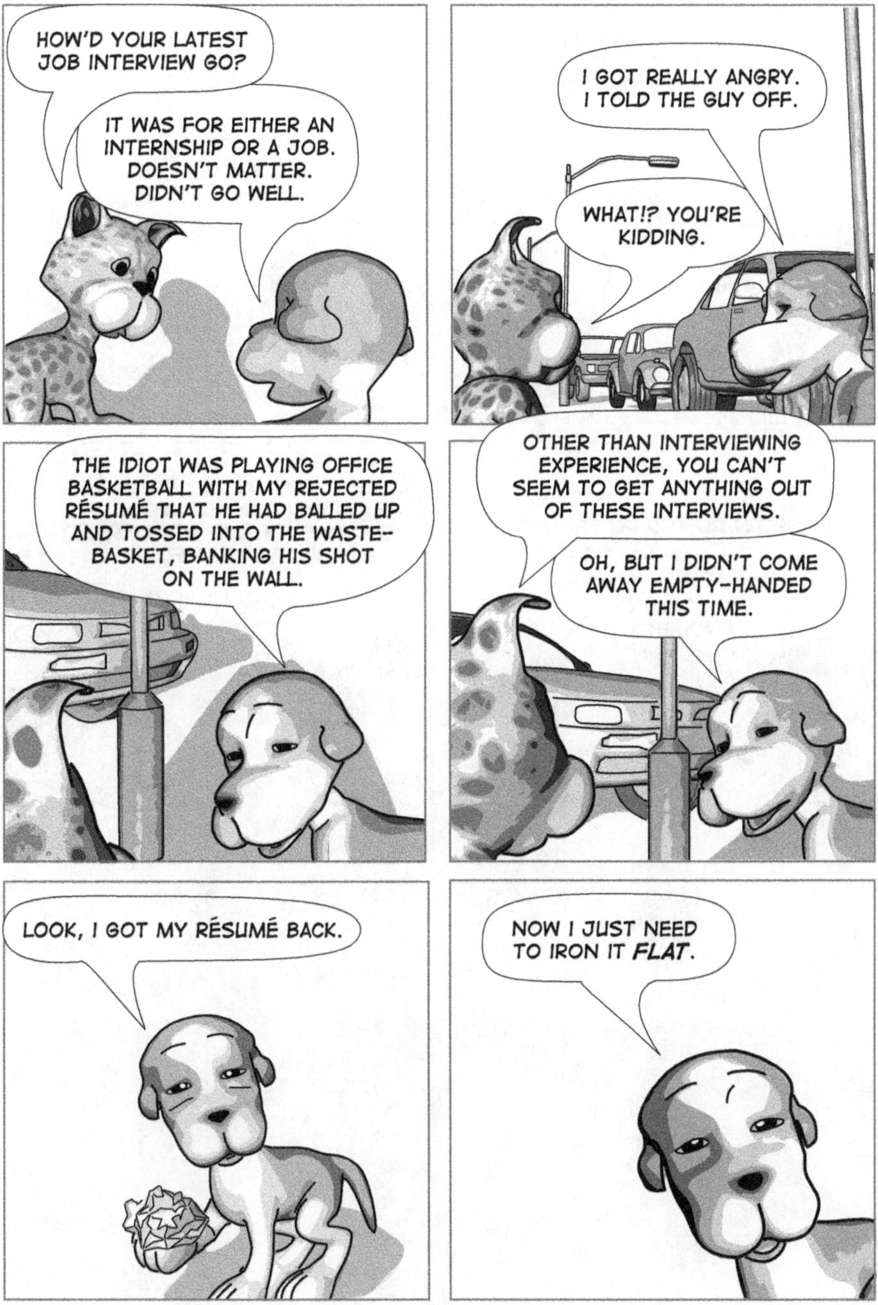
HOW'D YOUR LATEST JOB INTERVIEW GO?
IT WAS FOR EITHER AN INTERNSHIP OR A JOB. DOESN'T MATTER. DIDN'T GO WELL.
I GOT REALLY ANGRY. I TOLD THE GUY OFF.
WHAT!? YOU'RE KIDDING.
THE IDIOT WAS PLAYING OFFICE BASKETBALL WITH MY REJECTED RÉSUMÉ THAT HE HAD BALLED UP AND TOSSED INTO THE WASTE-BASKET, BANKING HIS SHOT ON THE WALL.
OTHER THAN INTERVIEWING EXPERIENCE, YOU CAN'T SEEM TO GET ANYTHING OUT OF THESE INTERVIEWS.
OH, BUT I DIDN'T COME AWAY EMPTY-HANDED THIS TIME.
LOOK, I GOT MY RÉSUMÉ BACK.
NOW I JUST NEED TO IRON IT *FLAT*.

ISN'T IT PRETTY UNUSUAL FOR A REJECTED RÉSUMÉ TO BE RETURNED TO THE APPLICANT?
WELL, YEAH. BUT I DON'T SEE ANYTHING WRONG WITH ASKING FOR IT BACK.
HOW OFTEN DO YOU DO THAT?
NOT OFTEN ENOUGH.
IF I SEND OUT MY RÉSUMÉ BY MAIL, I MAKE IT A POINT TO ENCLOSE A ***SELF-ADDRESSED STAMPED ENVELOPE***.

OH, C'MON. YOU ENCLOSE AN *SASE* EVERY TIME YOU MAIL OUT A COPY OF YOUR RÉSUMÉ?

THAT'S RIGHT, DUDE.

BUT DIDN'T YOU TELL ME THAT YOU DON'T HAVE A REAL MAILING ADDRESS?

I DID? WELL, MY MOM AND I, WE DO HAVE A MAILING ADDRESS. SORT OF. IT'S CARE OF APARTMENT BUILDING 709 C, BACKSTREET ALLEY.

SO IF YOU MAIL ME SOMETHING USING THAT ADDRESS, I'LL GET IT.

JUST MAKE SURE TO INSERT SOMEWHERE IN THE MAILING ADDRESS THE LINE "BY THE BIG RED DUMPSTER."

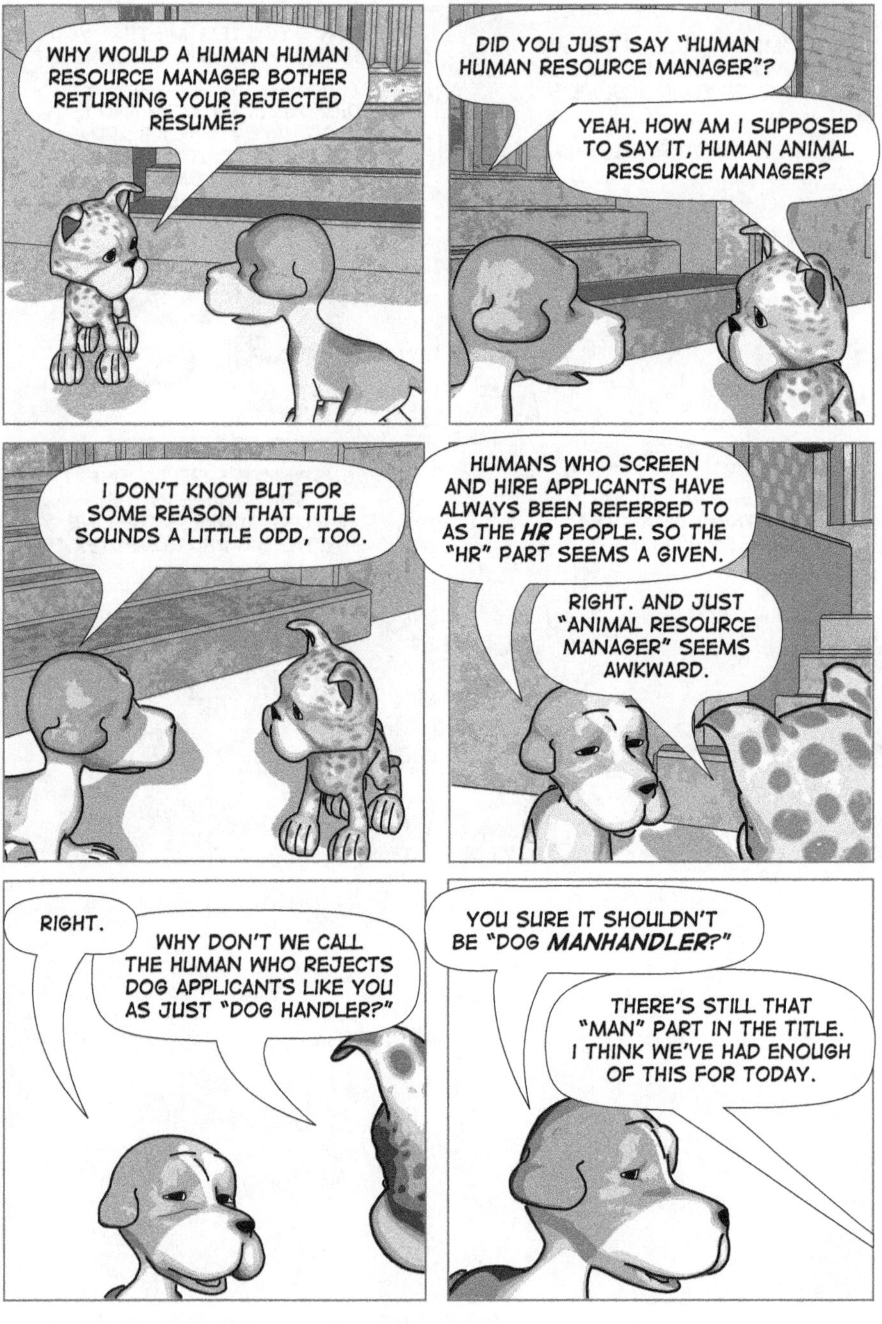
WHY WOULD A HUMAN HUMAN RESOURCE MANAGER BOTHER RETURNING YOUR REJECTED RÉSUMÉ?
DID YOU JUST SAY "HUMAN HUMAN RESOURCE MANAGER"?
YEAH. HOW AM I SUPPOSED TO SAY IT, HUMAN ANIMAL RESOURCE MANAGER?
I DON'T KNOW BUT FOR SOME REASON THAT TITLE SOUNDS A LITTLE ODD, TOO.
HUMANS WHO SCREEN AND HIRE APPLICANTS HAVE ALWAYS BEEN REFERRED TO AS THE HR PEOPLE. SO THE "HR" PART SEEMS A GIVEN.
RIGHT. AND JUST "ANIMAL RESOURCE MANAGER" SEEMS AWKWARD.
RIGHT.
WHY DON'T WE CALL THE HUMAN WHO REJECTS DOG APPLICANTS LIKE YOU AS JUST "DOG HANDLER?"
YOU SURE IT SHOULDN'T BE "DOG MANHANDLER?"
THERE'S STILL THAT "MAN" PART IN THE TITLE. I THINK WE'VE HAD ENOUGH OF THIS FOR TODAY.

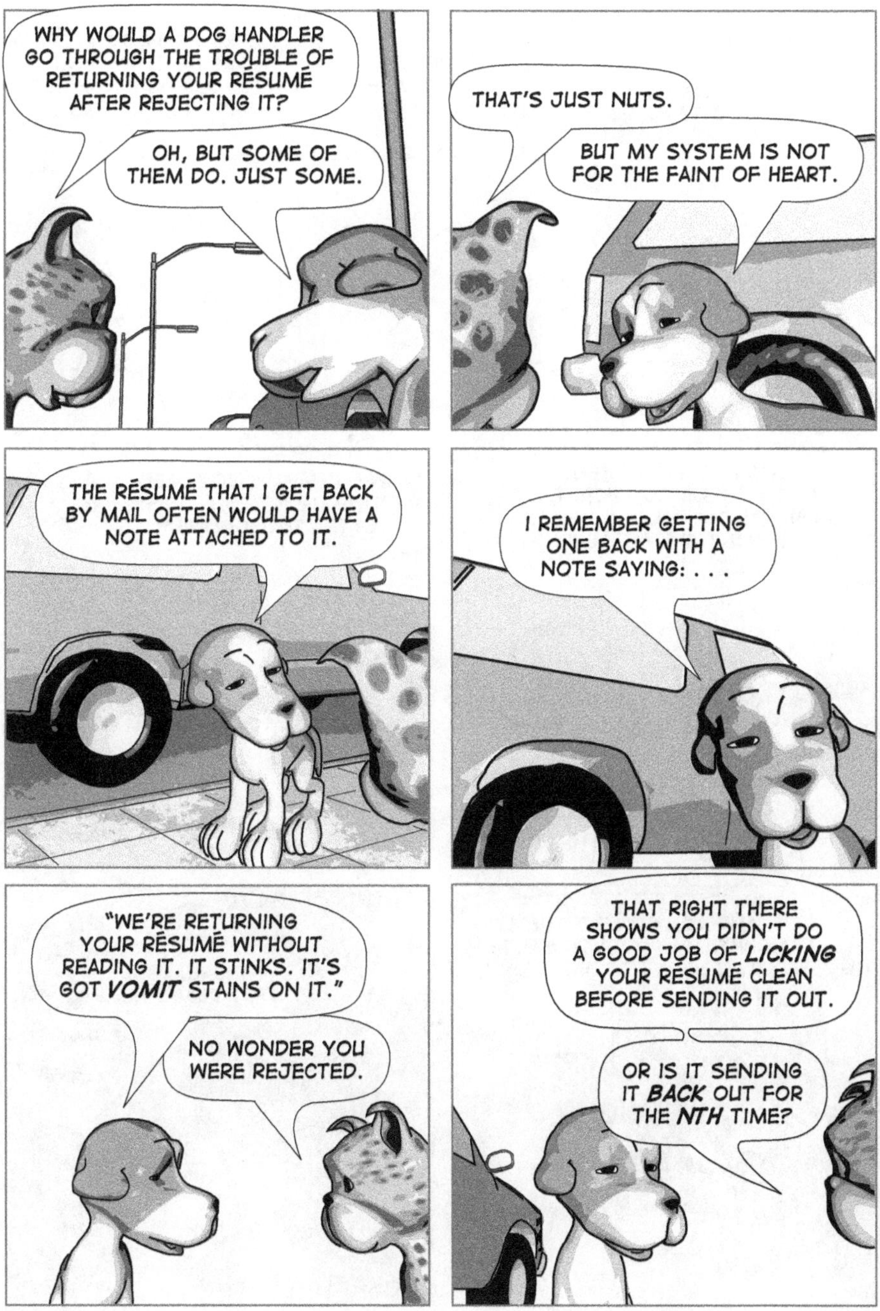
WHY WOULD A DOG HANDLER GO THROUGH THE TROUBLE OF RETURNING YOUR RÉSUMÉ AFTER REJECTING IT?
OH, BUT SOME OF THEM DO. JUST SOME.
THAT'S JUST NUTS.
BUT MY SYSTEM IS NOT FOR THE FAINT OF HEART.
THE RÉSUMÉ THAT I GET BACK BY MAIL OFTEN WOULD HAVE A NOTE ATTACHED TO IT.
I REMEMBER GETTING ONE BACK WITH A NOTE SAYING: . . .
"WE'RE RETURNING YOUR RÉSUMÉ WITHOUT READING IT. IT STINKS. IT'S GOT *VOMIT* STAINS ON IT."
NO WONDER YOU WERE REJECTED.
THAT RIGHT THERE SHOWS YOU DIDN'T DO A GOOD JOB OF *LICKING* YOUR RÉSUMÉ CLEAN BEFORE SENDING IT OUT.
OR IS IT SENDING IT *BACK* OUT FOR THE *NTH* TIME?

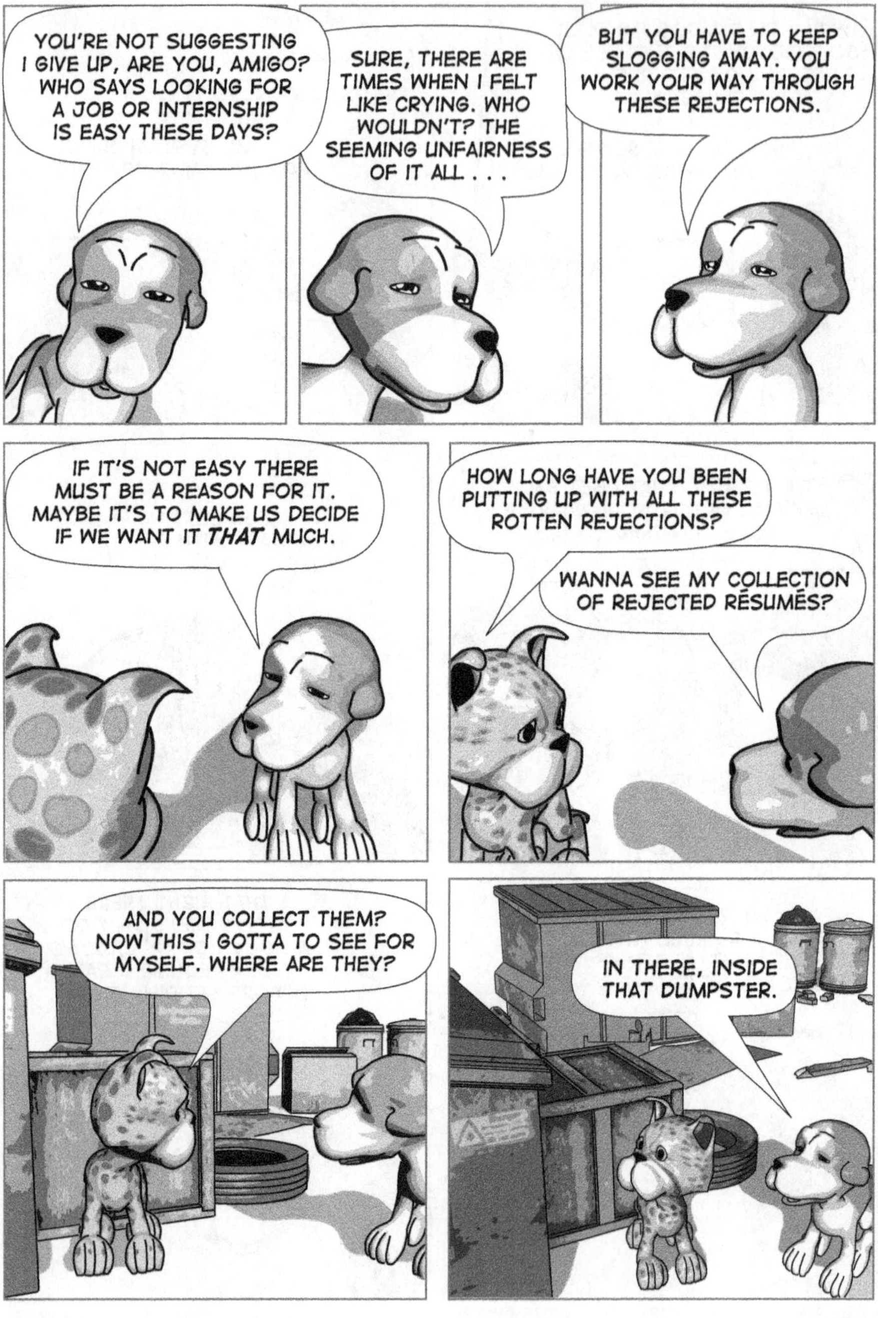
YOU'RE NOT SUGGESTING I GIVE UP, ARE YOU, AMIGO? WHO SAYS LOOKING FOR A JOB OR INTERNSHIP IS EASY THESE DAYS?
SURE, THERE ARE TIMES WHEN I FELT LIKE CRYING. WHO WOULDN'T? THE SEEMING UNFAIRNESS OF IT ALL . . .
BUT YOU HAVE TO KEEP SLOGGING AWAY. YOU WORK YOUR WAY THROUGH THESE REJECTIONS.
IF IT'S NOT EASY THERE MUST BE A REASON FOR IT. MAYBE IT'S TO MAKE US DECIDE IF WE WANT IT *THAT* MUCH.
HOW LONG HAVE YOU BEEN PUTTING UP WITH ALL THESE ROTTEN REJECTIONS?
WANNA SEE MY COLLECTION OF REJECTED RÉSUMÉS?
AND YOU COLLECT THEM? NOW THIS I GOTTA TO SEE FOR MYSELF. WHERE ARE THEY?
IN THERE, INSIDE THAT DUMPSTER.

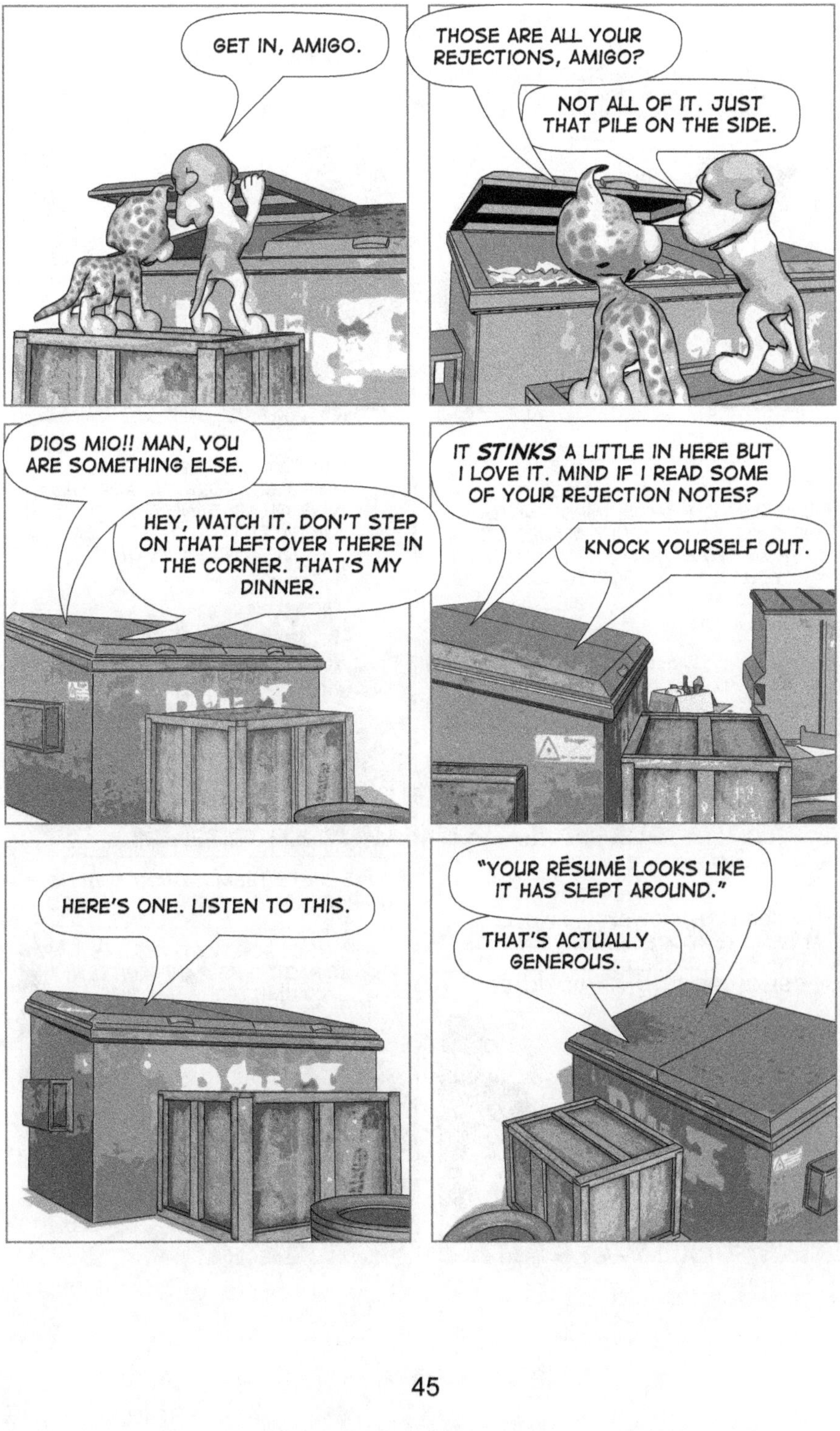
GET IN, AMIGO.
THOSE ARE ALL YOUR REJECTIONS, AMIGO?
NOT ALL OF IT. JUST THAT PILE ON THE SIDE.
DIOS MIO!! MAN, YOU ARE SOMETHING ELSE.
HEY, WATCH IT. DON'T STEP ON THAT LEFTOVER THERE IN THE CORNER. THAT'S MY DINNER.
IT *STINKS* A LITTLE IN HERE BUT I LOVE IT. MIND IF I READ SOME OF YOUR REJECTION NOTES?
KNOCK YOURSELF OUT.
HERE'S ONE. LISTEN TO THIS.
"YOUR RÉSUMÉ LOOKS LIKE IT HAS SLEPT AROUND."
THAT'S ACTUALLY GENEROUS.

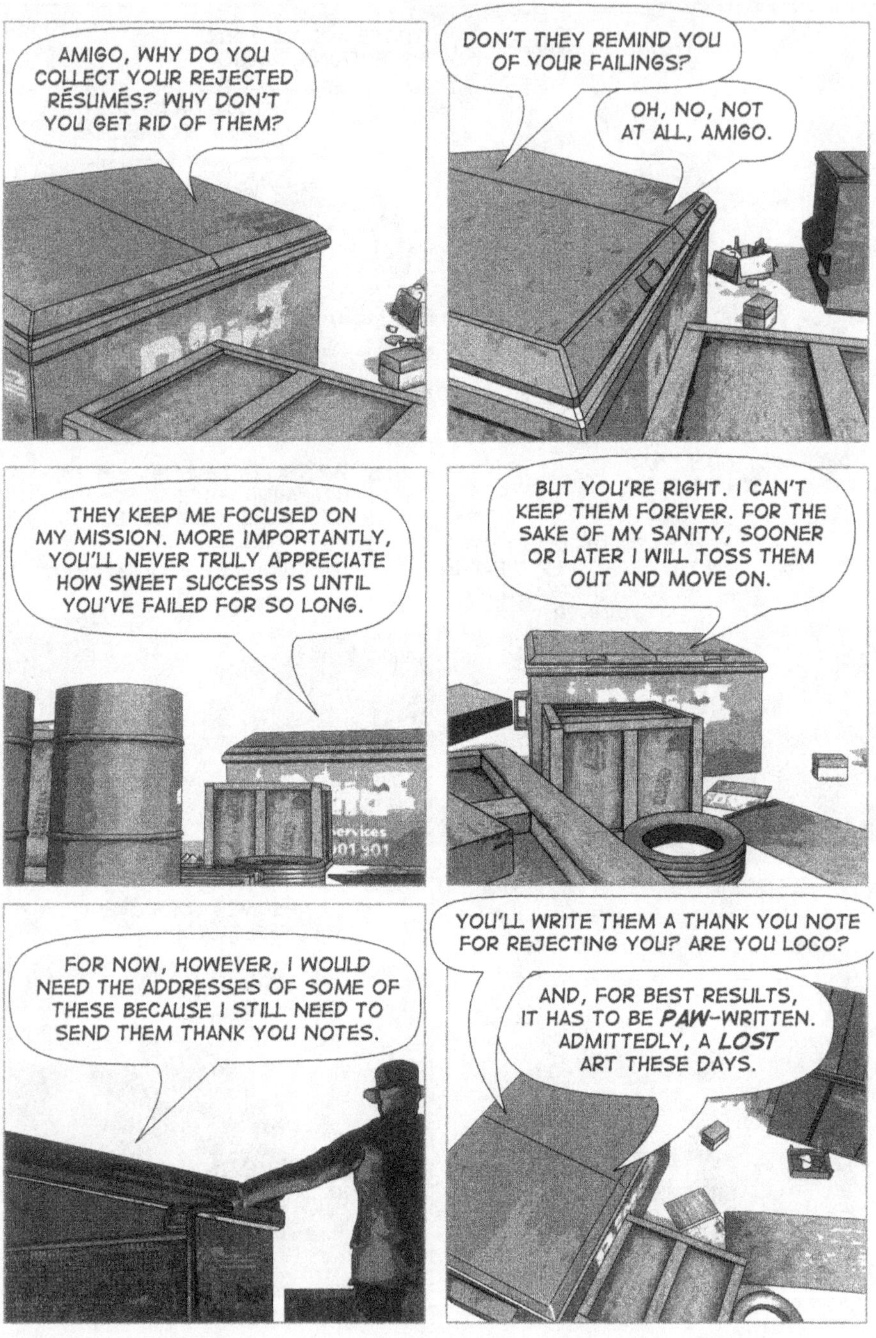
AMIGO, WHY DO YOU COLLECT YOUR REJECTED RÉSUMÉS? WHY DON'T YOU GET RID OF THEM?
DON'T THEY REMIND YOU OF YOUR FAILINGS?
OH, NO, NOT AT ALL, AMIGO.
THEY KEEP ME FOCUSED ON MY MISSION. MORE IMPORTANTLY, YOU'LL NEVER TRULY APPRECIATE HOW SWEET SUCCESS IS UNTIL YOU'VE FAILED FOR SO LONG.
BUT YOU'RE RIGHT. I CAN'T KEEP THEM FOREVER. FOR THE SAKE OF MY SANITY, SOONER OR LATER I WILL TOSS THEM OUT AND MOVE ON.
FOR NOW, HOWEVER, I WOULD NEED THE ADDRESSES OF SOME OF THESE BECAUSE I STILL NEED TO SEND THEM THANK YOU NOTES.
YOU'LL WRITE THEM A THANK YOU NOTE FOR REJECTING YOU? ARE YOU LOCO?
AND, FOR BEST RESULTS, IT HAS TO BE ***PAW***-WRITTEN. ADMITTEDLY, A ***LOST*** ART THESE DAYS.

Cloudy, with a 30 Per Cent Chance of an Asteroid Falling

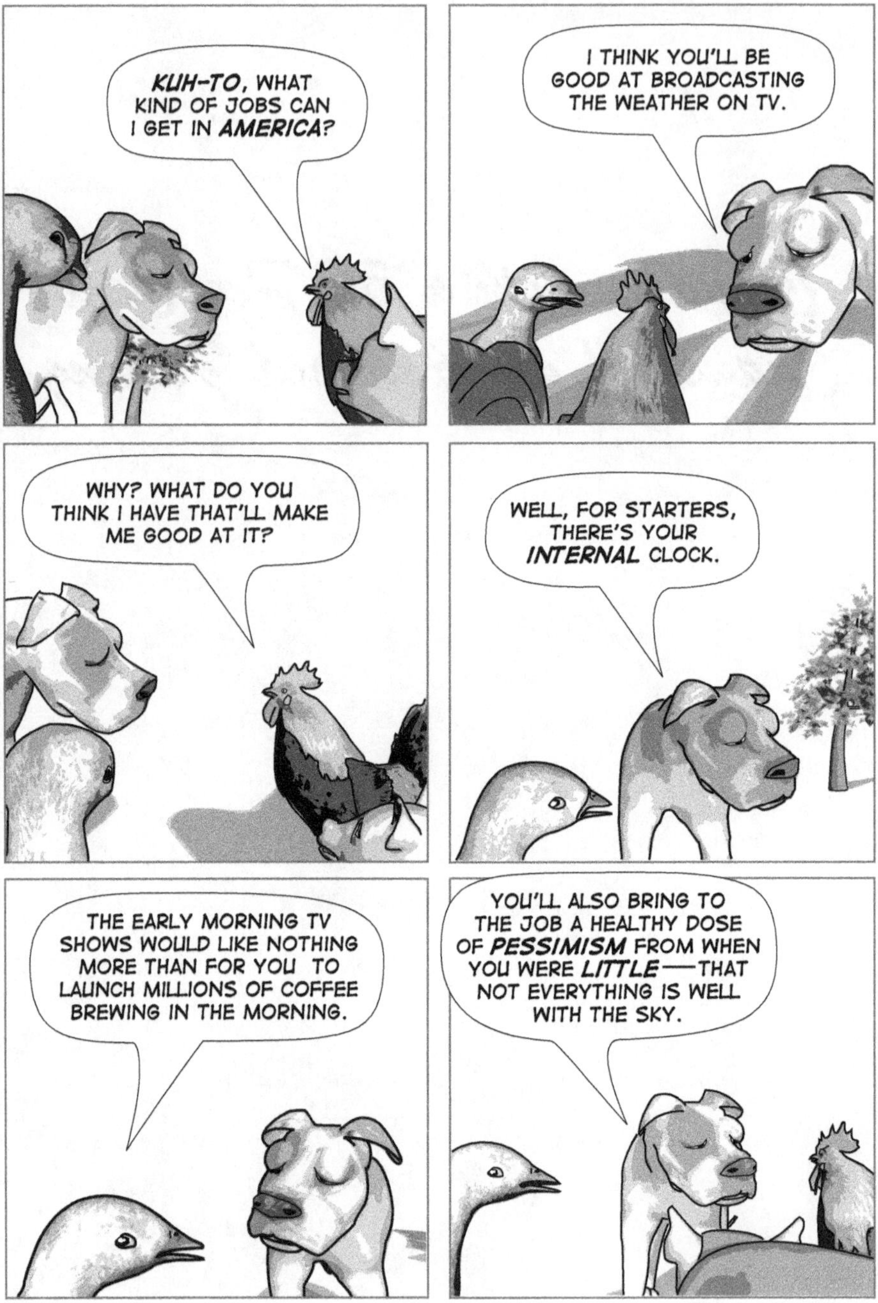
KUH-TO, WHAT KIND OF JOBS CAN I GET IN AMERICA?
I THINK YOU'LL BE GOOD AT BROADCASTING THE WEATHER ON TV.
WHY? WHAT DO YOU THINK I HAVE THAT'LL MAKE ME GOOD AT IT?
WELL, FOR STARTERS, THERE'S YOUR INTERNAL CLOCK.
THE EARLY MORNING TV SHOWS WOULD LIKE NOTHING MORE THAN FOR YOU TO LAUNCH MILLIONS OF COFFEE BREWING IN THE MORNING.
YOU'LL ALSO BRING TO THE JOB A HEALTHY DOSE OF PESSIMISM FROM WHEN YOU WERE LITTLE—THAT NOT EVERYTHING IS WELL WITH THE SKY.

Getting to Know Your Neighbor

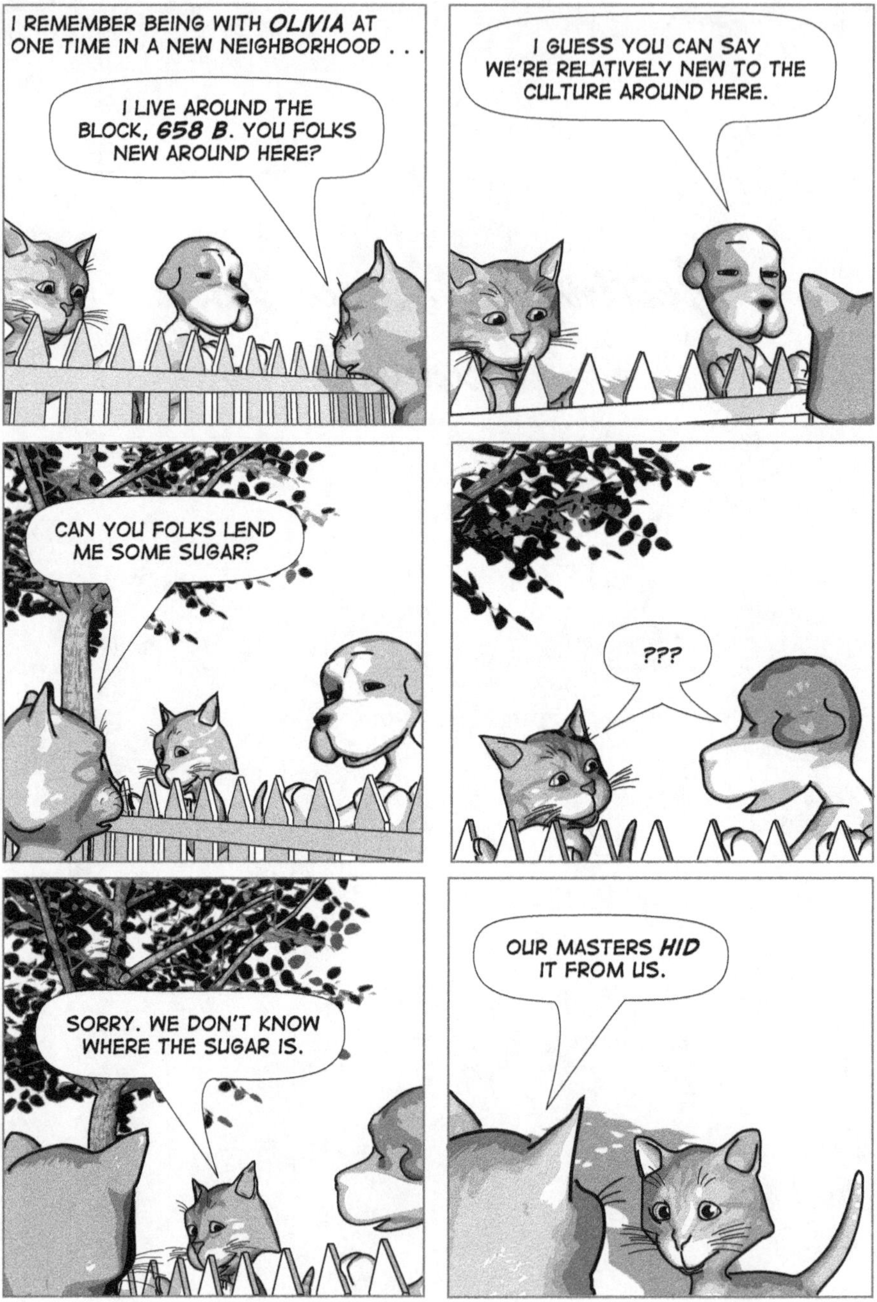
I REMEMBER BEING WITH OLIVIA AT ONE TIME IN A NEW NEIGHBORHOOD . . .
I LIVE AROUND THE BLOCK, 658 B. YOU FOLKS NEW AROUND HERE?
I GUESS YOU CAN SAY WE'RE RELATIVELY NEW TO THE CULTURE AROUND HERE.
CAN YOU FOLKS LEND ME SOME SUGAR?
???
SORRY. WE DON'T KNOW WHERE THE SUGAR IS.
OUR MASTERS HID IT FROM US.

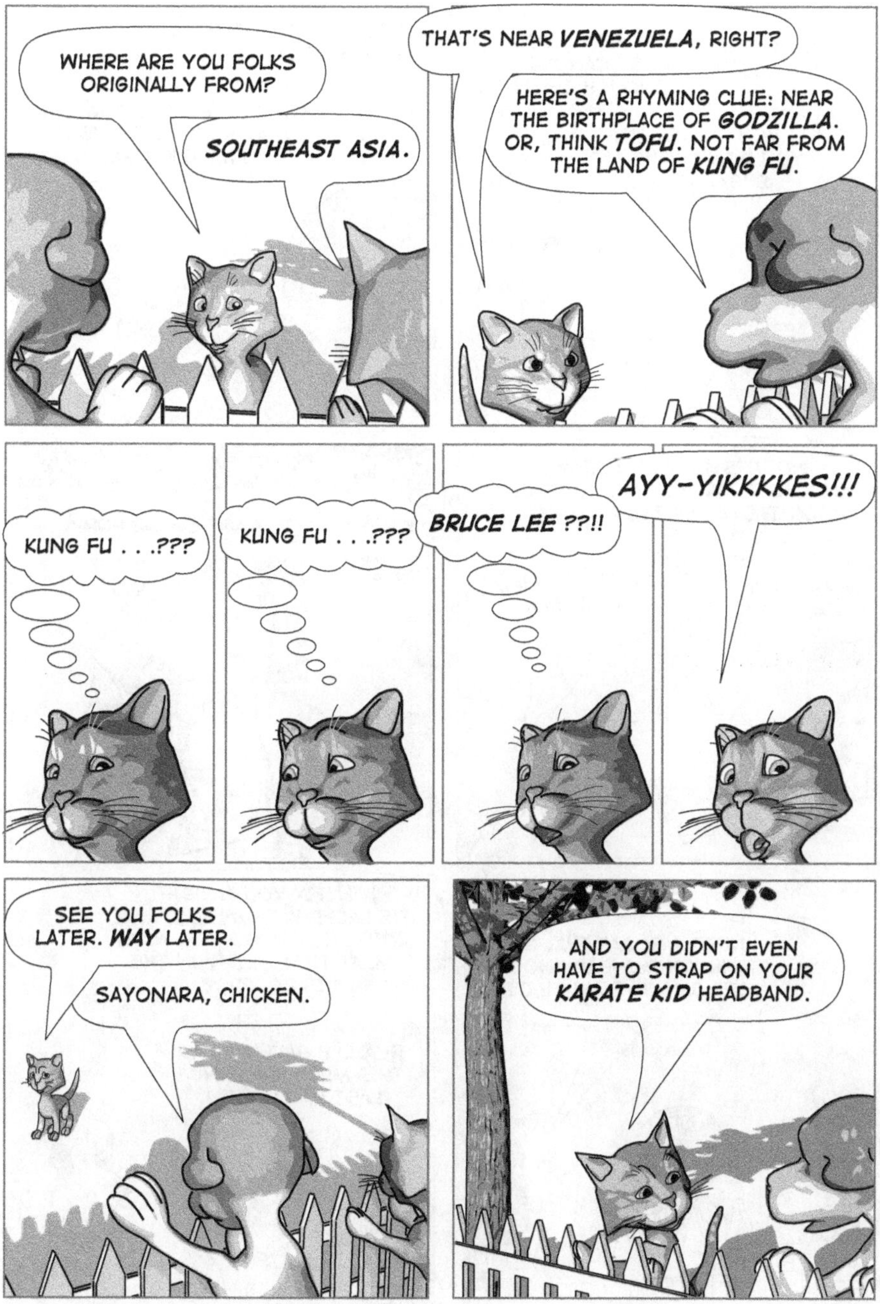
WHERE ARE YOU FOLKS ORIGINALLY FROM?
SOUTHEAST ASIA.
THAT'S NEAR VENEZUELA, RIGHT?
HERE'S A RHYMING CLUE: NEAR THE BIRTHPLACE OF GODZILLA. OR, THINK TOFU. NOT FAR FROM THE LAND OF KUNG FU.
KUNG FU . . .???
KUNG FU . . .???
BRUCE LEE ??!!
AYY-YIKKKKES!!!
SEE YOU FOLKS LATER. WAY LATER.
SAYONARA, CHICKEN.
AND YOU DIDN'T EVEN HAVE TO STRAP ON YOUR KARATE KID HEADBAND.

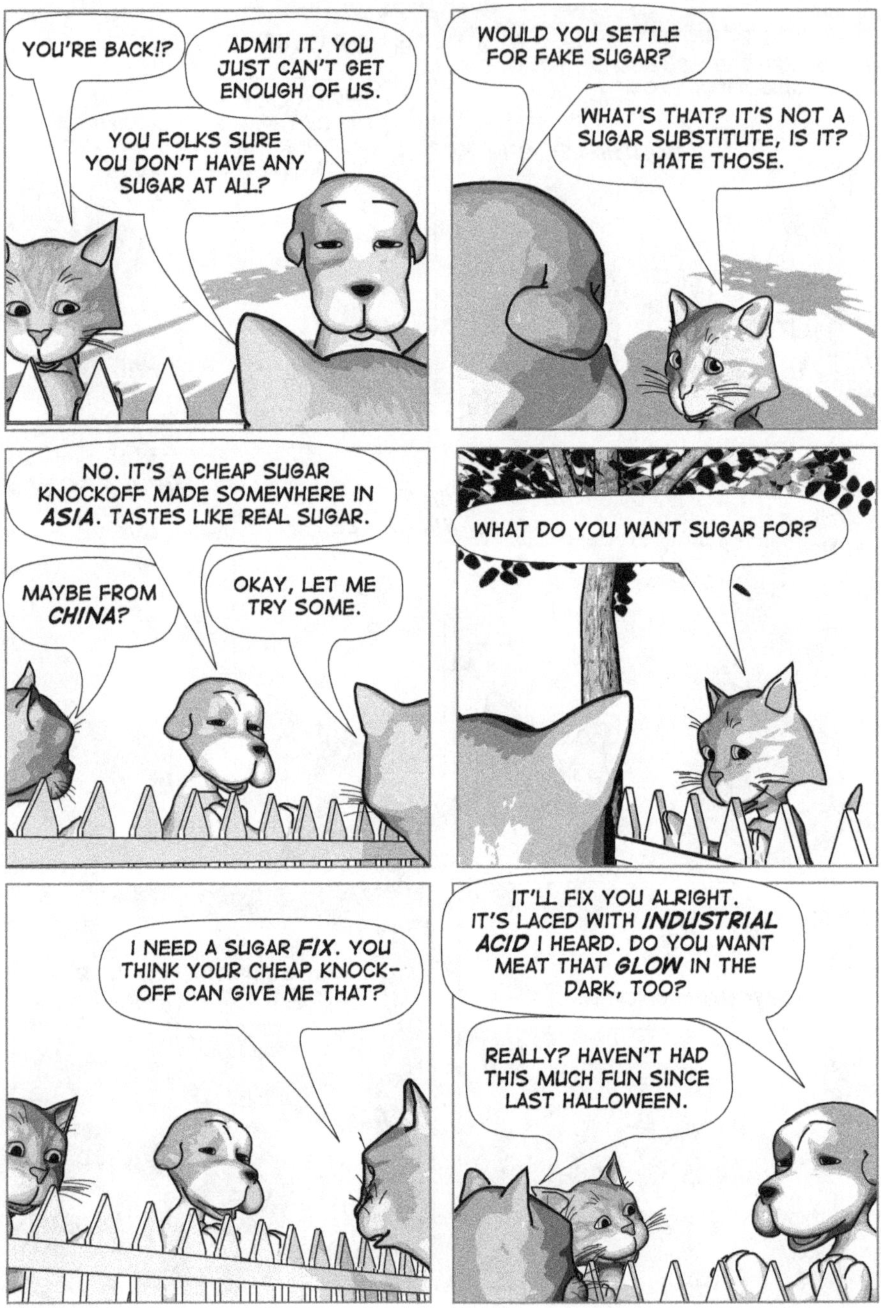

YOU'RE BACK!?
ADMIT IT. YOU JUST CAN'T GET ENOUGH OF US.
YOU FOLKS SURE YOU DON'T HAVE ANY SUGAR AT ALL?
WOULD YOU SETTLE FOR FAKE SUGAR?
WHAT'S THAT? IT'S NOT A SUGAR SUBSTITUTE, IS IT? I HATE THOSE.
NO. IT'S A CHEAP SUGAR KNOCKOFF MADE SOMEWHERE IN *ASIA*. TASTES LIKE REAL SUGAR.
MAYBE FROM *CHINA*?
OKAY, LET ME TRY SOME.
WHAT DO YOU WANT SUGAR FOR?
I NEED A SUGAR *FIX*. YOU THINK YOUR CHEAP KNOCK-OFF CAN GIVE ME THAT?
IT'LL FIX YOU ALRIGHT. IT'S LACED WITH *INDUSTRIAL ACID* I HEARD. DO YOU WANT MEAT THAT *GLOW* IN THE DARK, TOO?
REALLY? HAVEN'T HAD THIS MUCH FUN SINCE LAST HALLOWEEN.

The Allure of a PBS War Series for Pigeons

WINGPIGEON TO SQUADRON LEADER! WINGPIGEON TO SQUADRON LEADER!
REQUEST PERMISSION TO ABORT MISSION! REQUEST PERMISSION TO ABORT MISSION!
SQUADRON LEADER TO WINGPIGEON. YOU SOUND LIKE A BROKEN RECORD, LIKE A BROKEN RECORD.
WE GOT TO TURN BACK, SIR!
WHY? WHY DO YOU WANT US TO ABORT THIS BOMBING MISSION?
I FORGOT MY *KAMIKAZE* HEADBAND, SIR!

TARGETS AT SIX O'CLOCK. ZERO IN ON THE GARY LARSON BULLS-EYE.
ROGER, SQUADRON LEADER. GOT MY KAMIKAZE HEADBAND NOW, SIR.
DID YOU SEE THE MOVIE "PEARL HARBOR?"
IT'S A LOVE STORY, RIGHT?
I DON'T KNOW WHY, OLIVIA, BUT I HAVE A BAD FEELING ABOUT THAT MOVIE NOW THAT YOU ASK.
SPLAT!
SPLAAT!
OH, SH__!
WHAT THE—
I NEVER LIKED MOVIES ABOUT SNEAK ATTACKS.
ME NEITHER. I NEVER LIKED LOVE STORIES.

WINGPIGEON TO SQUADRON LEADER! WINGPIGEON TO SQUADRON LEADER!
REQUEST PERMISSION TO RETURN TO BASE RIGHT AWAY, SIR!
SQUADRON LEADER TO WINGPIGEON. TAKE IT EASY. WE'VE JUST COMPLETED A SUCCESSFUL BOMBING RUN.
WE GOT TO GET HOME NOW, SIR!
WHY? WHAT'S THE HURRY?
I DON'T WANNA MISS ON *PBS* THE *KEN BURNS* SERIES "THE WAR," SIR.

WINGPIGEON TO SQUADRON LEADER! WINGPIGEON TO SQUADRON LEADER!
REQUEST PERMISSION TO FLY FASTER, SIR!
SQUADRON LEADER TO WINGPIGEON. WE'RE ALREADY AT MAXIMUM SPEED. NOT EVEN THE *CONCORDE* CAN CATCH US NOW.
WITH ALL DUE RESPECT, SIR, THAT PLANE'S BEEN JUNKED.
BUMMER!
SEE, I TOLD YOU. WE NEEDED TO BE HERE EARLY TO GET *GOOD* SEATS, SIR.

Friends in High and Low Places as References, and the Debt of Gratitude

KAWAYANG CANE, MAY I USE YOU AS A REFERENCE?
SURE.
YOU DID WHAT!!?
HEY, YOU WERE MY FIRST CHOICE FOR A REFERENCE. BUT I NEEDED MORE THAN ONE.
I'VE ALSO ASKED A RABBIT FRIEND. AND A FEW FIRE ANTS.
IT DOESN'T HELP YOU NAIL THIS JOB TO PUT DOWN ON YOUR RÉSUMÉ THAT YOU HAVE FRIENDS IN LOW PLACES.

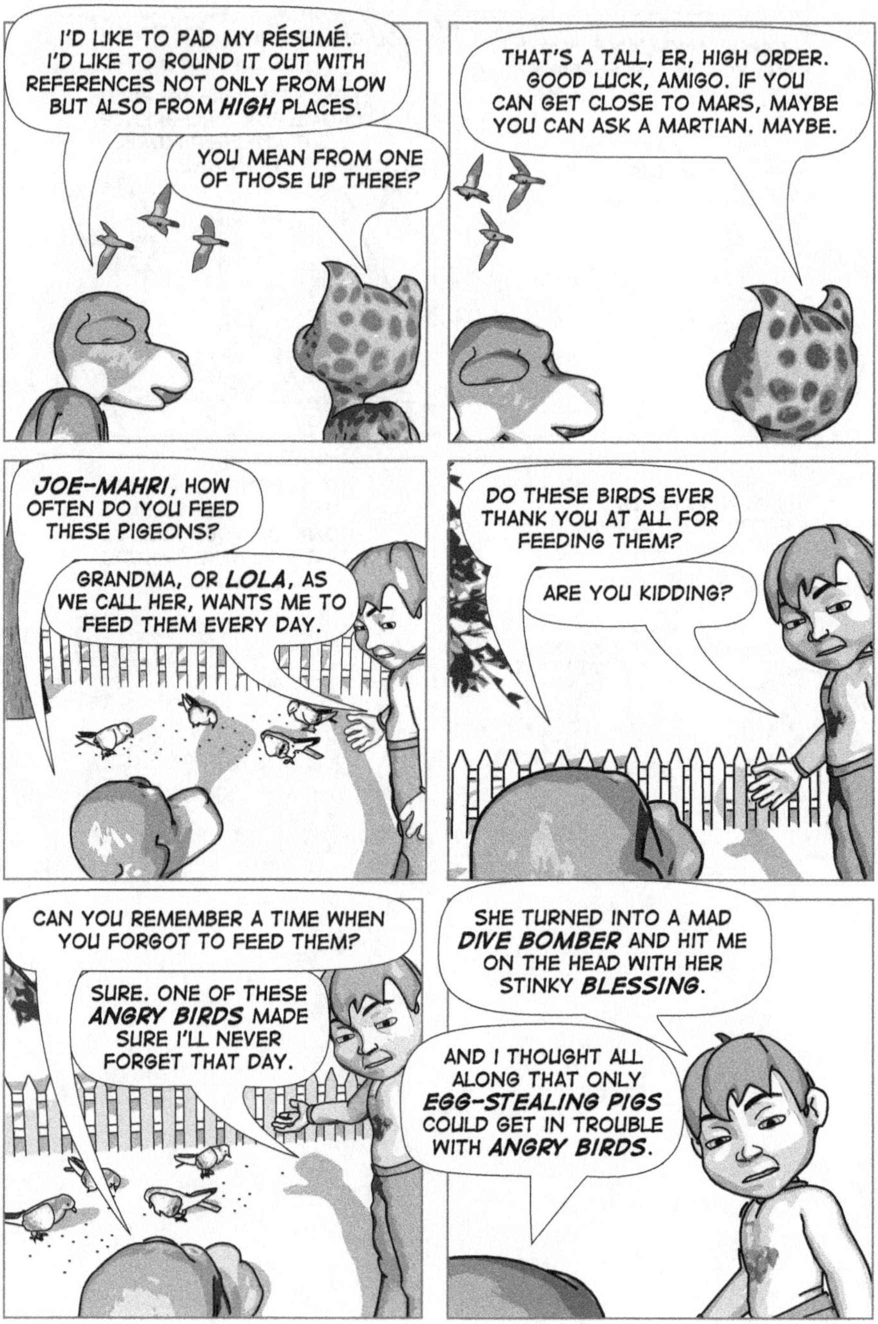
I'D LIKE TO PAD MY RÉSUMÉ. I'D LIKE TO ROUND IT OUT WITH REFERENCES NOT ONLY FROM LOW BUT ALSO FROM *HIGH* PLACES.
YOU MEAN FROM ONE OF THOSE UP THERE?
THAT'S A TALL, ER, HIGH ORDER. GOOD LUCK, AMIGO. IF YOU CAN GET CLOSE TO MARS, MAYBE YOU CAN ASK A MARTIAN. MAYBE.
JOE-MAHRI, HOW OFTEN DO YOU FEED THESE PIGEONS?
GRANDMA, OR *LOLA*, AS WE CALL HER, WANTS ME TO FEED THEM EVERY DAY.
DO THESE BIRDS EVER THANK YOU AT ALL FOR FEEDING THEM?
ARE YOU KIDDING?
CAN YOU REMEMBER A TIME WHEN YOU FORGOT TO FEED THEM?
SURE. ONE OF THESE *ANGRY BIRDS* MADE SURE I'LL NEVER FORGET THAT DAY.
SHE TURNED INTO A MAD *DIVE BOMBER* AND HIT ME ON THE HEAD WITH HER STINKY *BLESSING*.
AND I THOUGHT ALL ALONG THAT ONLY *EGG-STEALING PIGS* COULD GET IN TROUBLE WITH *ANGRY BIRDS*.

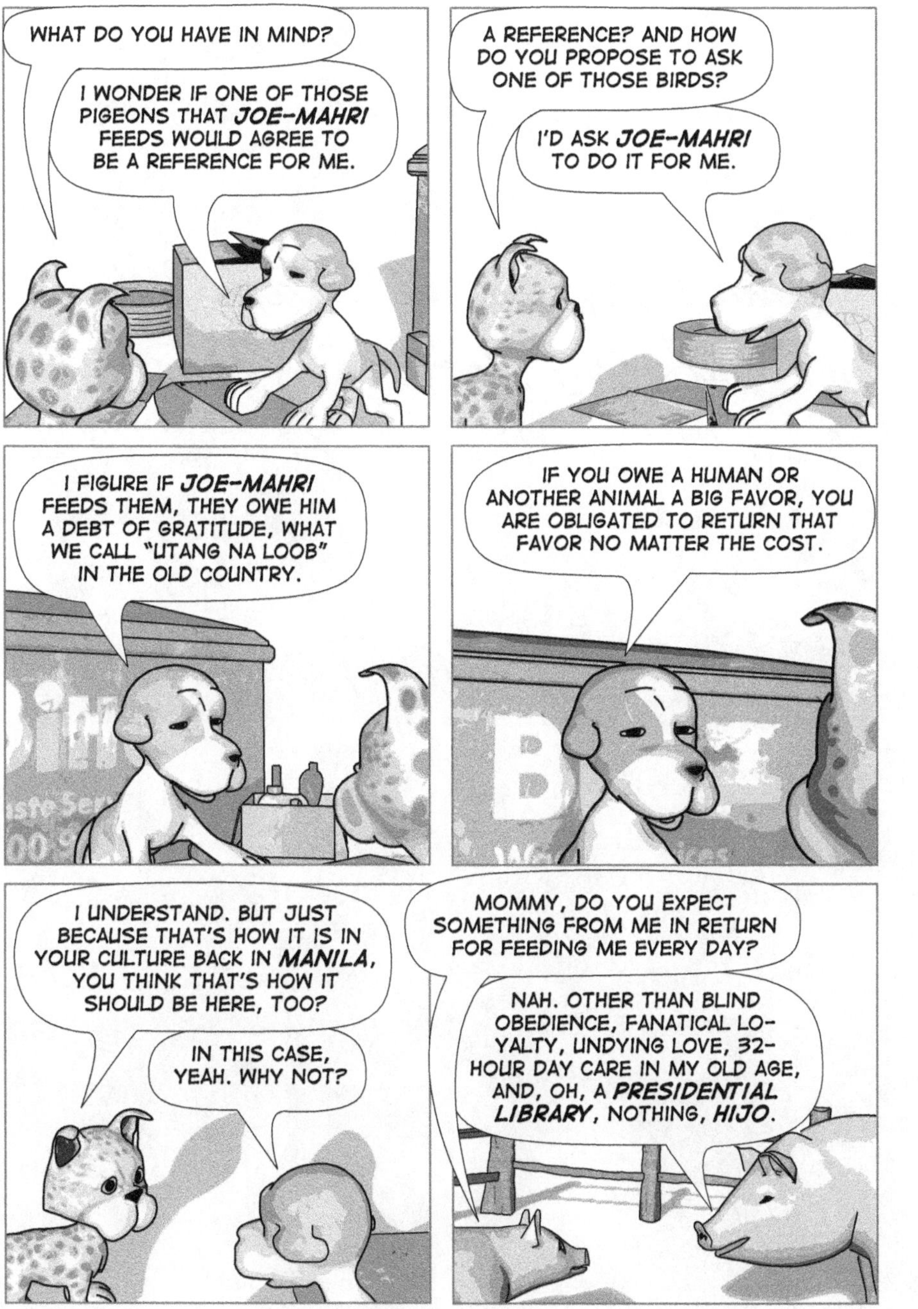
WHAT DO YOU HAVE IN MIND?
I WONDER IF ONE OF THOSE PIGEONS THAT JOE-MAHRI FEEDS WOULD AGREE TO BE A REFERENCE FOR ME.
A REFERENCE? AND HOW DO YOU PROPOSE TO ASK ONE OF THOSE BIRDS?
I'D ASK JOE-MAHRI TO DO IT FOR ME.
I FIGURE IF JOE-MAHRI FEEDS THEM, THEY OWE HIM A DEBT OF GRATITUDE, WHAT WE CALL "UTANG NA LOOB" IN THE OLD COUNTRY.
IF YOU OWE A HUMAN OR ANOTHER ANIMAL A BIG FAVOR, YOU ARE OBLIGATED TO RETURN THAT FAVOR NO MATTER THE COST.
I UNDERSTAND. BUT JUST BECAUSE THAT'S HOW IT IS IN YOUR CULTURE BACK IN MANILA, YOU THINK THAT'S HOW IT SHOULD BE HERE, TOO?
IN THIS CASE, YEAH. WHY NOT?
MOMMY, DO YOU EXPECT SOMETHING FROM ME IN RETURN FOR FEEDING ME EVERY DAY?
NAH. OTHER THAN BLIND OBEDIENCE, FANATICAL LOYALTY, UNDYING LOVE, 32-HOUR DAY CARE IN MY OLD AGE, AND, OH, A PRESIDENTIAL LIBRARY, NOTHING, HIJO.

Who's Afraid of Math When You Can Turn to Heaven?

MY DEFICIENCY IN MATH BECAME EVIDENT OVER TIME, AS IF THESE THINGS HAVE A WAY OF CATCHING UP WITH YOU.
KUH-TO, WILL YOU HELP ME WITH THIS CROSS-MULTIPLICATION PROBLEM?
UM, . . . SURE, ANITA.
GO AHEAD AND MULTIPLY THE NUMBERS ANY WAY YOU KNOW HOW TO.
ANY WAY?
YEP. IT DOESN'T REALLY MATTER HOW YOU DO IT AT THIS POINT.
THERE. I DID IT.
NOW MAKE THE SIGN OF THE CROSS.
ARE YOU SURE?
YOU MISSED A CRUCIAL STEP.
WHAT'S THAT?
YOU MUST FIRST DIP YOUR PAW IN HOLY WATER.

WHY? IS IT TO GET AN ACCURATE MATH ANSWER?
HUMANS, TO BE *MORE* ACCURATE, USE NOT ONE BUT *TWO* FINGERS.
I SUPPOSE YOU WOULD SAY THAT IT HELPS THEIR CALCULATION IF THEY GENUFLECT, TOO.
NOPE. THEY HAVE TO KNEEL ON *TWO* KNEES. CROSS MY HEART.

PATO-TEN, I'M DYING TO GO TO AMERICA BUT I'M SCARED AS HECK OF MATH IN DOG SCHOOL. YOU KNOW, THIS CROSS-MULTIPLICATION THING . . .
THAT SHOULDN'T HOLD BACK YOUR DREAM. PRAY OFTEN.
PRAY? YOU THINK THAT'LL WORK FOR ME?
DUH, HAVE FAITH. GO TO CHURCH.
RIGHT. YOU KNOW, IF IT EVER GETS DOWN TO THAT, I'LL TAKE IT REAL SLOW. ONE STEP AT A TIME.
IN AMERICA, DO YOU THINK THE CHURCHES THERE MIGHT HAVE SOMETHING LIKE A REMEDIAL PEW?

A Filipino Immigrant's Home in America

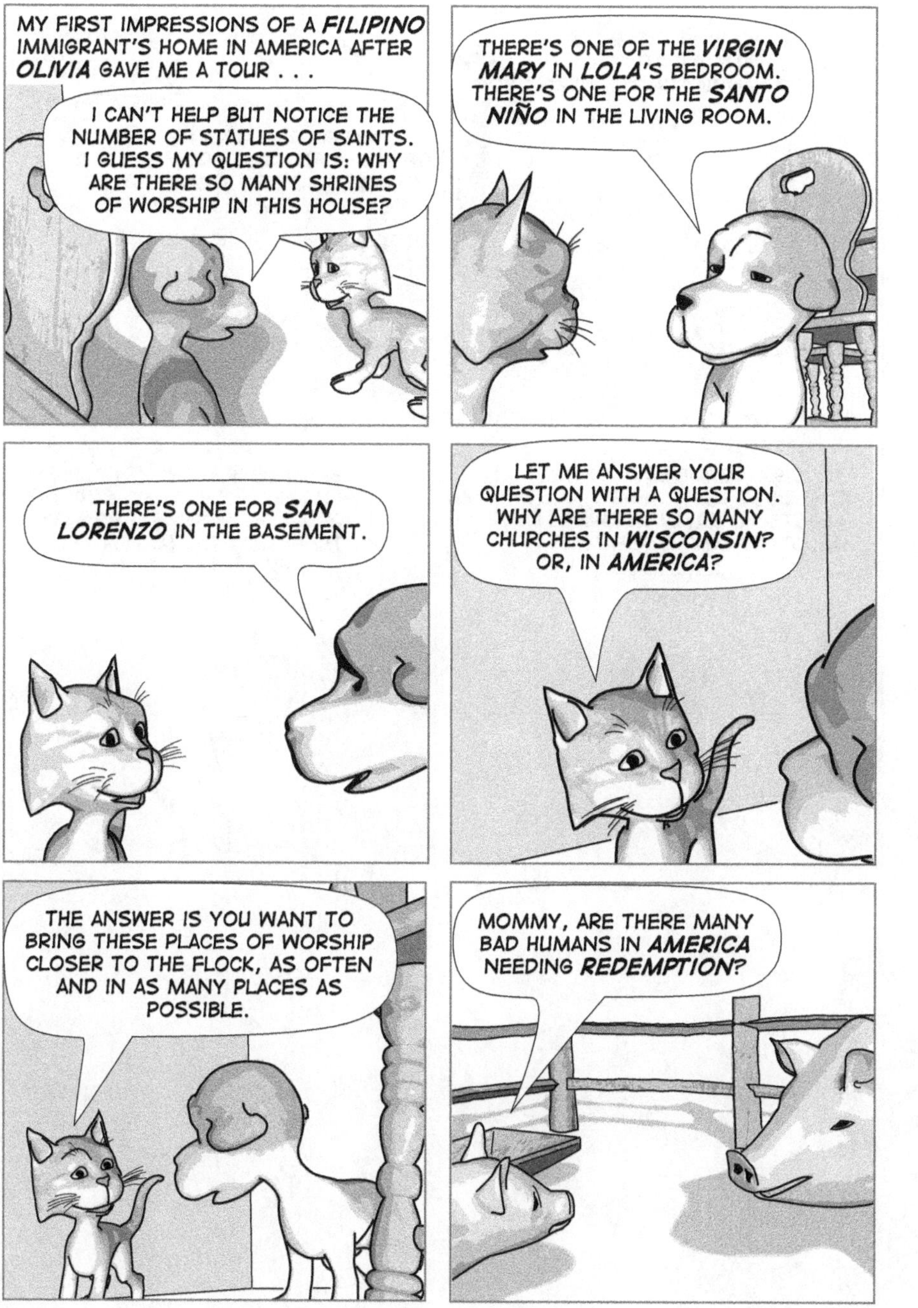
MY FIRST IMPRESSIONS OF A ***FILIPINO*** IMMIGRANT'S HOME IN AMERICA AFTER ***OLIVIA*** GAVE ME A TOUR . . .
I CAN'T HELP BUT NOTICE THE NUMBER OF STATUES OF SAINTS. I GUESS MY QUESTION IS: WHY ARE THERE SO MANY SHRINES OF WORSHIP IN THIS HOUSE?
THERE'S ONE OF THE ***VIRGIN MARY*** IN ***LOLA***'S BEDROOM. THERE'S ONE FOR THE ***SANTO NIÑO*** IN THE LIVING ROOM.
THERE'S ONE FOR ***SAN LORENZO*** IN THE BASEMENT.
LET ME ANSWER YOUR QUESTION WITH A QUESTION. WHY ARE THERE SO MANY CHURCHES IN ***WISCONSIN***? OR, IN ***AMERICA***?
THE ANSWER IS YOU WANT TO BRING THESE PLACES OF WORSHIP CLOSER TO THE FLOCK, AS OFTEN AND IN AS MANY PLACES AS POSSIBLE.
MOMMY, ARE THERE MANY BAD HUMANS IN ***AMERICA*** NEEDING ***REDEMPTION***?

NOW WHY WOULD THE LADY OF THE HOUSE WANT A PICTURE OF THE LAST SUPPER HANGING IN THE DINING ROOM?
MAYBE TO REMIND HERSELF OF THE IMPORTANT PROMISES THE CHRIST MADE TO THE APOSTLES IN HIS LAST MEAL WITH THEM.
MY GUESS IS THE LADY OF THE HOUSE JUST WANTS HER DINNER GUESTS TO SAY NICE THINGS ABOUT HER AND HER FAMILY.
WHY?
BECAUSE IF THEY DON'T, THE PICTURE OF THE LAST SUPPER WOULD DO NICELY TO REMIND THEM THAT THE DINNER THEY ARE HAVING COULD BE THEIR LAST.

OLIVIA, WHEN YOU FIRST CAME TO THIS HOUSE, HOW DID YOU KNOW THAT IT WAS OCCUPIED BY A NEWLY IMMIGRANT FILIPINO FAMILY?
I DIDN'T. BUT THE SIGNS WERE EVERYWHERE.
OLIVIA WAS RIGHT. THE SIGNS WERE UNMISTAKABLE, IN ALMOST EVERY . . .
. . . ROOM AND LIVING AREA. IF YOU'RE INTO THIS THING, WHY GO TO CHURCH TO DO THE STATIONS OF THE CROSS?
YOU COULD DO IT RIGHT THERE IN THE COMFORT OF YOUR HOME.

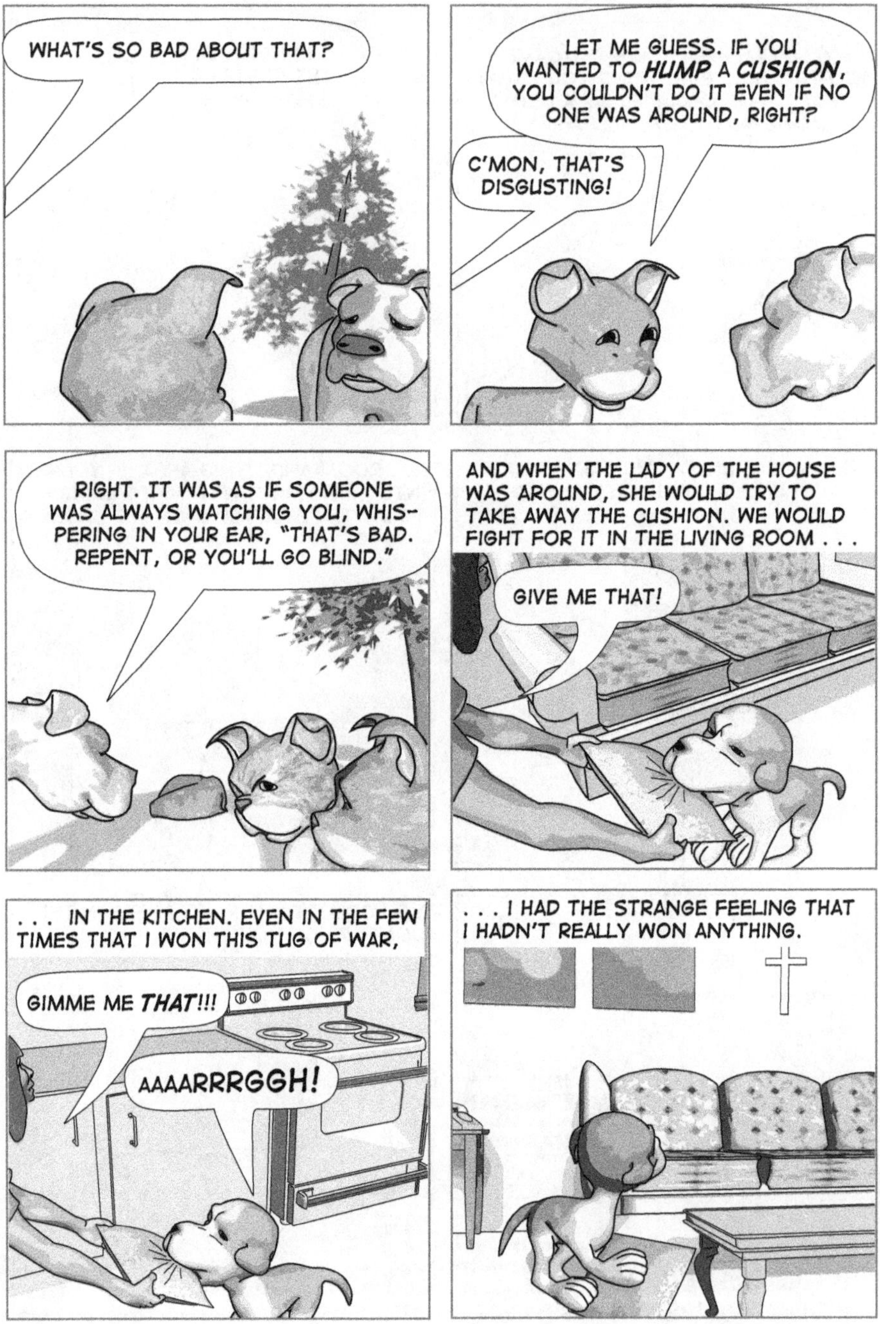
WHAT'S SO BAD ABOUT THAT?
LET ME GUESS. IF YOU WANTED TO HUMP A CUSHION, YOU COULDN'T DO IT EVEN IF NO ONE WAS AROUND, RIGHT?
C'MON, THAT'S DISGUSTING!
RIGHT. IT WAS AS IF SOMEONE WAS ALWAYS WATCHING YOU, WHIS-PERING IN YOUR EAR, "THAT'S BAD. REPENT, OR YOU'LL GO BLIND."
AND WHEN THE LADY OF THE HOUSE WAS AROUND, SHE WOULD TRY TO TAKE AWAY THE CUSHION. WE WOULD FIGHT FOR IT IN THE LIVING ROOM . . .
GIVE ME THAT!
. . . IN THE KITCHEN. EVEN IN THE FEW TIMES THAT I WON THIS TUG OF WAR,
GIMME ME THAT!!!
AAAARRRGGH!
. . . I HAD THE STRANGE FEELING THAT I HADN'T REALLY WON ANYTHING.

HOW ABOUT YOU, GUYS? HOW WAS IT LIKE GROWING UP HERE IN THIS BELOVED COUNTRY OF OURS?
IN THE BIG CITIES, YES, BUT OUT HERE, WE DON'T HAVE THE KIND OF FANCY, CUSHY FURNITURE THAT YOU HAVE IN AMERICA.
WE HAVE NO CUSHIONS OR ANYTHING LIKE THAT. NOT EVEN A WHOOPEE CUSHION.
WE HAVE ROCKS.
YOU SHOULD KNOW THIS. MANY OF OUR FURNITURE COME FROM NATIVE MATERIALS LIKE RATTAN OR BAMBOO.
RIGHT. HUMPING IT CAN BE A PROBLEM.

Failing a Class? Legislate Parenting

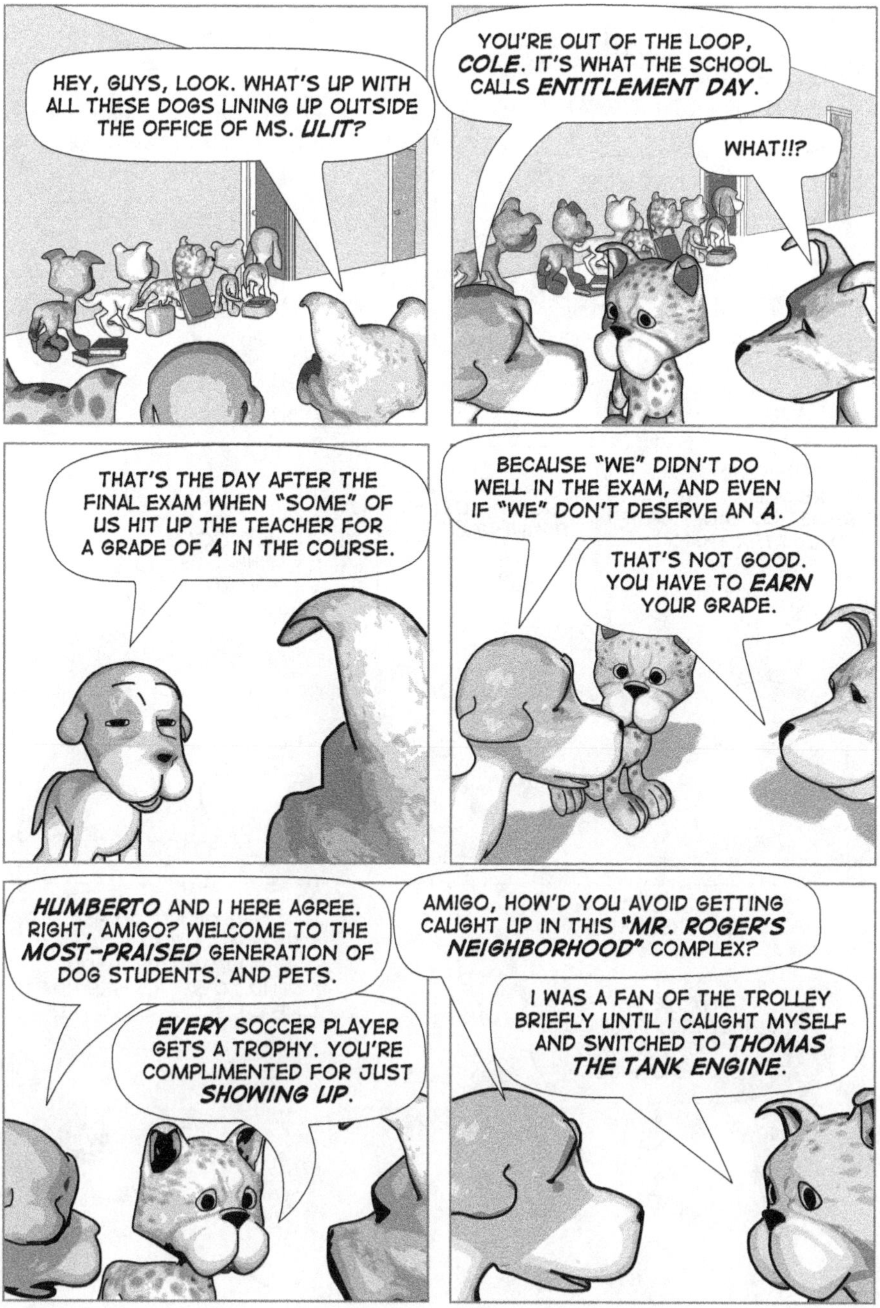
HEY, GUYS, LOOK. WHAT'S UP WITH ALL THESE DOGS LINING UP OUTSIDE THE OFFICE OF MS. *ULIT?*
YOU'RE OUT OF THE LOOP, *COLE*. IT'S WHAT THE SCHOOL CALLS *ENTITLEMENT DAY*.
WHAT!!?
THAT'S THE DAY AFTER THE FINAL EXAM WHEN "SOME" OF US HIT UP THE TEACHER FOR A GRADE OF *A* IN THE COURSE.
BECAUSE "WE" DIDN'T DO WELL IN THE EXAM, AND EVEN IF "WE" DON'T DESERVE AN *A*.
THAT'S NOT GOOD. YOU HAVE TO *EARN* YOUR GRADE.
HUMBERTO AND I HERE AGREE. RIGHT, AMIGO? WELCOME TO THE *MOST-PRAISED* GENERATION OF DOG STUDENTS. AND PETS.
EVERY SOCCER PLAYER GETS A TROPHY. YOU'RE COMPLIMENTED FOR JUST *SHOWING UP*.
AMIGO, HOW'D YOU AVOID GETTING CAUGHT UP IN THIS *"MR. ROGER'S NEIGHBORHOOD"* COMPLEX?
I WAS A FAN OF THE TROLLEY BRIEFLY UNTIL I CAUGHT MYSELF AND SWITCHED TO *THOMAS THE TANK ENGINE*.

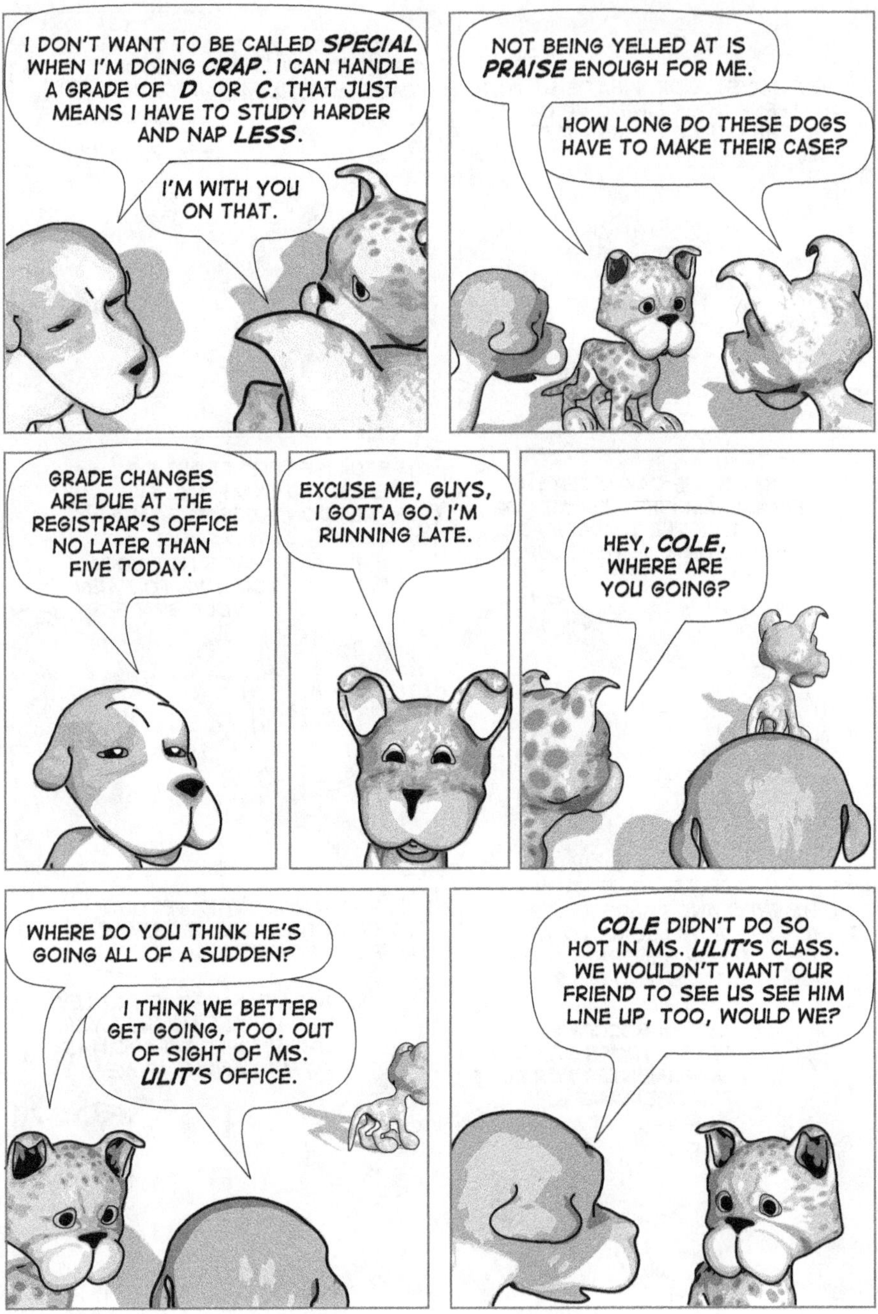
I DON'T WANT TO BE CALLED SPECIAL WHEN I'M DOING CRAP. I CAN HANDLE A GRADE OF D OR C. THAT JUST MEANS I HAVE TO STUDY HARDER AND NAP LESS.
I'M WITH YOU ON THAT.
NOT BEING YELLED AT IS PRAISE ENOUGH FOR ME.
HOW LONG DO THESE DOGS HAVE TO MAKE THEIR CASE?
GRADE CHANGES ARE DUE AT THE REGISTRAR'S OFFICE NO LATER THAN FIVE TODAY.
EXCUSE ME, GUYS, I GOTTA GO. I'M RUNNING LATE.
HEY, COLE, WHERE ARE YOU GOING?
WHERE DO YOU THINK HE'S GOING ALL OF A SUDDEN?
I THINK WE BETTER GET GOING, TOO. OUT OF SIGHT OF MS. ULIT'S OFFICE.
COLE DIDN'T DO SO HOT IN MS. ULIT'S CLASS. WE WOULDN'T WANT OUR FRIEND TO SEE US SEE HIM LINE UP, TOO, WOULD WE?

WOULD YOU CONDEMN A FRIEND, AMIGO?

NO. NEVER.

I'LL SEE YOU LATER, *KUH-TO*. HASTA LUEGO.

HEY, WHERE ARE YOU GOING?

I'M CAMPING OUT BY MS. *ULIT*'S OFFICE.

YOU, TOO!!? OH, NO! HEY, WAIT UP.

IT WAS ONE OF THOSE MOMENTS I SUDDENLY FELT ODD, MAYBE ODDLY OLD.

C'MON, *HUMBERTO*. YOU'RE— YOU'RE NOT SELLING OUT, ARE YOU?

SILLY, NO, BUT I NEED TO CATCH UP ON THE LATEST CARTOON CLIPPINGS POSTED OUTSIDE THE OFFICE OF MS. *ULIT*.

Generation Gap and the Age of Big Data

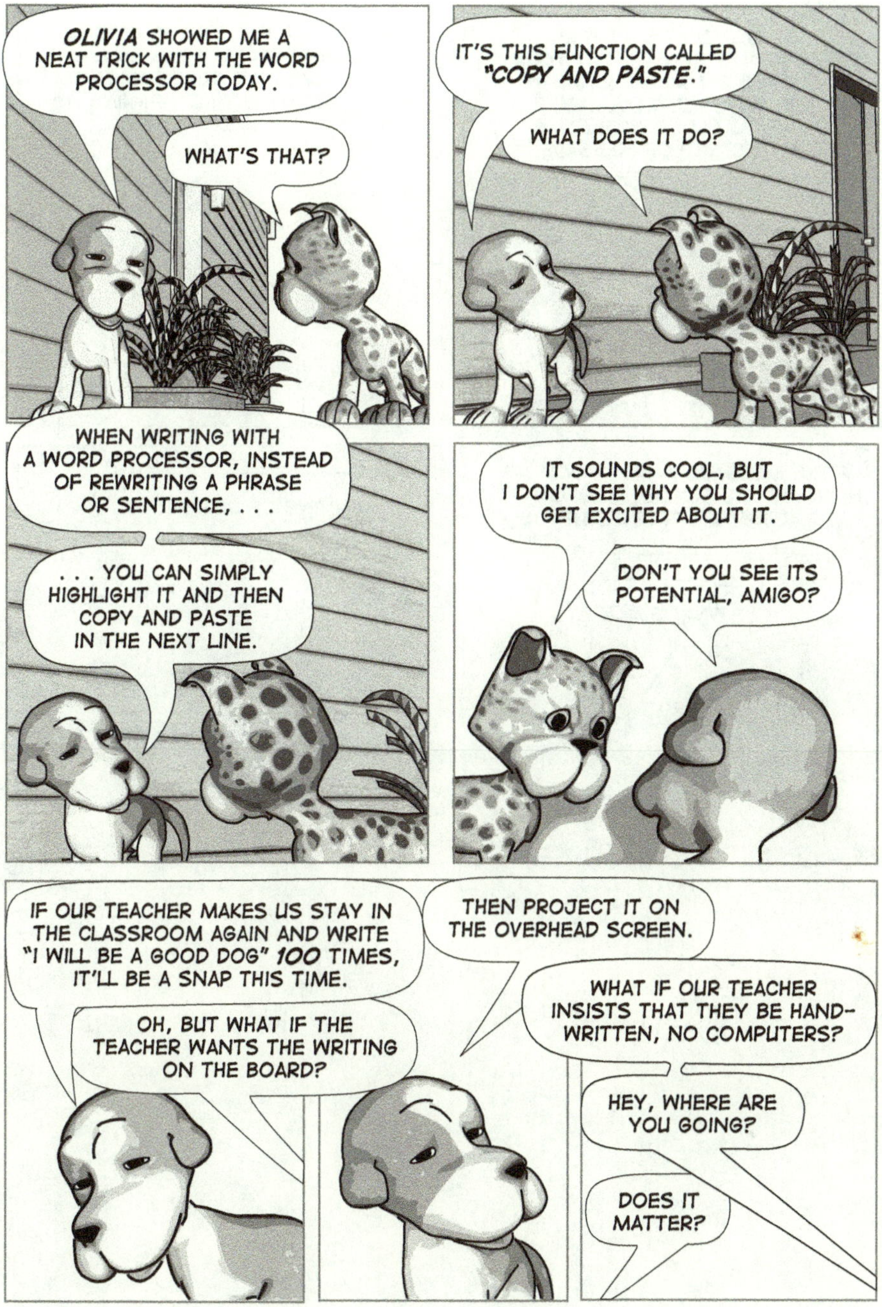
OLIVIA SHOWED ME A NEAT TRICK WITH THE WORD PROCESSOR TODAY.
WHAT'S THAT?
IT'S THIS FUNCTION CALLED "COPY AND PASTE."
WHAT DOES IT DO?
WHEN WRITING WITH A WORD PROCESSOR, INSTEAD OF REWRITING A PHRASE OR SENTENCE, . . .
. . . YOU CAN SIMPLY HIGHLIGHT IT AND THEN COPY AND PASTE IN THE NEXT LINE.
IT SOUNDS COOL, BUT I DON'T SEE WHY YOU SHOULD GET EXCITED ABOUT IT.
DON'T YOU SEE ITS POTENTIAL, AMIGO?
IF OUR TEACHER MAKES US STAY IN THE CLASSROOM AGAIN AND WRITE "I WILL BE A GOOD DOG" 100 TIMES, IT'LL BE A SNAP THIS TIME.
OH, BUT WHAT IF THE TEACHER WANTS THE WRITING ON THE BOARD?
THEN PROJECT IT ON THE OVERHEAD SCREEN.
WHAT IF OUR TEACHER INSISTS THAT THEY BE HAND-WRITTEN, NO COMPUTERS?
HEY, WHERE ARE YOU GOING?
DOES IT MATTER?

IF, AND THAT'S A BIG IF, YOU REALLY HAVE TO PUT YOUR *ENTIRE* E-MAIL MESSAGE IN THE *SUBJECT LINE*, MAKE SURE TO CLOSE WITH *EOM*, THAT IS, "END OF MESSAGE."
WHY?
IT'S GOOD E-MAIL ETIQUETTE. YOU'RE BEING UPFRONT, CANDID. IT SAVES THE RECIPIENT FROM WASTING TIME OPENING YOUR *EMPTY* E-MAIL.
IF THE MESSAGE IS NOT GOOD NEWS, IS THE SENDER ALLOWED TO ADD *BOD* AFTER *EOM*?
WHAT'S *BOD*?
"BEGINNING OF DESPAIR."

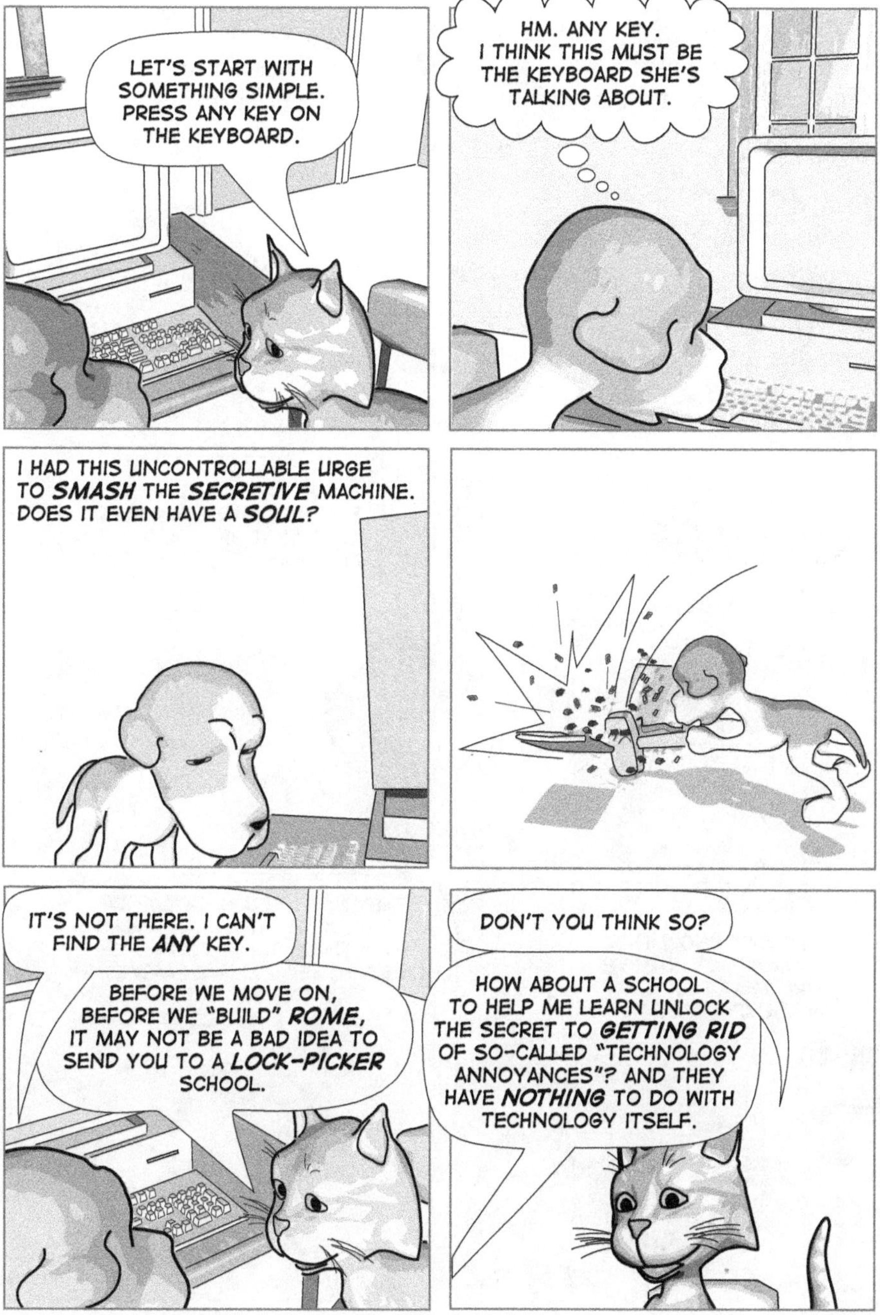
LET'S START WITH SOMETHING SIMPLE. PRESS ANY KEY ON THE KEYBOARD.
HM. ANY KEY. I THINK THIS MUST BE THE KEYBOARD SHE'S TALKING ABOUT.
I HAD THIS UNCONTROLLABLE URGE TO SMASH THE SECRETIVE MACHINE. DOES IT EVEN HAVE A SOUL?
IT'S NOT THERE. I CAN'T FIND THE ANY KEY.
BEFORE WE MOVE ON, BEFORE WE "BUILD" ROME, IT MAY NOT BE A BAD IDEA TO SEND YOU TO A LOCK-PICKER SCHOOL.
DON'T YOU THINK SO?
HOW ABOUT A SCHOOL TO HELP ME LEARN UNLOCK THE SECRET TO GETTING RID OF SO-CALLED "TECHNOLOGY ANNOYANCES"? AND THEY HAVE NOTHING TO DO WITH TECHNOLOGY ITSELF.

HOW ABOUT THE SPACE BAR?
THE SPACE BAR? IS IT ON THE KEYBOARD?
NOPE. I DON'T SEE IT, OLIVIA.
YOU HAVE NEITHER THE YIN NOR YANG FOR IT. SO JUST WHAT, IF ANY, DO YOU KNOW ABOUT COMPUTERS?
I DON'T KNOW THIS FOR A FACT BUT I'VE HEARD THAT THEY LACK AN INSTANT-ON FEATURE.
THEY HAVE A LONG BOOT-UP SEQUENCE THAT HUMAN MALES SOMETIMES REFER TO IN DES-CRIBING THEIR FEMALE PARTNERS DURING INTIMACY.

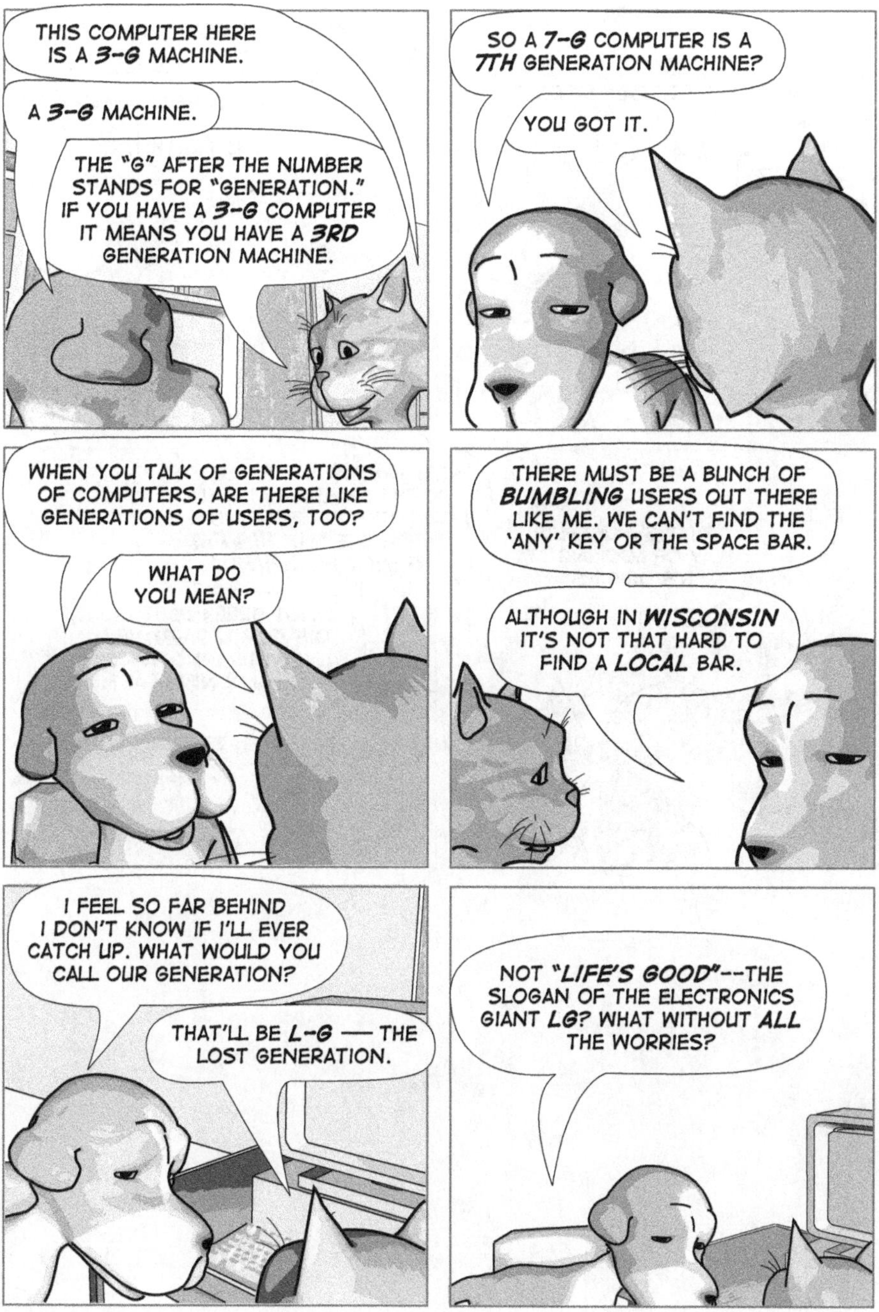
THIS COMPUTER HERE IS A 3-G MACHINE.
A 3-G MACHINE.
THE "G" AFTER THE NUMBER STANDS FOR "GENERATION." IF YOU HAVE A 3-G COMPUTER IT MEANS YOU HAVE A 3RD GENERATION MACHINE.
SO A 7-G COMPUTER IS A 7TH GENERATION MACHINE?
YOU GOT IT.
WHEN YOU TALK OF GENERATIONS OF COMPUTERS, ARE THERE LIKE GENERATIONS OF USERS, TOO?
WHAT DO YOU MEAN?
THERE MUST BE A BUNCH OF BUMBLING USERS OUT THERE LIKE ME. WE CAN'T FIND THE 'ANY' KEY OR THE SPACE BAR.
ALTHOUGH IN WISCONSIN IT'S NOT THAT HARD TO FIND A LOCAL BAR.
I FEEL SO FAR BEHIND I DON'T KNOW IF I'LL EVER CATCH UP. WHAT WOULD YOU CALL OUR GENERATION?
THAT'LL BE L-G — THE LOST GENERATION.
NOT "LIFE'S GOOD"--THE SLOGAN OF THE ELECTRONICS GIANT LG? WHAT WITHOUT ALL THE WORRIES?

WHAT'S A *TROJAN HORSE?*
I KEPT TELLING MYSELF IT WAS NOT A TRICK QUESTION.
DOES IT HAVE SOME-THING TO DO WITH *GREEKS* AND PRESENTS?
THAT'S A USEFUL WAY OF LOOKING AT ITS ORIGINS.
WITH GREEKS AND PRESENTS IN THE SAME BREATH, ALL I CAN THINK OF RIGHT NOW IS THE MOVIE *"MY BIG FAT GREEK WEDDING."*
NOT GREEK DEBT IN THE *EUROZONE?* YES, LIKE YOUR IGNORANCE, IT'S BALOONING FAST.

A TROJAN HORSE IS A COMPUTER VIRUS. AVOID IT AT ALL COST.
HUMBERTO, NEVER ACCEPT A TROJAN HORSE FOR A WEDDING GIFT.
PORQUE, NO? WHY NOT, AMIGO?
IS IT BECAUSE YOU CAN'T LOOK A GIFT HORSE IN THE MOUTH?
AND WHAT IF IT WERE A GIFT PONY? WHAT IF THEY SEND IT HIDDEN IN A PILE OF MANURE FROM WHICH I HAVE TO DIG IT OUT OF TO SHOW I'M AN OPTIMIST?
I WAS JUST TELLING YOU ABOUT COMPUTER VIRUSES. I WASN'T ASKING IF YOU WERE AN OPTIMIST. BESIDES, I NEVER SAID YOU DIDN'T LIKE POOP.

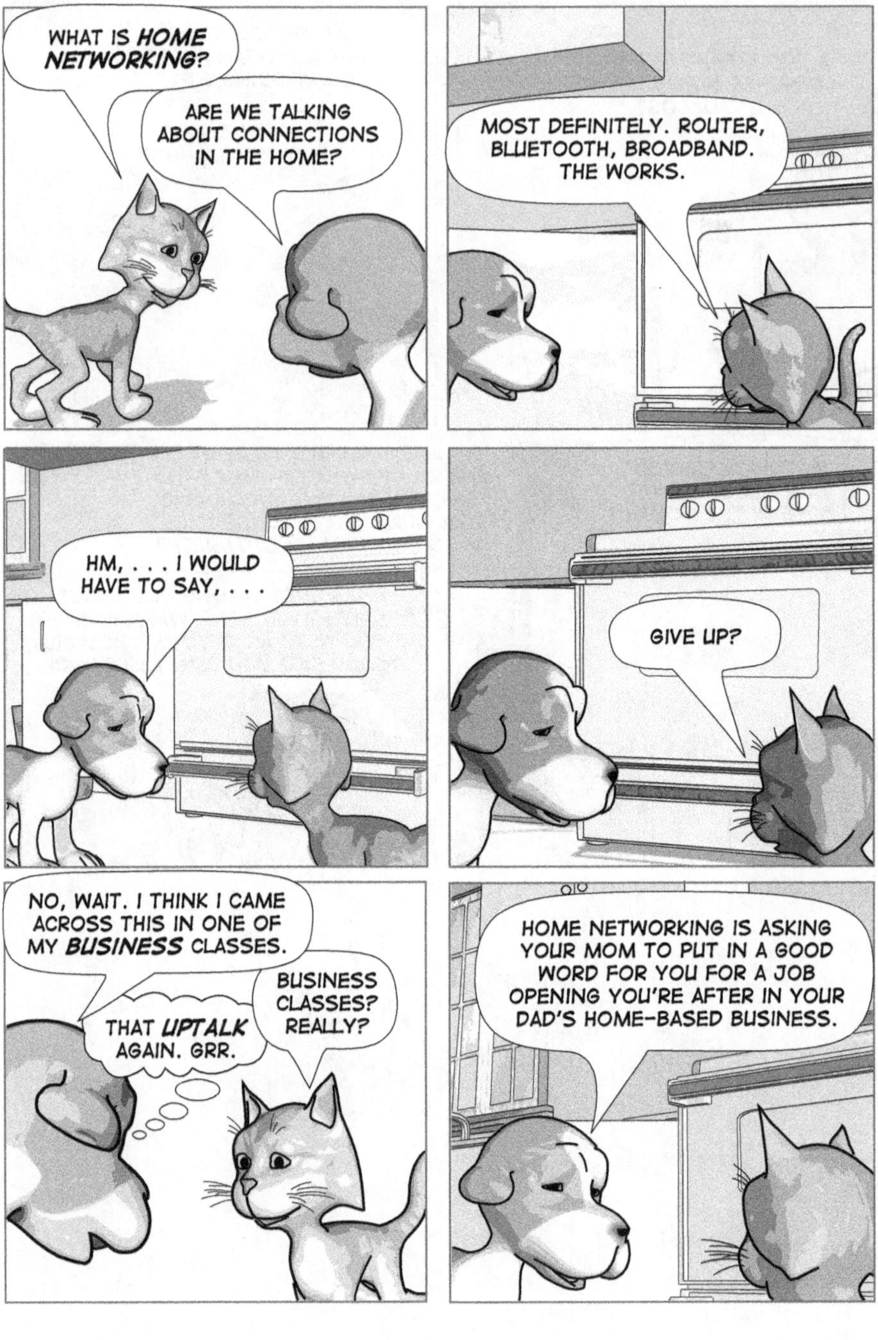
WHAT IS *HOME NETWORKING*?
ARE WE TALKING ABOUT CONNECTIONS IN THE HOME?
MOST DEFINITELY. ROUTER, BLUETOOTH, BROADBAND. THE WORKS.
HM, . . . I WOULD HAVE TO SAY, . . .
GIVE UP?
NO, WAIT. I THINK I CAME ACROSS THIS IN ONE OF MY *BUSINESS* CLASSES.
THAT *UPTALK* AGAIN. GRR.
BUSINESS CLASSES? REALLY?
HOME NETWORKING IS ASKING YOUR MOM TO PUT IN A GOOD WORD FOR YOU FOR A JOB OPENING YOU'RE AFTER IN YOUR DAD'S HOME-BASED BUSINESS.

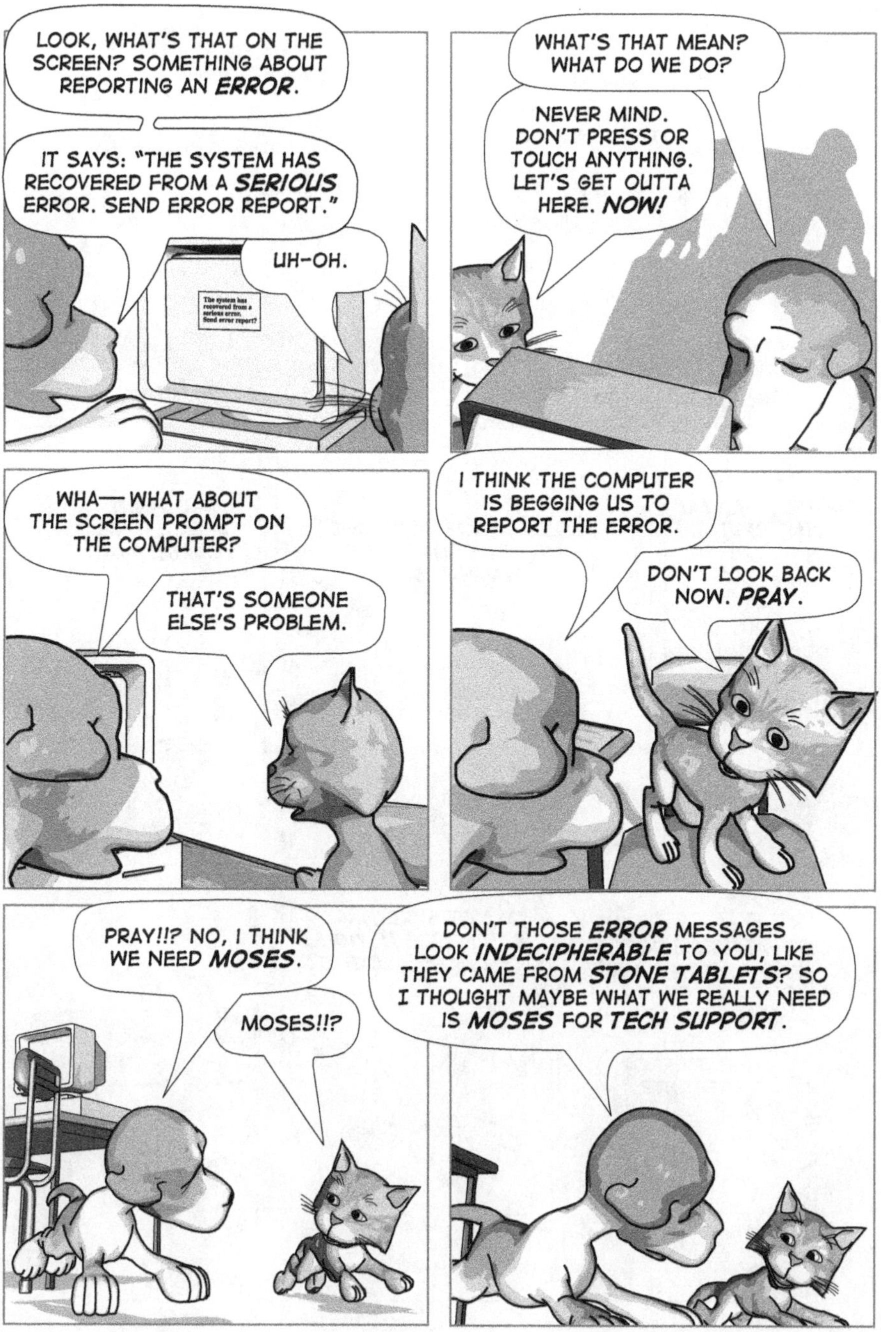
LOOK, WHAT'S THAT ON THE SCREEN? SOMETHING ABOUT REPORTING AN ERROR.
IT SAYS: "THE SYSTEM HAS RECOVERED FROM A SERIOUS ERROR. SEND ERROR REPORT."
The system has recovered from a serious error. Send error report?
UH-OH.
WHAT'S THAT MEAN? WHAT DO WE DO?
NEVER MIND. DON'T PRESS OR TOUCH ANYTHING. LET'S GET OUTTA HERE. NOW!
WHA— WHAT ABOUT THE SCREEN PROMPT ON THE COMPUTER?
THAT'S SOMEONE ELSE'S PROBLEM.
I THINK THE COMPUTER IS BEGGING US TO REPORT THE ERROR.
DON'T LOOK BACK NOW. PRAY.
PRAY!!? NO, I THINK WE NEED MOSES.
MOSES!!?
DON'T THOSE ERROR MESSAGES LOOK INDECIPHERABLE TO YOU, LIKE THEY CAME FROM STONE TABLETS? SO I THOUGHT MAYBE WHAT WE REALLY NEED IS MOSES FOR TECH SUPPORT.

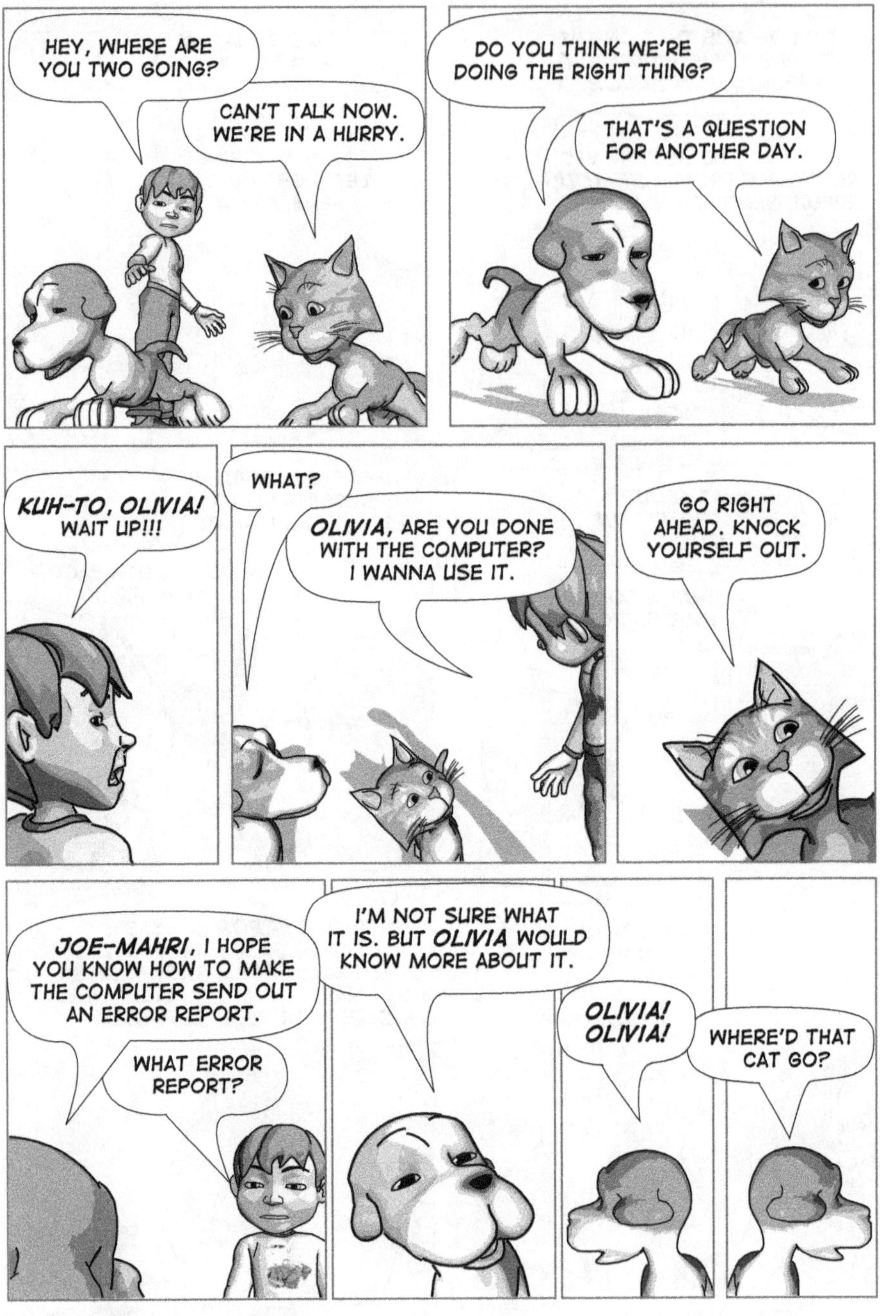
HEY, WHERE ARE YOU TWO GOING?
CAN'T TALK NOW. WE'RE IN A HURRY.
DO YOU THINK WE'RE DOING THE RIGHT THING?
THAT'S A QUESTION FOR ANOTHER DAY.
KUH-TO, OLIVIA! WAIT UP!!!
WHAT?
OLIVIA, ARE YOU DONE WITH THE COMPUTER? I WANNA USE IT.
GO RIGHT AHEAD. KNOCK YOURSELF OUT.
JOE-MAHRI, I HOPE YOU KNOW HOW TO MAKE THE COMPUTER SEND OUT AN ERROR REPORT.
WHAT ERROR REPORT?
I'M NOT SURE WHAT IT IS. BUT OLIVIA WOULD KNOW MORE ABOUT IT.
OLIVIA! OLIVIA!
WHERE'D THAT CAT GO?

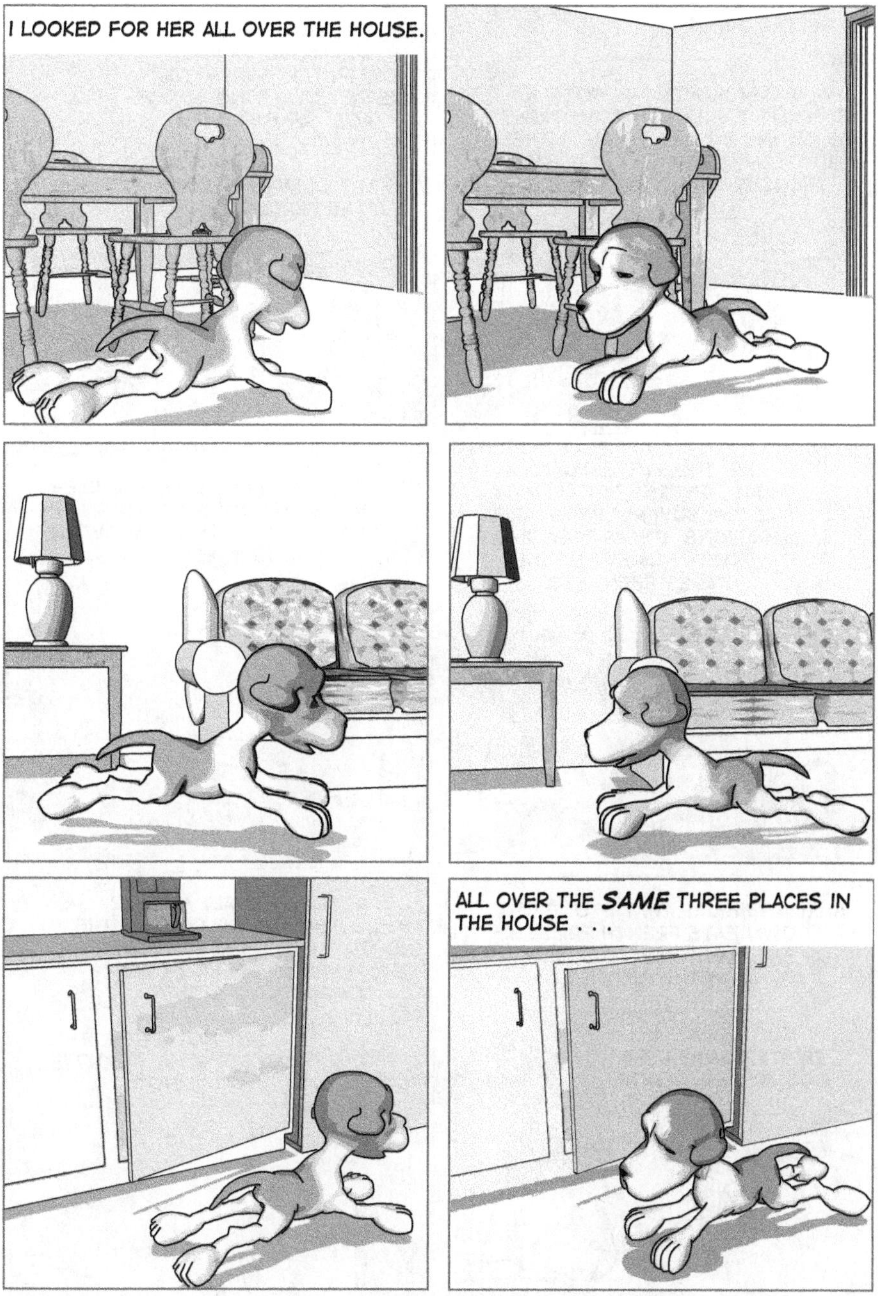
I LOOKED FOR HER ALL OVER THE HOUSE.
ALL OVER THE SAME THREE PLACES IN THE HOUSE . . .

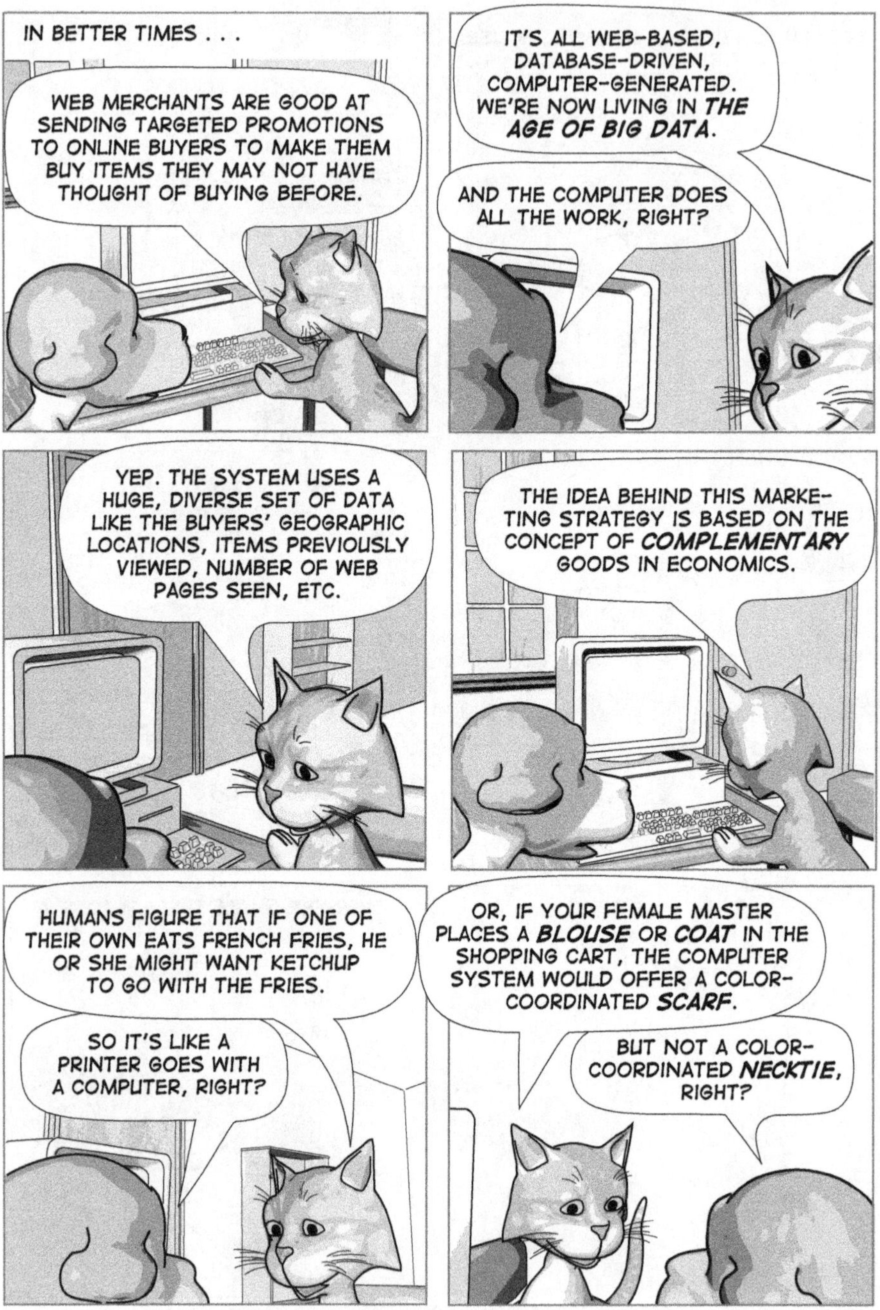
IN BETTER TIMES . . .
WEB MERCHANTS ARE GOOD AT SENDING TARGETED PROMOTIONS TO ONLINE BUYERS TO MAKE THEM BUY ITEMS THEY MAY NOT HAVE THOUGHT OF BUYING BEFORE.
IT'S ALL WEB-BASED, DATABASE-DRIVEN, COMPUTER-GENERATED. WE'RE NOW LIVING IN ***THE AGE OF BIG DATA***.
AND THE COMPUTER DOES ALL THE WORK, RIGHT?
YEP. THE SYSTEM USES A HUGE, DIVERSE SET OF DATA LIKE THE BUYERS' GEOGRAPHIC LOCATIONS, ITEMS PREVIOUSLY VIEWED, NUMBER OF WEB PAGES SEEN, ETC.
THE IDEA BEHIND THIS MARKETING STRATEGY IS BASED ON THE CONCEPT OF ***COMPLEMENTARY*** GOODS IN ECONOMICS.
HUMANS FIGURE THAT IF ONE OF THEIR OWN EATS FRENCH FRIES, HE OR SHE MIGHT WANT KETCHUP TO GO WITH THE FRIES.
SO IT'S LIKE A PRINTER GOES WITH A COMPUTER, RIGHT?
OR, IF YOUR FEMALE MASTER PLACES A ***BLOUSE*** OR ***COAT*** IN THE SHOPPING CART, THE COMPUTER SYSTEM WOULD OFFER A COLOR-COORDINATED ***SCARF***.
BUT NOT A COLOR-COORDINATED ***NECKTIE***, RIGHT?

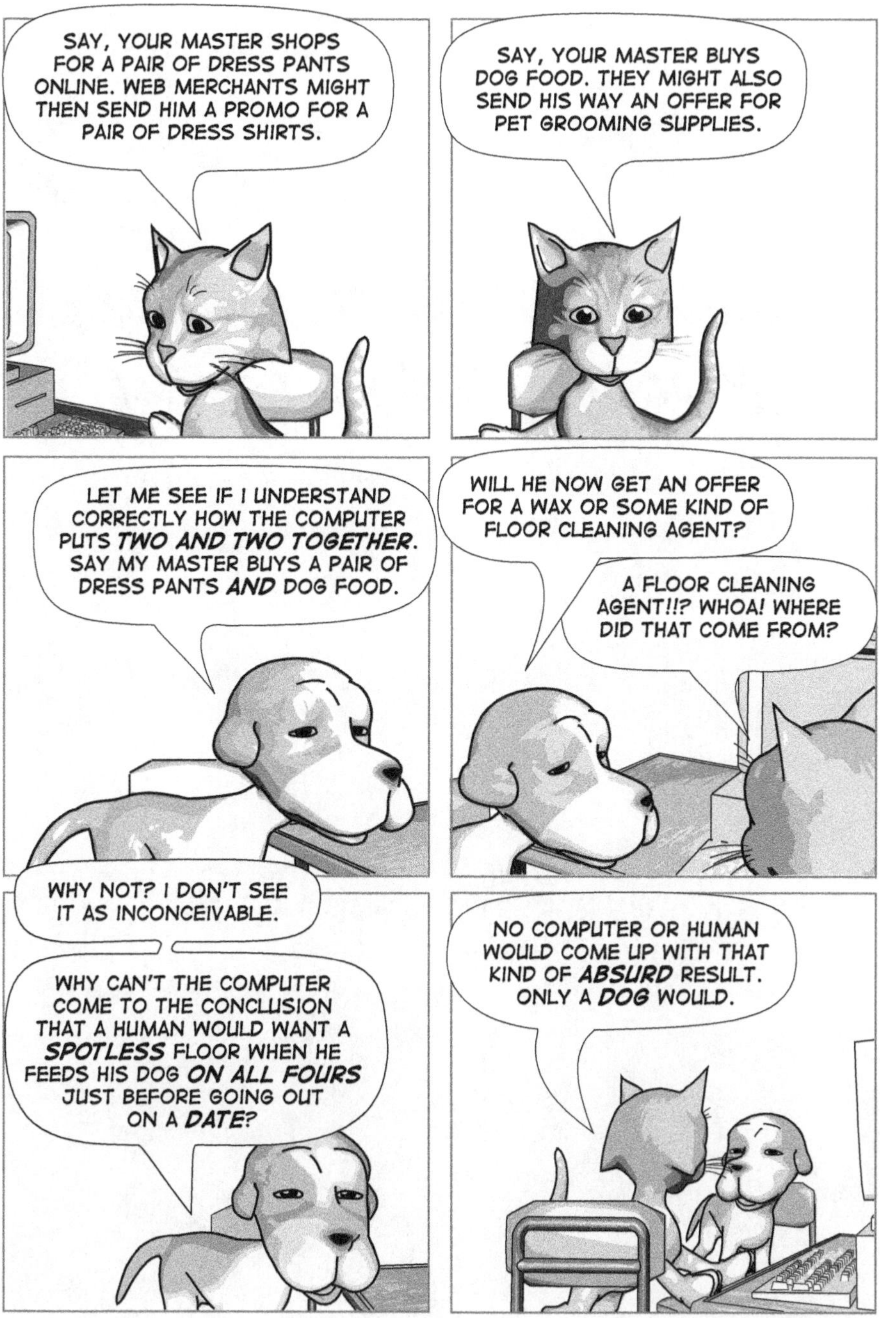
SAY, YOUR MASTER SHOPS FOR A PAIR OF DRESS PANTS ONLINE. WEB MERCHANTS MIGHT THEN SEND HIM A PROMO FOR A PAIR OF DRESS SHIRTS.
SAY, YOUR MASTER BUYS DOG FOOD. THEY MIGHT ALSO SEND HIS WAY AN OFFER FOR PET GROOMING SUPPLIES.
LET ME SEE IF I UNDERSTAND CORRECTLY HOW THE COMPUTER PUTS *TWO AND TWO TOGETHER*. SAY MY MASTER BUYS A PAIR OF DRESS PANTS *AND* DOG FOOD.
WILL HE NOW GET AN OFFER FOR A WAX OR SOME KIND OF FLOOR CLEANING AGENT?
A FLOOR CLEANING AGENT!!? WHOA! WHERE DID THAT COME FROM?
WHY NOT? I DON'T SEE IT AS INCONCEIVABLE.
WHY CAN'T THE COMPUTER COME TO THE CONCLUSION THAT A HUMAN WOULD WANT A *SPOTLESS* FLOOR WHEN HE FEEDS HIS DOG *ON ALL FOURS* JUST BEFORE GOING OUT ON A *DATE*?
NO COMPUTER OR HUMAN WOULD COME UP WITH THAT KIND OF *ABSURD* RESULT. ONLY A *DOG* WOULD.

Rubrics and the Opportunity Cost of a School Project

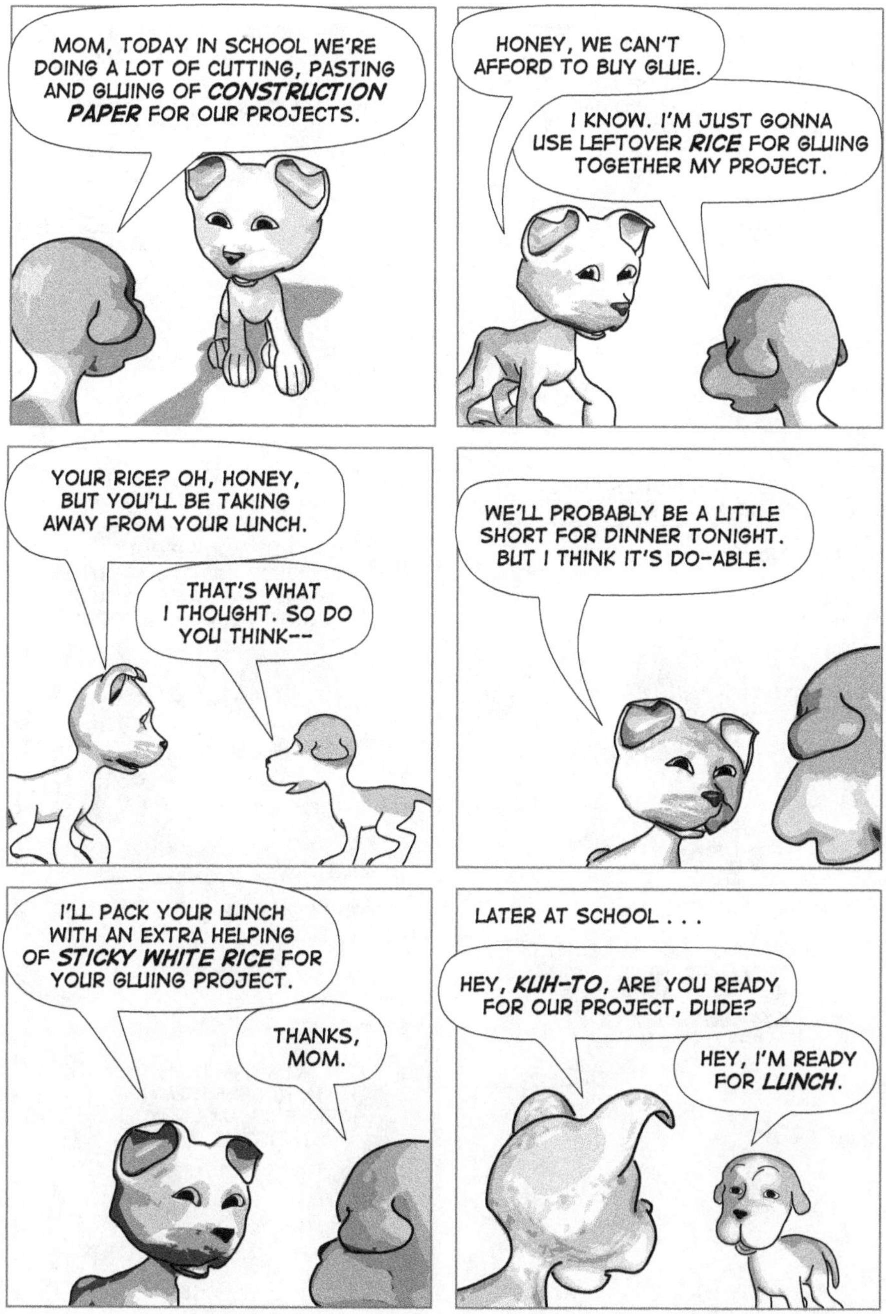
MOM, TODAY IN SCHOOL WE'RE DOING A LOT OF CUTTING, PASTING AND GLUING OF CONSTRUCTION PAPER FOR OUR PROJECTS.
HONEY, WE CAN'T AFFORD TO BUY GLUE.
I KNOW. I'M JUST GONNA USE LEFTOVER RICE FOR GLUING TOGETHER MY PROJECT.
YOUR RICE? OH, HONEY, BUT YOU'LL BE TAKING AWAY FROM YOUR LUNCH.
THAT'S WHAT I THOUGHT. SO DO YOU THINK--
WE'LL PROBABLY BE A LITTLE SHORT FOR DINNER TONIGHT. BUT I THINK IT'S DO-ABLE.
I'LL PACK YOUR LUNCH WITH AN EXTRA HELPING OF STICKY WHITE RICE FOR YOUR GLUING PROJECT.
THANKS, MOM.
LATER AT SCHOOL . . .
HEY, KUH-TO, ARE YOU READY FOR OUR PROJECT, DUDE?
HEY, I'M READY FOR LUNCH.

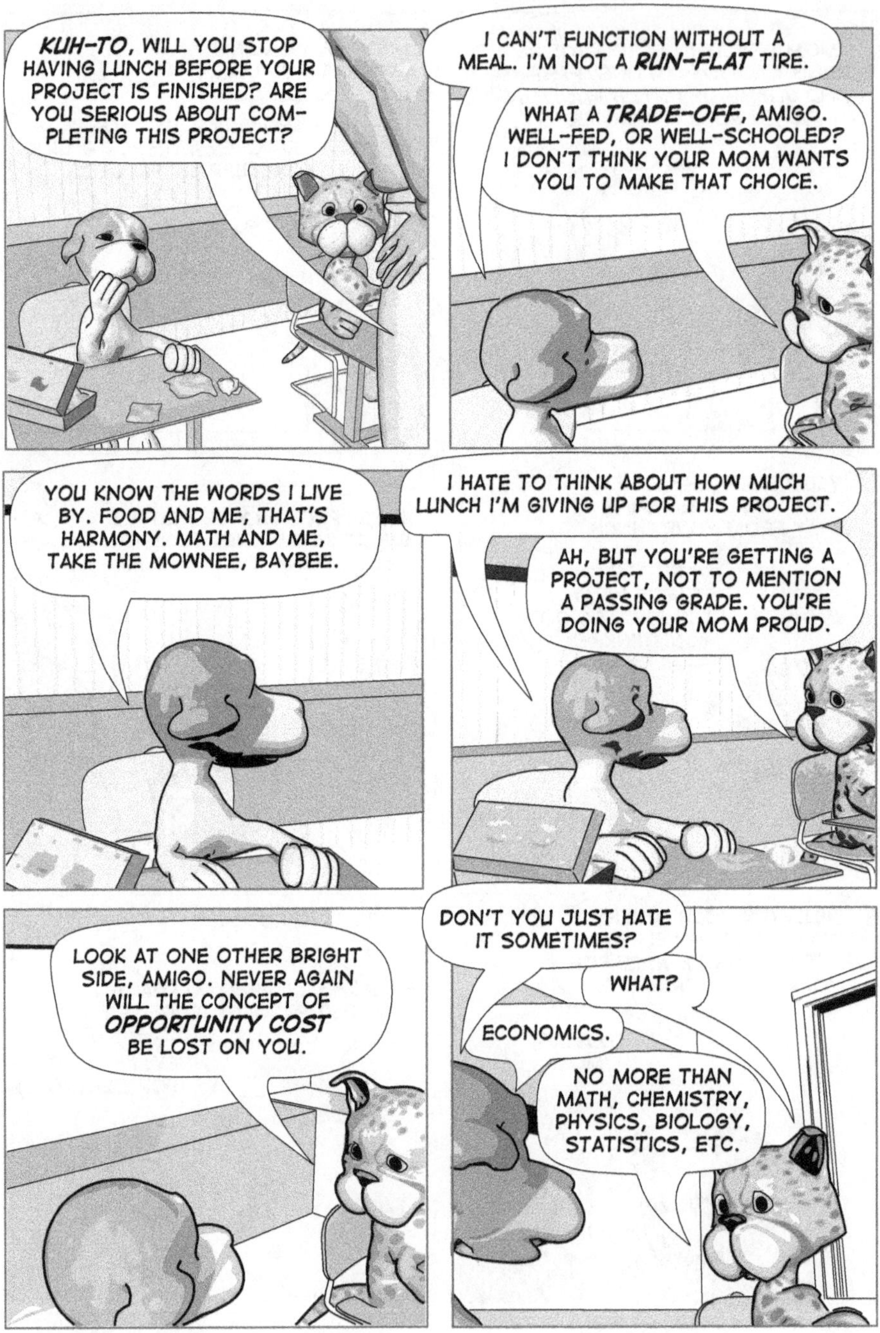
KUH-TO, WILL YOU STOP HAVING LUNCH BEFORE YOUR PROJECT IS FINISHED? ARE YOU SERIOUS ABOUT COMPLETING THIS PROJECT?
I CAN'T FUNCTION WITHOUT A MEAL. I'M NOT A RUN-FLAT TIRE.
WHAT A TRADE-OFF, AMIGO. WELL-FED, OR WELL-SCHOOLED? I DON'T THINK YOUR MOM WANTS YOU TO MAKE THAT CHOICE.
YOU KNOW THE WORDS I LIVE BY. FOOD AND ME, THAT'S HARMONY. MATH AND ME, TAKE THE MOWNEE, BAYBEE.
I HATE TO THINK ABOUT HOW MUCH LUNCH I'M GIVING UP FOR THIS PROJECT.
AH, BUT YOU'RE GETTING A PROJECT, NOT TO MENTION A PASSING GRADE. YOU'RE DOING YOUR MOM PROUD.
LOOK AT ONE OTHER BRIGHT SIDE, AMIGO. NEVER AGAIN WILL THE CONCEPT OF OPPORTUNITY COST BE LOST ON YOU.
DON'T YOU JUST HATE IT SOMETIMES?
WHAT?
ECONOMICS.
NO MORE THAN MATH, CHEMISTRY, PHYSICS, BIOLOGY, STATISTICS, ETC.

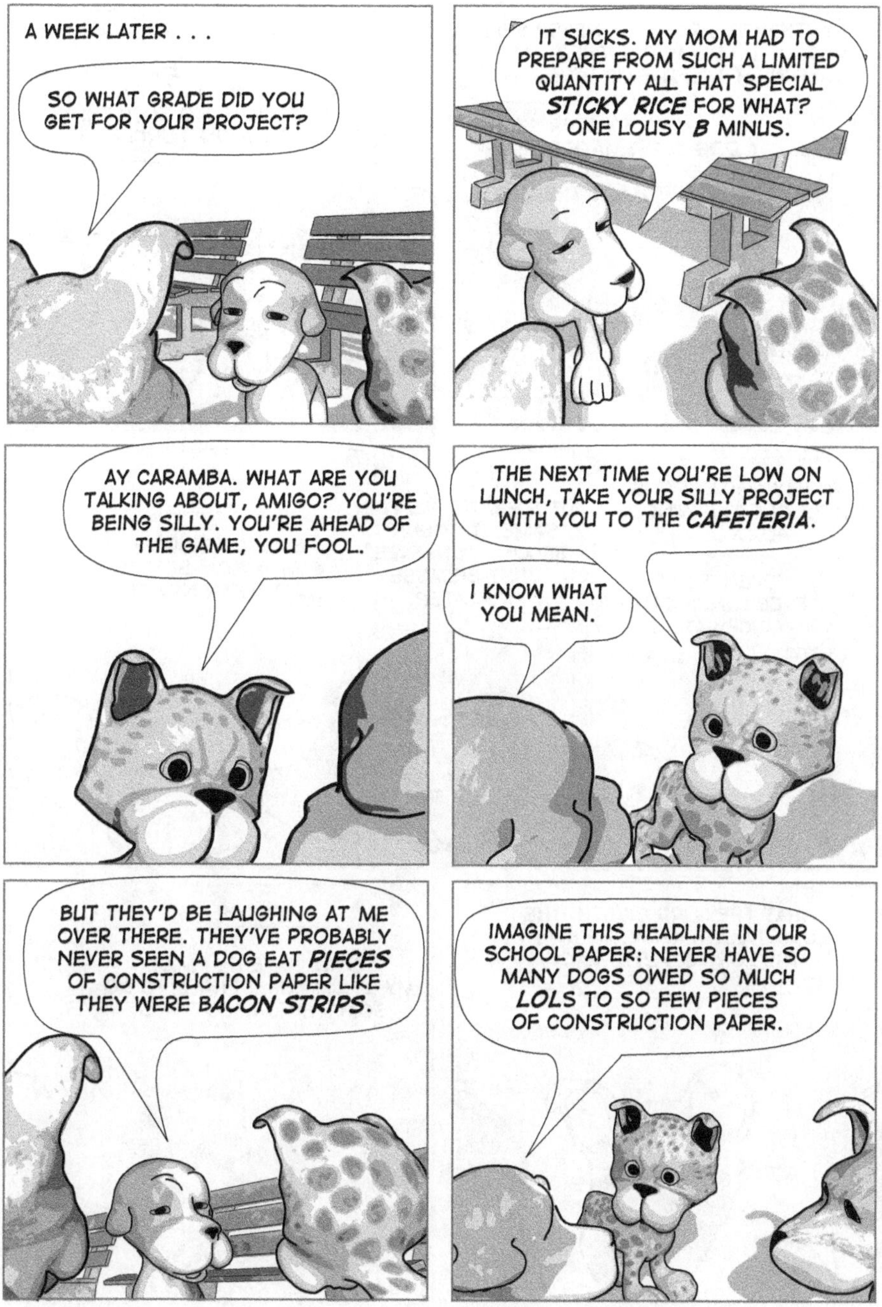
A WEEK LATER . . .
SO WHAT GRADE DID YOU GET FOR YOUR PROJECT?
IT SUCKS. MY MOM HAD TO PREPARE FROM SUCH A LIMITED QUANTITY ALL THAT SPECIAL STICKY RICE FOR WHAT? ONE LOUSY B MINUS.
AY CARAMBA. WHAT ARE YOU TALKING ABOUT, AMIGO? YOU'RE BEING SILLY. YOU'RE AHEAD OF THE GAME, YOU FOOL.
THE NEXT TIME YOU'RE LOW ON LUNCH, TAKE YOUR SILLY PROJECT WITH YOU TO THE CAFETERIA.
I KNOW WHAT YOU MEAN.
BUT THEY'D BE LAUGHING AT ME OVER THERE. THEY'VE PROBABLY NEVER SEEN A DOG EAT PIECES OF CONSTRUCTION PAPER LIKE THEY WERE BACON STRIPS.
IMAGINE THIS HEADLINE IN OUR SCHOOL PAPER: NEVER HAVE SO MANY DOGS OWED SO MUCH LOLS TO SO FEW PIECES OF CONSTRUCTION PAPER.

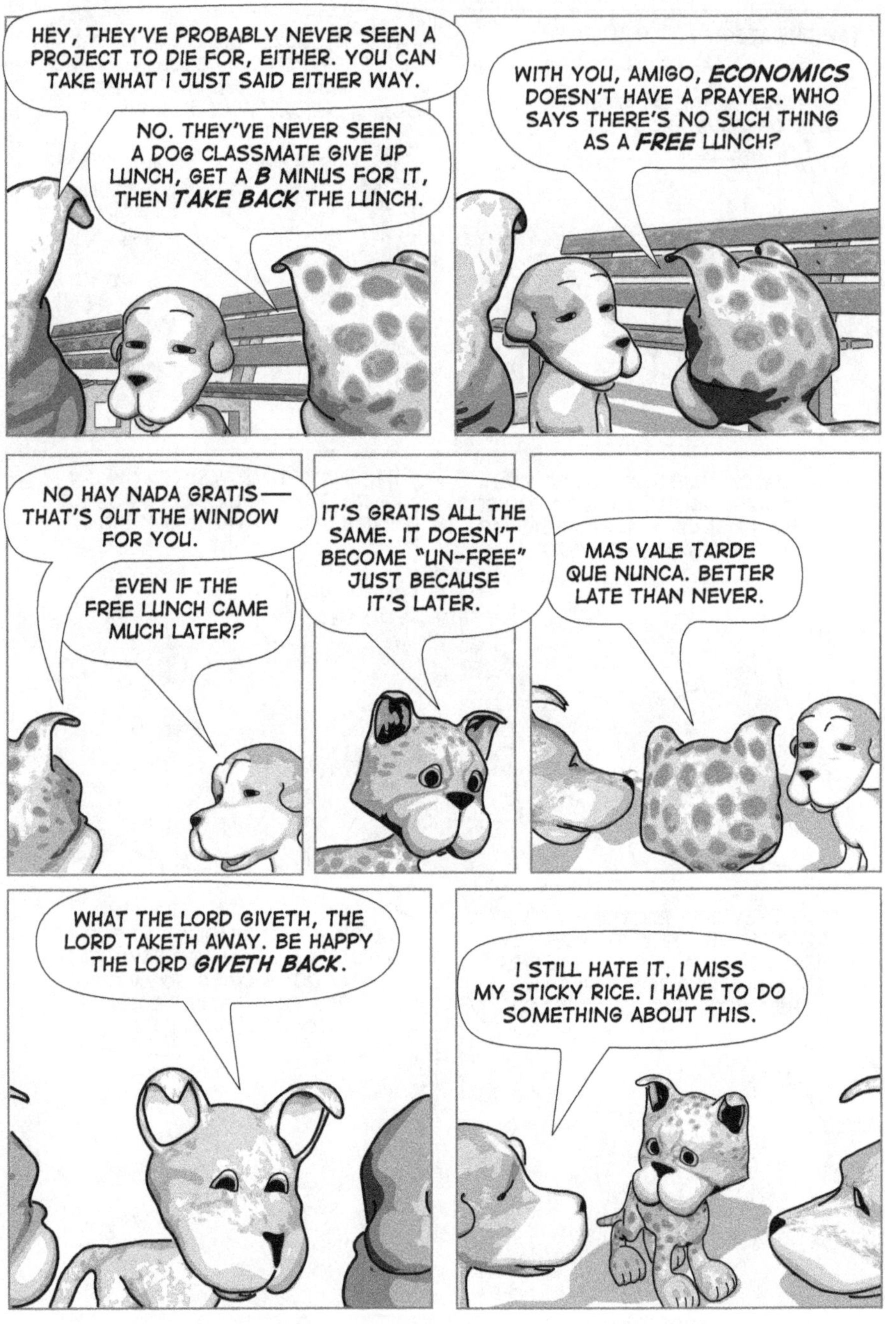
HEY, THEY'VE PROBABLY NEVER SEEN A PROJECT TO DIE FOR, EITHER. YOU CAN TAKE WHAT I JUST SAID EITHER WAY.
NO. THEY'VE NEVER SEEN A DOG CLASSMATE GIVE UP LUNCH, GET A *B* MINUS FOR IT, THEN *TAKE BACK* THE LUNCH.
WITH YOU, AMIGO, *ECONOMICS* DOESN'T HAVE A PRAYER. WHO SAYS THERE'S NO SUCH THING AS A *FREE* LUNCH?
NO HAY NADA GRATIS— THAT'S OUT THE WINDOW FOR YOU.
EVEN IF THE FREE LUNCH CAME MUCH LATER?
IT'S GRATIS ALL THE SAME. IT DOESN'T BECOME "UN-FREE" JUST BECAUSE IT'S LATER.
MAS VALE TARDE QUE NUNCA. BETTER LATE THAN NEVER.
WHAT THE LORD GIVETH, THE LORD TAKETH AWAY. BE HAPPY THE LORD *GIVETH BACK*.
I STILL HATE IT. I MISS MY STICKY RICE. I HAVE TO DO SOMETHING ABOUT THIS.

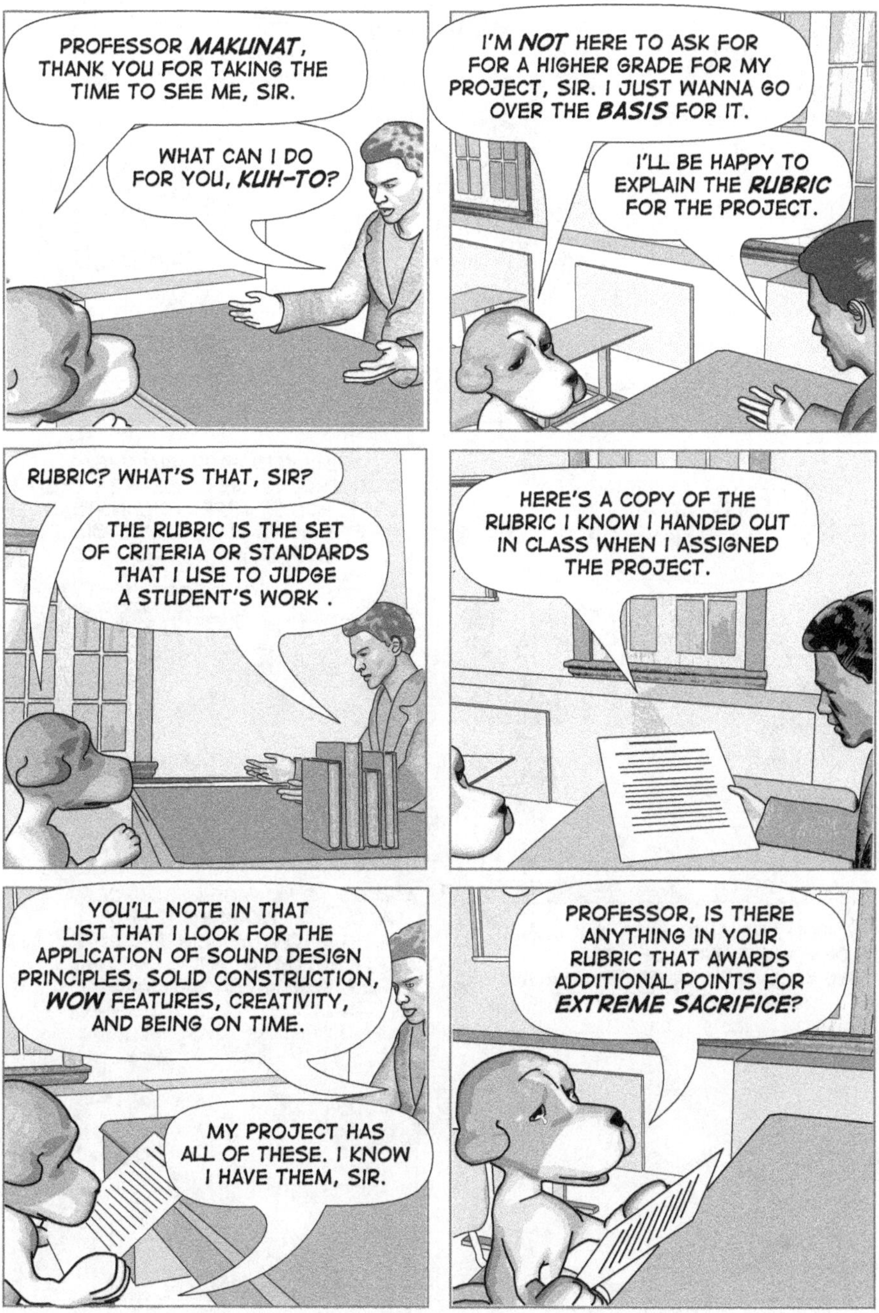
PROFESSOR MAKUNAT, THANK YOU FOR TAKING THE TIME TO SEE ME, SIR.
WHAT CAN I DO FOR YOU, KUH-TO?
I'M NOT HERE TO ASK FOR FOR A HIGHER GRADE FOR MY PROJECT, SIR. I JUST WANNA GO OVER THE BASIS FOR IT.
I'LL BE HAPPY TO EXPLAIN THE RUBRIC FOR THE PROJECT.
RUBRIC? WHAT'S THAT, SIR?
THE RUBRIC IS THE SET OF CRITERIA OR STANDARDS THAT I USE TO JUDGE A STUDENT'S WORK .
HERE'S A COPY OF THE RUBRIC I KNOW I HANDED OUT IN CLASS WHEN I ASSIGNED THE PROJECT.
YOU'LL NOTE IN THAT LIST THAT I LOOK FOR THE APPLICATION OF SOUND DESIGN PRINCIPLES, SOLID CONSTRUCTION, WOW FEATURES, CREATIVITY, AND BEING ON TIME.
MY PROJECT HAS ALL OF THESE. I KNOW I HAVE THEM, SIR.
PROFESSOR, IS THERE ANYTHING IN YOUR RUBRIC THAT AWARDS ADDITIONAL POINTS FOR EXTREME SACRIFICE?

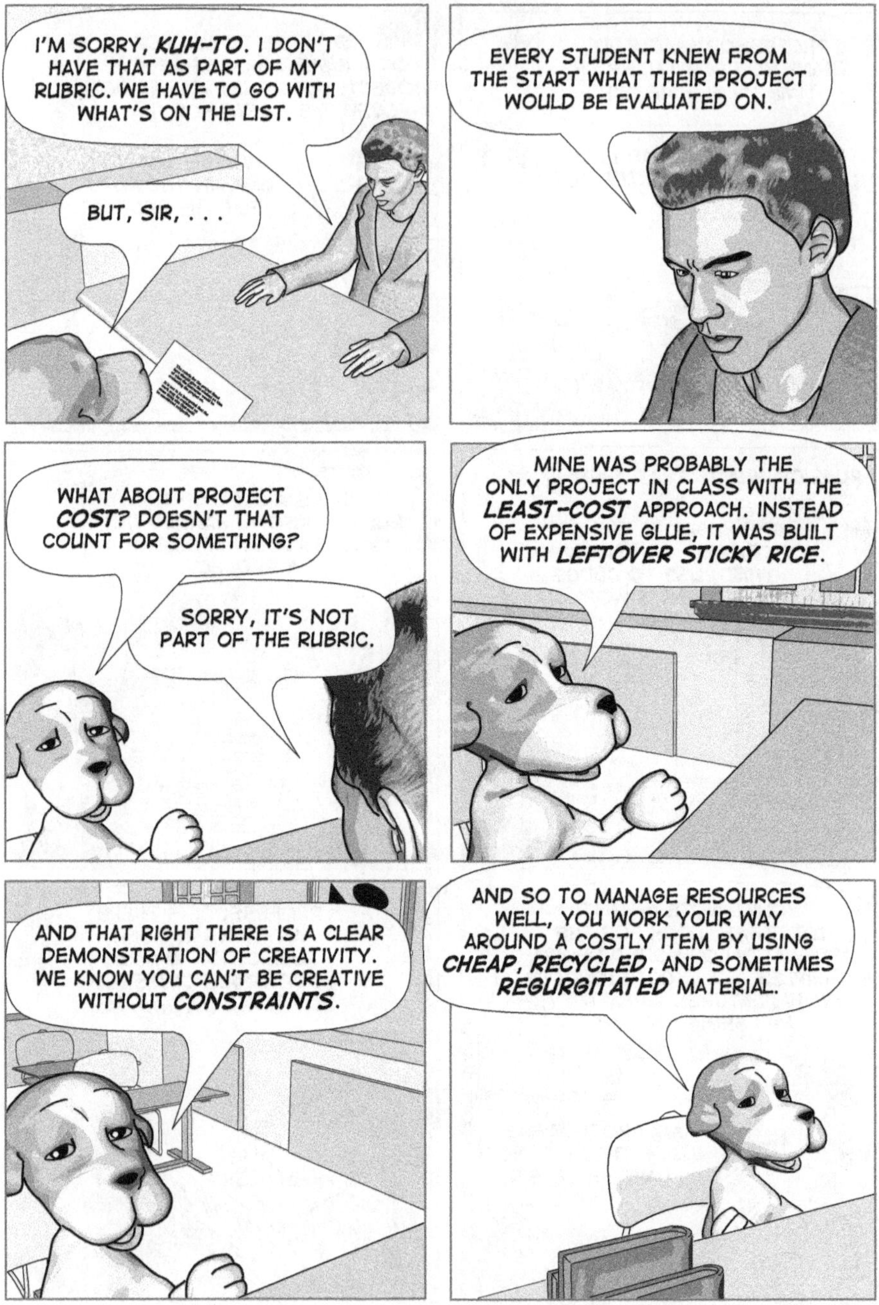
I'M SORRY, KUH-TO. I DON'T HAVE THAT AS PART OF MY RUBRIC. WE HAVE TO GO WITH WHAT'S ON THE LIST.
BUT, SIR, . . .
EVERY STUDENT KNEW FROM THE START WHAT THEIR PROJECT WOULD BE EVALUATED ON.
WHAT ABOUT PROJECT COST? DOESN'T THAT COUNT FOR SOMETHING?
SORRY, IT'S NOT PART OF THE RUBRIC.
MINE WAS PROBABLY THE ONLY PROJECT IN CLASS WITH THE LEAST-COST APPROACH. INSTEAD OF EXPENSIVE GLUE, IT WAS BUILT WITH LEFTOVER STICKY RICE.
AND THAT RIGHT THERE IS A CLEAR DEMONSTRATION OF CREATIVITY. WE KNOW YOU CAN'T BE CREATIVE WITHOUT CONSTRAINTS.
AND SO TO MANAGE RESOURCES WELL, YOU WORK YOUR WAY AROUND A COSTLY ITEM BY USING CHEAP, RECYCLED, AND SOMETIMES REGURGITATED MATERIAL.

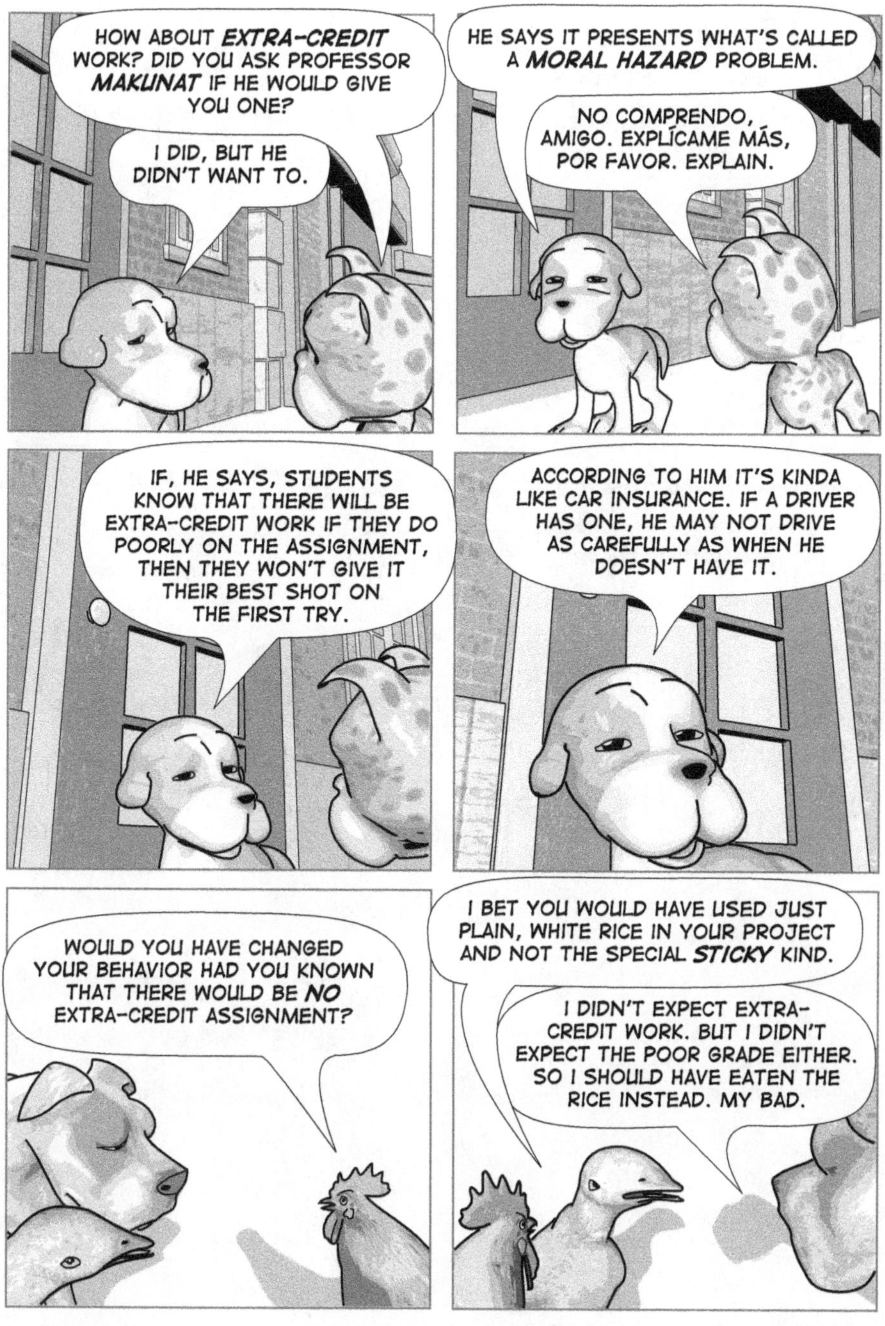
HOW ABOUT EXTRA-CREDIT WORK? DID YOU ASK PROFESSOR MAKUNAT IF HE WOULD GIVE YOU ONE?
I DID, BUT HE DIDN'T WANT TO.
HE SAYS IT PRESENTS WHAT'S CALLED A MORAL HAZARD PROBLEM.
NO COMPRENDO, AMIGO. EXPLÍCAME MÁS, POR FAVOR. EXPLAIN.
IF, HE SAYS, STUDENTS KNOW THAT THERE WILL BE EXTRA-CREDIT WORK IF THEY DO POORLY ON THE ASSIGNMENT, THEN THEY WON'T GIVE IT THEIR BEST SHOT ON THE FIRST TRY.
ACCORDING TO HIM IT'S KINDA LIKE CAR INSURANCE. IF A DRIVER HAS ONE, HE MAY NOT DRIVE AS CAREFULLY AS WHEN HE DOESN'T HAVE IT.
WOULD YOU HAVE CHANGED YOUR BEHAVIOR HAD YOU KNOWN THAT THERE WOULD BE NO EXTRA-CREDIT ASSIGNMENT?
I BET YOU WOULD HAVE USED JUST PLAIN, WHITE RICE IN YOUR PROJECT AND NOT THE SPECIAL STICKY KIND.
I DIDN'T EXPECT EXTRA-CREDIT WORK. BUT I DIDN'T EXPECT THE POOR GRADE EITHER. SO I SHOULD HAVE EATEN THE RICE INSTEAD. MY BAD.

I ASKED TO MEET WITH HIM AGAIN TO DISCUSS MY PROJECT SOME MORE BUT HE SAID HE WOULDN'T BE AVAILABLE.
SOMETIMES I'M AT A LOSS AS TO WHAT PROFESSORS REALLY DO.
YOU MEAN OTHER THAN TEACH?
WHAT ELSE IS THERE?
I HEARD THEY ALSO HAVE TO PUBLISH ***AND*** PERISH.
HOW SOON?

WHAT WAS THIS CLASS PROJECT THAT YOU WERE SO WORKED UP ABOUT?
IT WAS A MINIATURE DOGHOUSE. A MODEL.
A MINIATURE DOGHOUSE?
IT WAS NO ORDINARY MINIATURE DOGHOUSE.
UP UNTIL THAT TIME I'VE NEVER HAD A REAL DOGHOUSE. THE MODEL WAS FOR ME A SYMBOLIC EMBODIMENT OF THE AMERICAN DREAM OF HOMEOWNERSHIP.
WITH SO MANY HUMAN HOMES UNDERWATER IN THE U.S., I KNOW IT'S KINDA IRONIC TO THINK OF HOMEOWNERSHIP.
BUT IT'S GOT A UNIQUELY RETRO FEEL PREVIOUSLY UNHEARD OF IN THE ANNALS OF DOGHOUSE DESIGN WHICH THE PROFESSOR NEVER QUITE APPRECIATED.
ITS BAHAY-KUBO* DESIGN LENT IT SIMPLICITY AND A CULTURAL WOW FACTOR.
AND THIS LAST ONE IS WHAT STILL GETS A RISE OUT OF ME AFTER ALL THESE YEARS.
MY MINIATURE DOGHOUSE CAME WITH ITS OWN OUTHOUSE.

* Built as a single-room dwelling, a traditional *bahay kubo* is a thatched-roof hut, cubic in shape and uses native Philippine materials like bamboo and nipa palm.

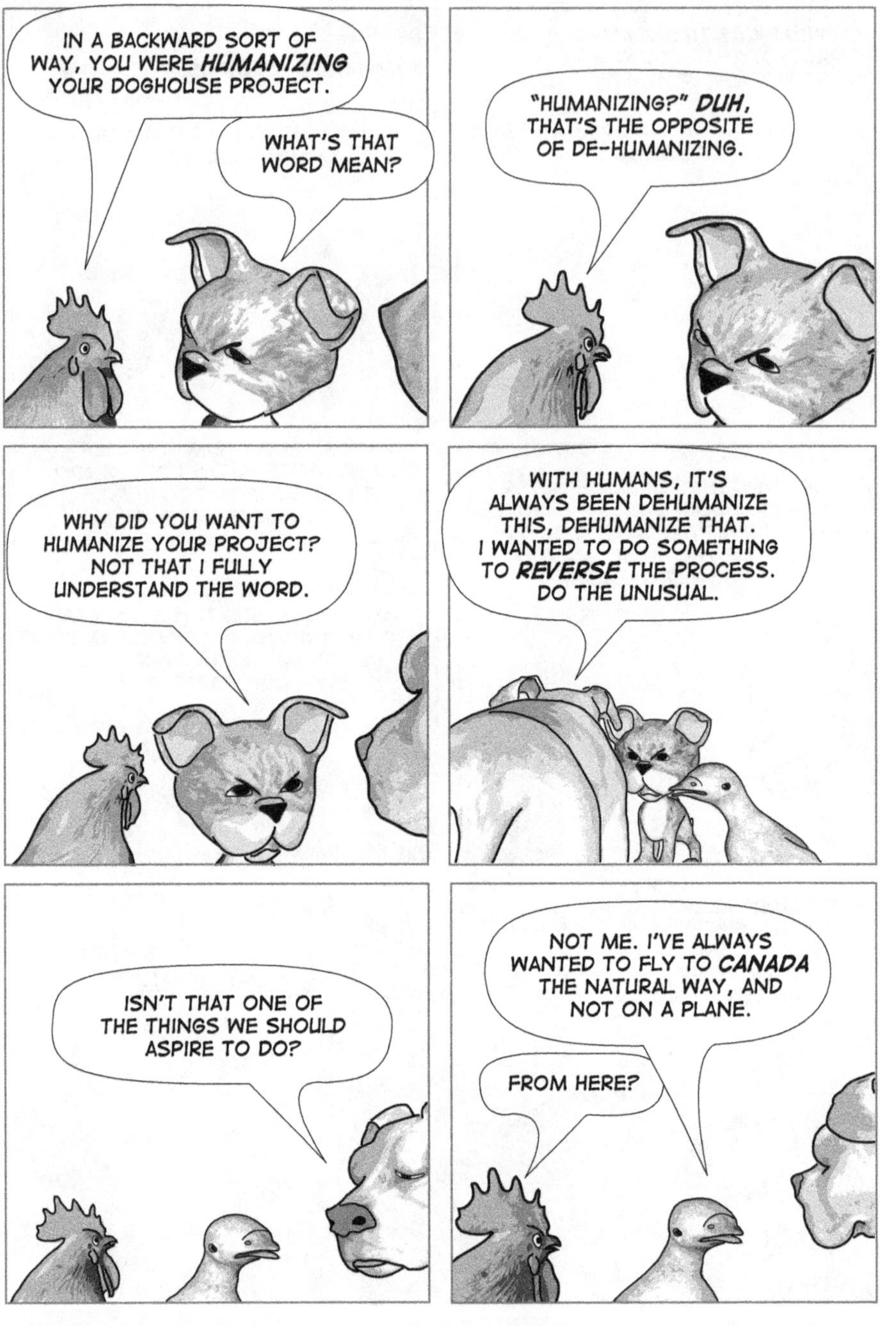
IN A BACKWARD SORT OF WAY, YOU WERE *HUMANIZING* YOUR DOGHOUSE PROJECT.
WHAT'S THAT WORD MEAN?
"HUMANIZING?" *DUH*, THAT'S THE OPPOSITE OF DE-HUMANIZING.
WHY DID YOU WANT TO HUMANIZE YOUR PROJECT? NOT THAT I FULLY UNDERSTAND THE WORD.
WITH HUMANS, IT'S ALWAYS BEEN DEHUMANIZE THIS, DEHUMANIZE THAT. I WANTED TO DO SOMETHING TO *REVERSE* THE PROCESS. DO THE UNUSUAL.
ISN'T THAT ONE OF THE THINGS WE SHOULD ASPIRE TO DO?
NOT ME. I'VE ALWAYS WANTED TO FLY TO *CANADA* THE NATURAL WAY, AND NOT ON A PLANE.
FROM HERE?

South Korea, North Korea, and an Incentive System for U.N. Inspectors

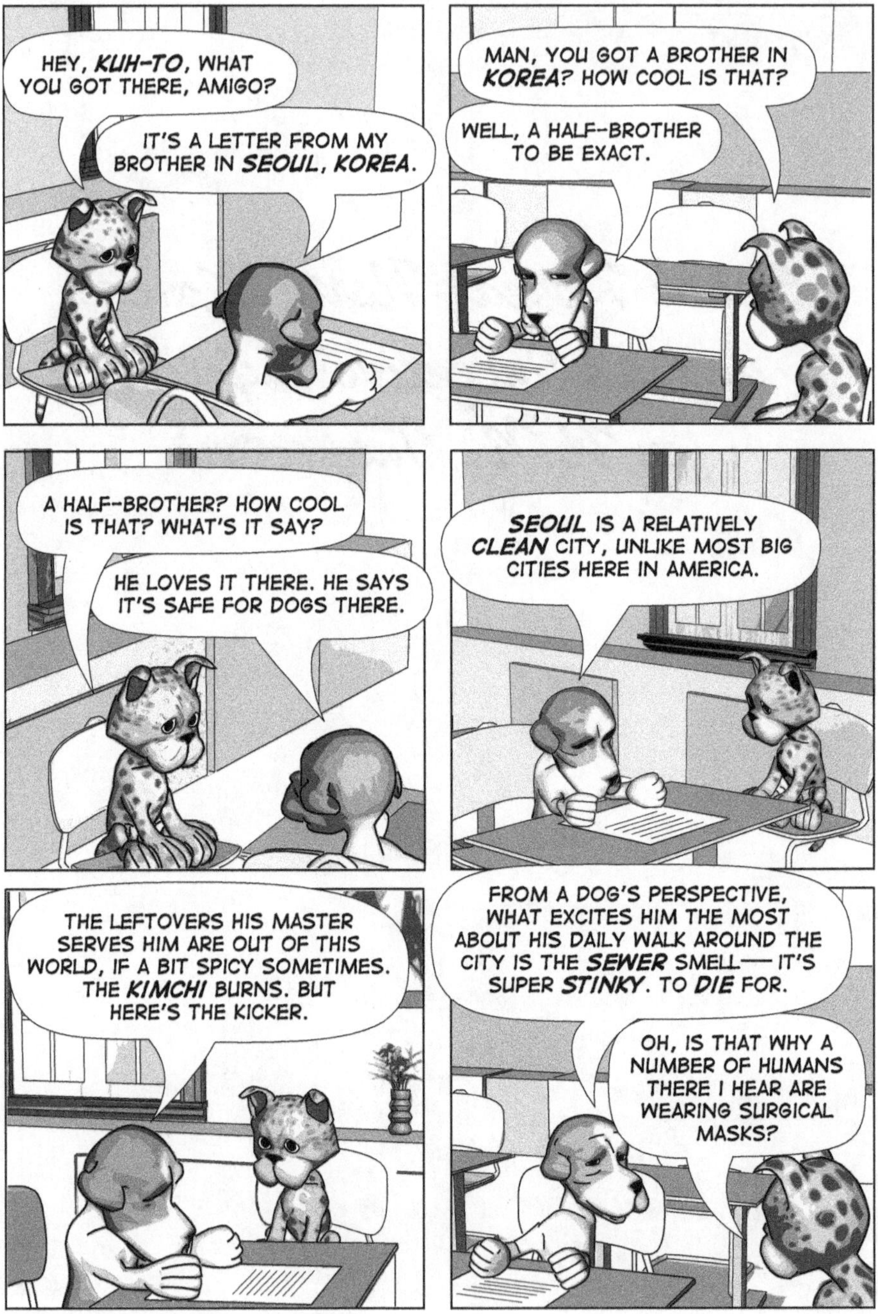
HEY, ***KUH-TO***, WHAT YOU GOT THERE, AMIGO?
IT'S A LETTER FROM MY BROTHER IN ***SEOUL, KOREA***.
MAN, YOU GOT A BROTHER IN ***KOREA***? HOW COOL IS THAT?
WELL, A HALF-BROTHER TO BE EXACT.
A HALF-BROTHER? HOW COOL IS THAT? WHAT'S IT SAY?
HE LOVES IT THERE. HE SAYS IT'S SAFE FOR DOGS THERE.
SEOUL IS A RELATIVELY ***CLEAN*** CITY, UNLIKE MOST BIG CITIES HERE IN AMERICA.
THE LEFTOVERS HIS MASTER SERVES HIM ARE OUT OF THIS WORLD, IF A BIT SPICY SOMETIMES. THE ***KIMCHI*** BURNS. BUT HERE'S THE KICKER.
FROM A DOG'S PERSPECTIVE, WHAT EXCITES HIM THE MOST ABOUT HIS DAILY WALK AROUND THE CITY IS THE ***SEWER*** SMELL— IT'S SUPER ***STINKY***. TO ***DIE*** FOR.
OH, IS THAT WHY A NUMBER OF HUMANS THERE I HEAR ARE WEARING SURGICAL MASKS?

MY HALF--BROTHER IN SOUTH KOREA WRITES THAT NORTH KOREA RECENTLY OPENED ITS FIRST FAST FOOD RESTAURANT.
REALLY? THE FIRST FAST FOOD RESTAURANT EVER IN COMMUNIST NORTH KOREA?
YEP, BUT HE SAYS IT DOESN'T SELL "HAMBURGERS."
WHY NOT?
IT SELLS WHAT IT CALLS "MINCED BEEF AND BREAD," WHICH, MY HALF--BROTHER SAYS, LOOKS SUSPCIOUSLY LIKE A HAMBURGER.
WAY CALL IT THAT? WHY NOT CALL A SPADE A SPADE, AND A HAMBURGER A HAMBURGER?
THE ISOLATIONIST COUNTRY DOESN'T WANT TO GIVE THE IMPRESSION THAT IT HAS EMBRACED THE AMERICAN WAY OF FINE DINING.
I WONDER WHAT WORDS THE NORTH KOREANS WOULD USE TO DISGUISE GAINING WEIGHT.

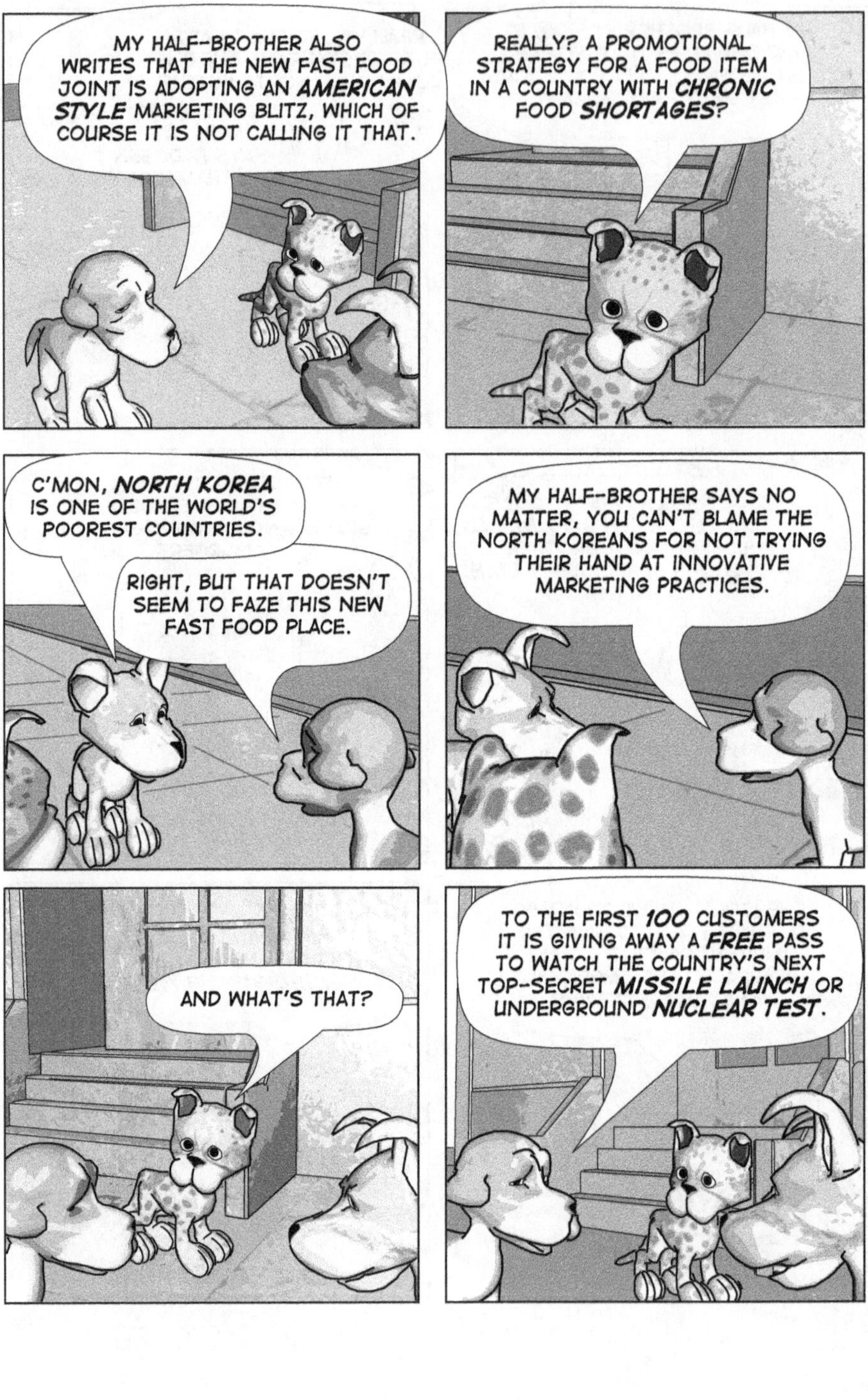
MY HALF-BROTHER ALSO WRITES THAT THE NEW FAST FOOD JOINT IS ADOPTING AN AMERICAN STYLE MARKETING BLITZ, WHICH OF COURSE IT IS NOT CALLING IT THAT.
REALLY? A PROMOTIONAL STRATEGY FOR A FOOD ITEM IN A COUNTRY WITH CHRONIC FOOD SHORTAGES?
C'MON, NORTH KOREA IS ONE OF THE WORLD'S POOREST COUNTRIES.
RIGHT, BUT THAT DOESN'T SEEM TO FAZE THIS NEW FAST FOOD PLACE.
MY HALF-BROTHER SAYS NO MATTER, YOU CAN'T BLAME THE NORTH KOREANS FOR NOT TRYING THEIR HAND AT INNOVATIVE MARKETING PRACTICES.
AND WHAT'S THAT?
TO THE FIRST 100 CUSTOMERS IT IS GIVING AWAY A FREE PASS TO WATCH THE COUNTRY'S NEXT TOP-SECRET MISSILE LAUNCH OR UNDERGROUND NUCLEAR TEST.

MY HALF--BROTHER IN SOUTH KOREA SAYS WEIGHT GAIN MAY NOT BE AN ISSUE WITH THE HAMBURGERS SERVED BY THIS NEW FAST FOOD JOINT.
WHY NOT?
IT'S PARTLY BECAUSE OF THE FAMINE IN THAT COUNTRY, BUT HE ALSO SAYS THE JOINT OFFERS REALLY LEAN BEEF PATTIES THAT COME FROM COWS GRAZING NEAR THE MISSILE LAUNCH SITE.
MOMMY, WHY WOULD COWS GRAZING NEAR A MISSILE LAUNCH SITE HAVE EXTRA LEAN MEAT?
HIJO, EVERY TIME A MISSILE IS LAUNCHED, THE COWS GET VERY NERVOUS. THEY LOOK UP TO THE HEAVENS AND PRAY FOR PEACE IN THE KOREAN PENINSULA.
YOU CAN'T BLAME THE POOR COWS. IT IS A HEART-STOPPING MOMENT FOR THEM EVERY TIME.
AND SO THEY EAT LESS AND LESS, AND PRETTY SOON THEY GET DEPRESSED, MALNOURISHED, SKINNY. SKINNY COWS YIELD LEAN MEAT. GET IT, HIJO?
BUT ONLY WHEN IN A PENINSULA, RIGHT, MOMMY?

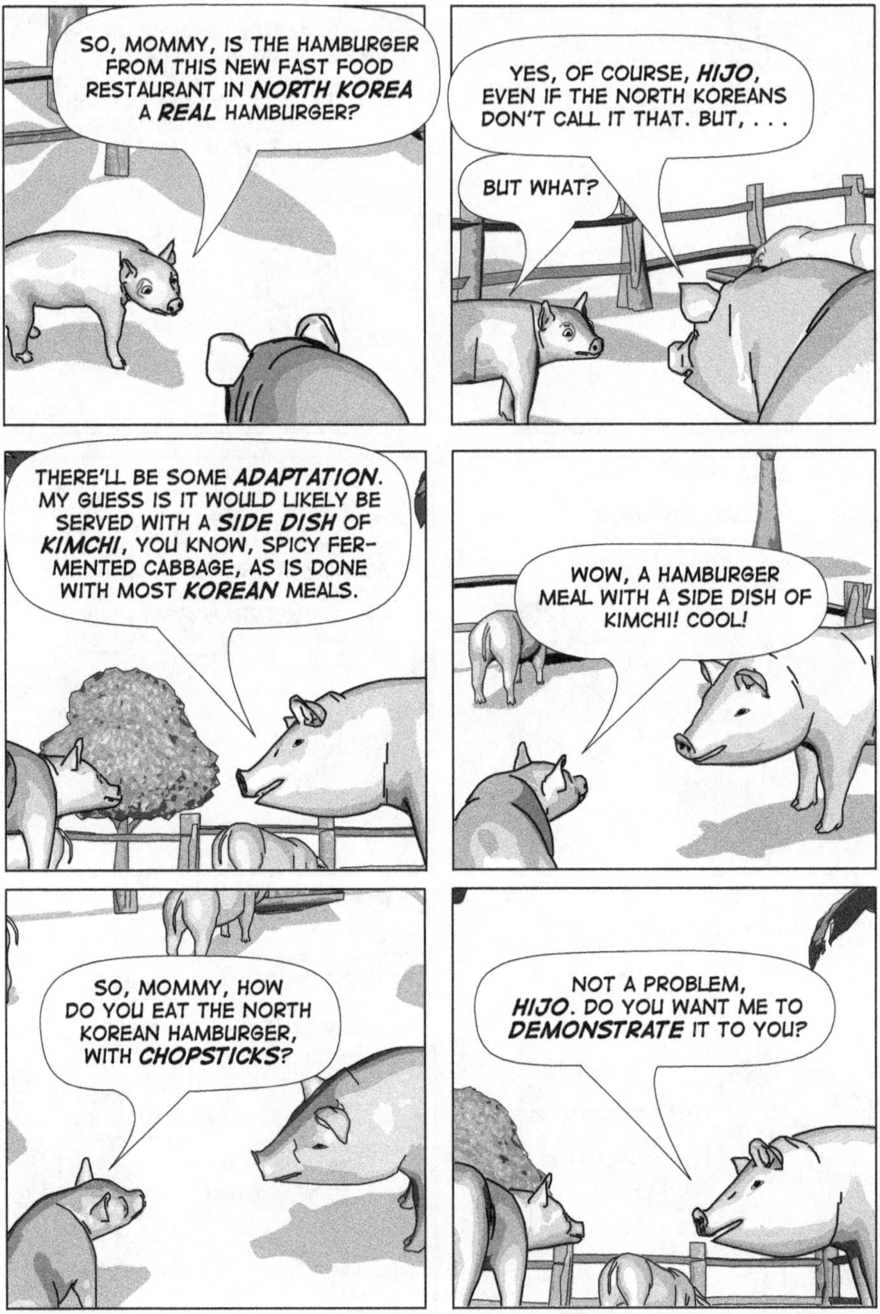
SO, MOMMY, IS THE HAMBURGER FROM THIS NEW FAST FOOD RESTAURANT IN NORTH KOREA A REAL HAMBURGER?
YES, OF COURSE, HIJO, EVEN IF THE NORTH KOREANS DON'T CALL IT THAT. BUT, . . .
BUT WHAT?
THERE'LL BE SOME ADAPTATION. MY GUESS IS IT WOULD LIKELY BE SERVED WITH A SIDE DISH OF KIMCHI, YOU KNOW, SPICY FERMENTED CABBAGE, AS IS DONE WITH MOST KOREAN MEALS.
WOW, A HAMBURGER MEAL WITH A SIDE DISH OF KIMCHI! COOL!
SO, MOMMY, HOW DO YOU EAT THE NORTH KOREAN HAMBURGER, WITH CHOPSTICKS?
NOT A PROBLEM, HIJO. DO YOU WANT ME TO DEMONSTRATE IT TO YOU?

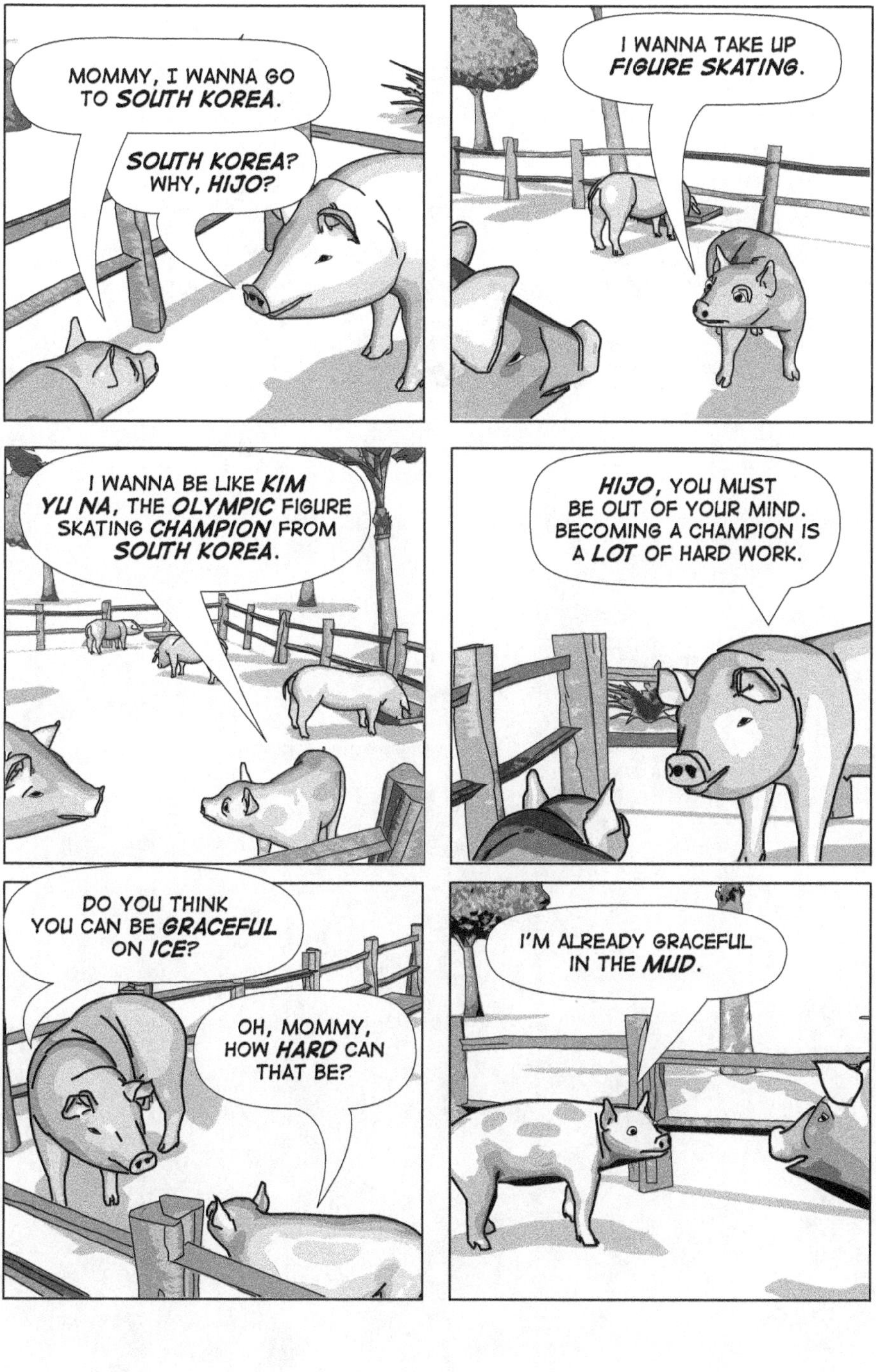
MOMMY, I WANNA GO TO SOUTH KOREA.
SOUTH KOREA? WHY, HIJO?
I WANNA TAKE UP FIGURE SKATING.
I WANNA BE LIKE KIM YU NA, THE OLYMPIC FIGURE SKATING CHAMPION FROM SOUTH KOREA.
HIJO, YOU MUST BE OUT OF YOUR MIND. BECOMING A CHAMPION IS A LOT OF HARD WORK.
DO YOU THINK YOU CAN BE GRACEFUL ON ICE?
OH, MOMMY, HOW HARD CAN THAT BE?
I'M ALREADY GRACEFUL IN THE MUD.

GDP and Well-Being: A Doggone Issue

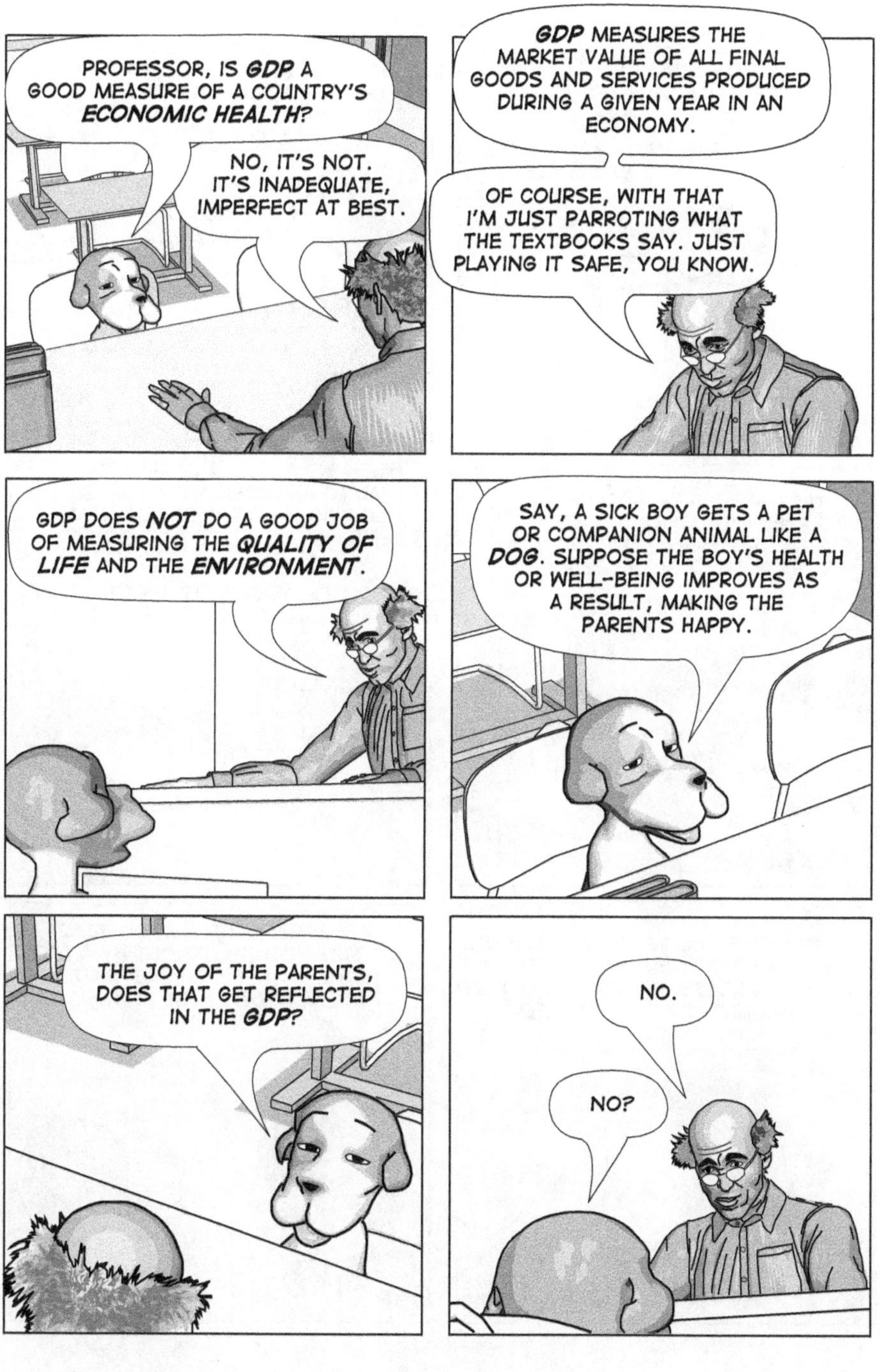
PROFESSOR, IS GDP A GOOD MEASURE OF A COUNTRY'S ECONOMIC HEALTH?
NO, IT'S NOT. IT'S INADEQUATE, IMPERFECT AT BEST.
GDP MEASURES THE MARKET VALUE OF ALL FINAL GOODS AND SERVICES PRODUCED DURING A GIVEN YEAR IN AN ECONOMY.
OF COURSE, WITH THAT I'M JUST PARROTING WHAT THE TEXTBOOKS SAY. JUST PLAYING IT SAFE, YOU KNOW.
GDP DOES NOT DO A GOOD JOB OF MEASURING THE QUALITY OF LIFE AND THE ENVIRONMENT.
SAY, A SICK BOY GETS A PET OR COMPANION ANIMAL LIKE A DOG. SUPPOSE THE BOY'S HEALTH OR WELL-BEING IMPROVES AS A RESULT, MAKING THE PARENTS HAPPY.
THE JOY OF THE PARENTS, DOES THAT GET REFLECTED IN THE GDP?
NO.
NO?

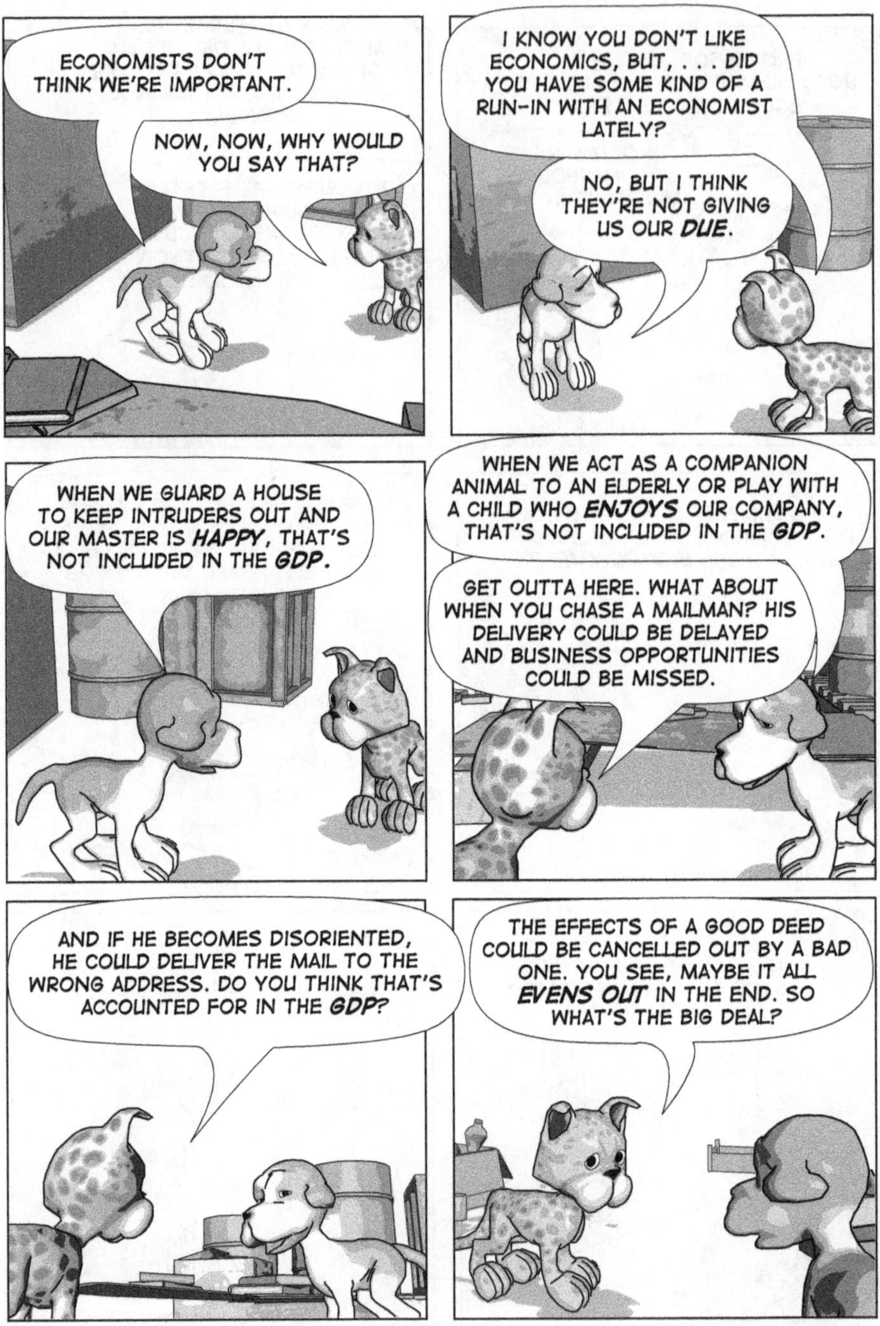
ECONOMISTS DON'T THINK WE'RE IMPORTANT.
NOW, NOW, WHY WOULD YOU SAY THAT?
I KNOW YOU DON'T LIKE ECONOMICS, BUT, . . . DID YOU HAVE SOME KIND OF A RUN-IN WITH AN ECONOMIST LATELY?
NO, BUT I THINK THEY'RE NOT GIVING US OUR *DUE*.
WHEN WE GUARD A HOUSE TO KEEP INTRUDERS OUT AND OUR MASTER IS *HAPPY*, THAT'S NOT INCLUDED IN THE *GDP*.
WHEN WE ACT AS A COMPANION ANIMAL TO AN ELDERLY OR PLAY WITH A CHILD WHO *ENJOYS* OUR COMPANY, THAT'S NOT INCLUDED IN THE *GDP*.
GET OUTTA HERE. WHAT ABOUT WHEN YOU CHASE A MAILMAN? HIS DELIVERY COULD BE DELAYED AND BUSINESS OPPORTUNITIES COULD BE MISSED.
AND IF HE BECOMES DISORIENTED, HE COULD DELIVER THE MAIL TO THE WRONG ADDRESS. DO YOU THINK THAT'S ACCOUNTED FOR IN THE *GDP*?
THE EFFECTS OF A GOOD DEED COULD BE CANCELLED OUT BY A BAD ONE. YOU SEE, MAYBE IT ALL *EVENS OUT* IN THE END. SO WHAT'S THE BIG DEAL?

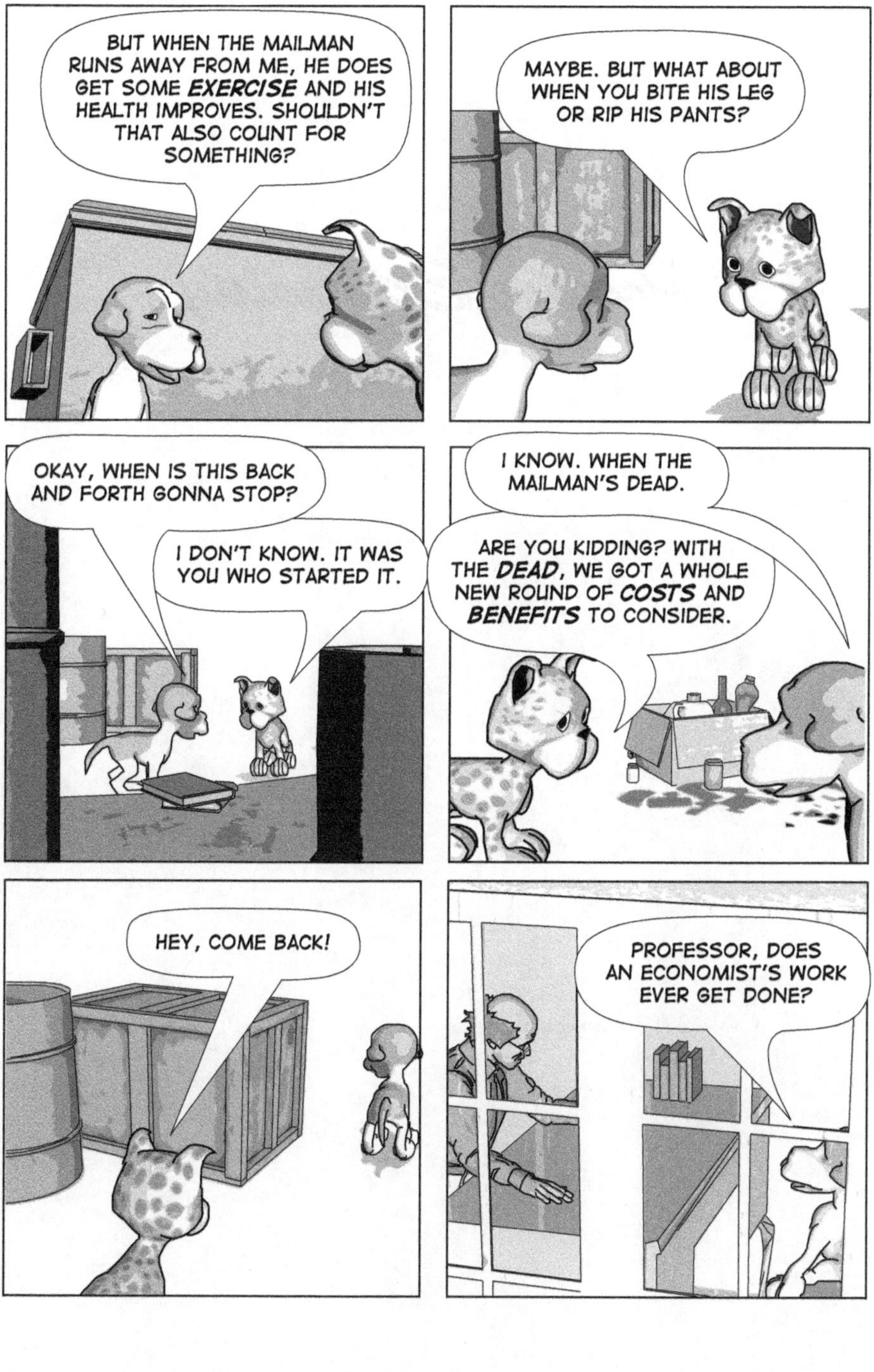
BUT WHEN THE MAILMAN RUNS AWAY FROM ME, HE DOES GET SOME *EXERCISE* AND HIS HEALTH IMPROVES. SHOULDN'T THAT ALSO COUNT FOR SOMETHING?
MAYBE. BUT WHAT ABOUT WHEN YOU BITE HIS LEG OR RIP HIS PANTS?
OKAY, WHEN IS THIS BACK AND FORTH GONNA STOP?
I DON'T KNOW. IT WAS YOU WHO STARTED IT.
I KNOW. WHEN THE MAILMAN'S DEAD.
ARE YOU KIDDING? WITH THE *DEAD*, WE GOT A WHOLE NEW ROUND OF *COSTS* AND *BENEFITS* TO CONSIDER.
HEY, COME BACK!
PROFESSOR, DOES AN ECONOMIST'S WORK EVER GET DONE?

Positive Externality

I'M STILL PUZZLED. NOW WHY WOULD A DOG BE A ***POSITIVE EXTERNALITY*** ACCORDING TO THE PROFESSOR? NOT THAT I MIND.
NOT ALL THE TIME BUT HERE'S WHY. YOU HAVE THE DOG OWNER ENJOYING THE BENEFITS OF OWNING YOU. AND RIGHTLY SO BECAUSE HE OR SHE IS FEEDING YOU.
WHEN YOU KEEP WATCH OVER YOUR MASTER'S PROPERTY, YOU DETER CRIMINALS.
AND BECAUSE YOUR PRESENCE IS MAKING THE NEIGHBORHOOD SAFER AND HOMES MORE VALUABLE, THE COMMUNITY ALSO BENEFITS IF INDIRECTLY.
NOT MEANING TO BEAT A DEAD HORSE BUT, WHAT IF I BARK AT THE MAILMAN AND CHASE THE POOR GUY?
THEN YOU'RE CREATING A ***NEGATIVE*** EXTERNALITY. YOU'RE MAKING NOISE, DISRUP-TING MAIL DELIVERY, AND CREATING A WHOLE HOSTS OF NEGATIVE EFFECTS ON THE COMMUNITY, WHICH COULD LATER PROVE COSTLY WHEN CORRECTED.
AM I RIGHT, ***HUMBERTO***?
SI. AND YOU'RE ALSO PROBABLY DISRUPTING HIS LUNCH, WHICH COULD BE VERY, VERY DISRUPTIVE.
HOW WOULD YOU FEEL IF THE MAILMAN DOES THAT TO YOU— DISRUPT YOUR LUNCH?
THEN THAT MEANS ***WAR***, NOT EXTERNALITY.

Frictional Unemployment

DO YOU THINK IT'S GONNA BE ON THE TEST?
WHICH ONE?
FRICTIONAL UNEMPLOYMENT.
YEP, I WOULD THINK SO.
FRICTIONAL UNEMPLOYMENT? WHAT'S THAT?
I DON'T REMEMBER THAT BEING COVERED IN CLASS.
OH, YEAH, IT WAS COVERED.
IF I REMEMBER RIGHT, YOU SKIPPED CLASS THAT DAY.
DARN!
FRICTIONAL UNEMPLOYMENT IS UNEMPLOYMENT DUE TO A TEMPORARY MISMATCH BETWEEN THE SKILLS AND EXPERIENCE OF JOB SEEKERS AND THOSE WANTED BY EMPLOYERS.

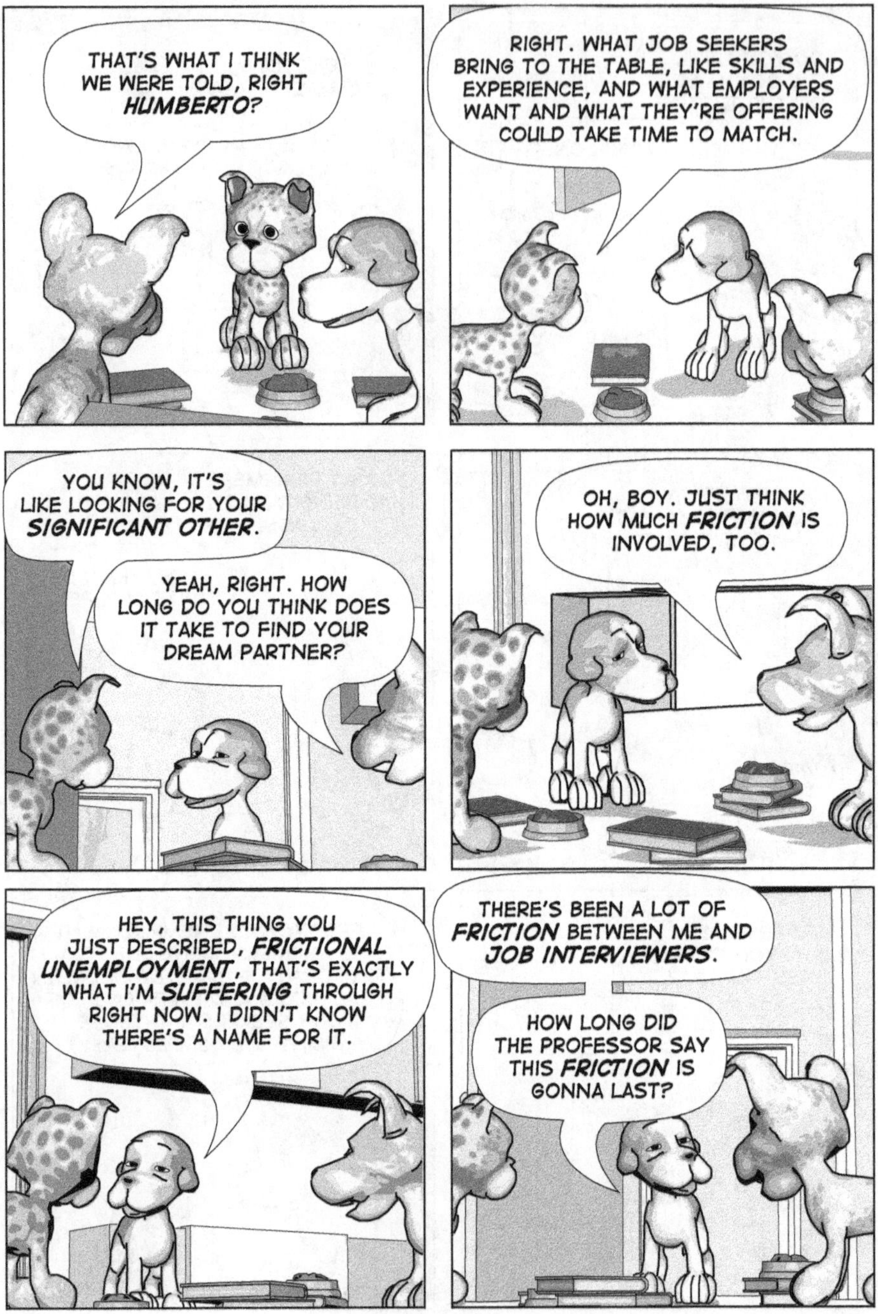
THAT'S WHAT I THINK WE WERE TOLD, RIGHT HUMBERTO?
RIGHT. WHAT JOB SEEKERS BRING TO THE TABLE, LIKE SKILLS AND EXPERIENCE, AND WHAT EMPLOYERS WANT AND WHAT THEY'RE OFFERING COULD TAKE TIME TO MATCH.
YOU KNOW, IT'S LIKE LOOKING FOR YOUR SIGNIFICANT OTHER.
YEAH, RIGHT. HOW LONG DO YOU THINK DOES IT TAKE TO FIND YOUR DREAM PARTNER?
OH, BOY. JUST THINK HOW MUCH FRICTION IS INVOLVED, TOO.
HEY, THIS THING YOU JUST DESCRIBED, FRICTIONAL UNEMPLOYMENT, THAT'S EXACTLY WHAT I'M SUFFERING THROUGH RIGHT NOW. I DIDN'T KNOW THERE'S A NAME FOR IT.
THERE'S BEEN A LOT OF FRICTION BETWEEN ME AND JOB INTERVIEWERS.
HOW LONG DID THE PROFESSOR SAY THIS FRICTION IS GONNA LAST?

A Boomer Master Works on His Set (Not Jump) Shot

THE AGING BOOMER MASTER NO LONGER PLAYS BASKETBALL IN HIS BACKYARD OR HUNTS DOWN A PICKUP GAME IN THE STREET.
BUT HIS FANTASY ABOUT DRILLING THE WINNING BASKET IN THE WANING SECONDS OF AN NBA GAME LIVES ON.
SO EVERY TIME HE GETS AN OPPORTUNITY, HE PRETENDS TO SINK A BASKETBALL SHOT INTO THE TRASH WITH A BALLED-UP PIECE OF PAPER.
SO FOR HIM NO MORE FANCY FADEAWAY SHOTS WITH A REAL BASKETBALL?
NO, HE'S JUST FAAADING AWAY.

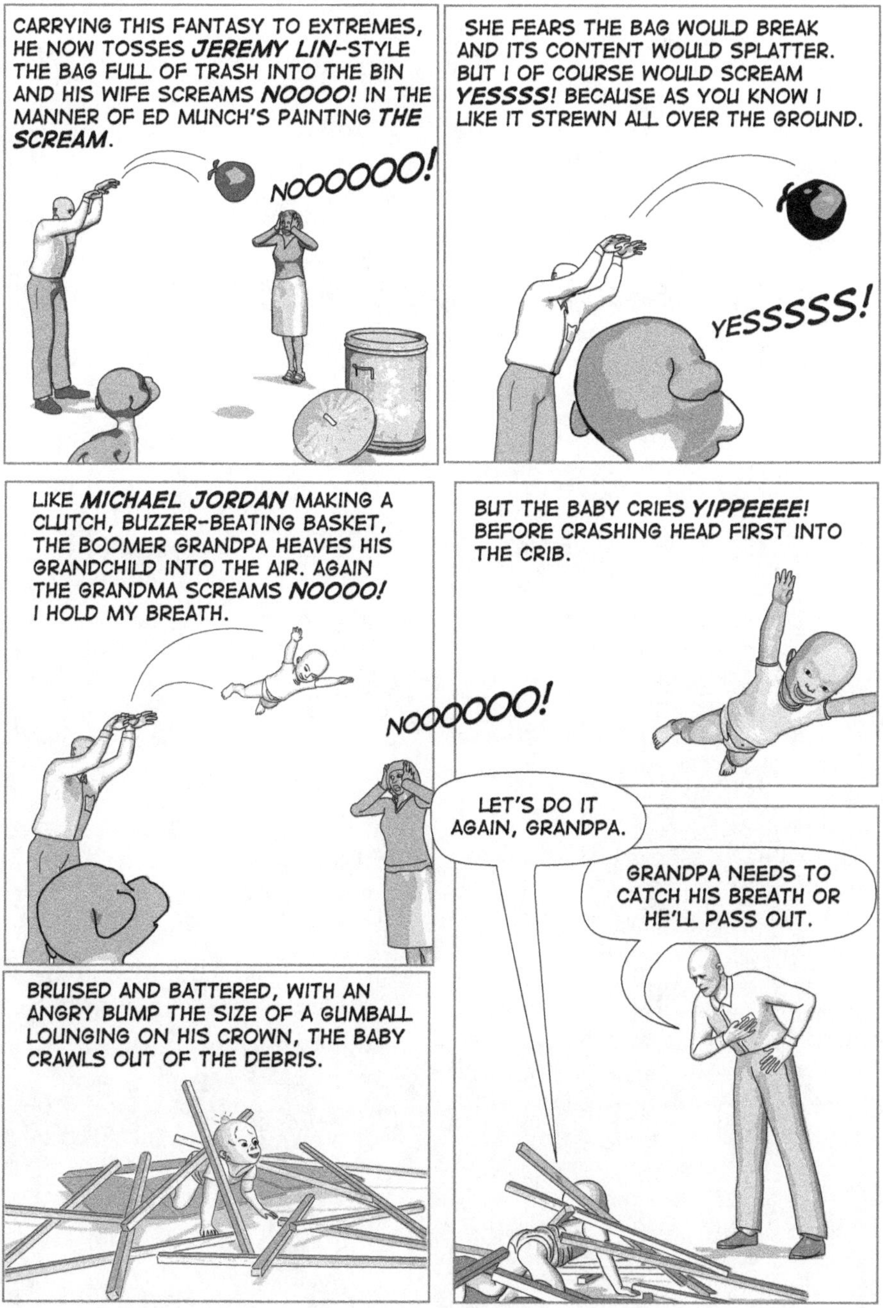
CARRYING THIS FANTASY TO EXTREMES, HE NOW TOSSES JEREMY LIN-STYLE THE BAG FULL OF TRASH INTO THE BIN AND HIS WIFE SCREAMS NOOOO! IN THE MANNER OF ED MUNCH'S PAINTING THE SCREAM.
NOOOOOO!
SHE FEARS THE BAG WOULD BREAK AND ITS CONTENT WOULD SPLATTER. BUT I OF COURSE WOULD SCREAM YESSSS! BECAUSE AS YOU KNOW I LIKE IT STREWN ALL OVER THE GROUND.
YESSSSS!
LIKE MICHAEL JORDAN MAKING A CLUTCH, BUZZER-BEATING BASKET, THE BOOMER GRANDPA HEAVES HIS GRANDCHILD INTO THE AIR. AGAIN THE GRANDMA SCREAMS NOOOO! I HOLD MY BREATH.
NOOOOOO!
BUT THE BABY CRIES YIPPEEEE! BEFORE CRASHING HEAD FIRST INTO THE CRIB.
BRUISED AND BATTERED, WITH AN ANGRY BUMP THE SIZE OF A GUMBALL LOUNGING ON HIS CROWN, THE BABY CRAWLS OUT OF THE DEBRIS.
LET'S DO IT AGAIN, GRANDPA.
GRANDPA NEEDS TO CATCH HIS BREATH OR HE'LL PASS OUT.

Memories and Pledges

KUH-TO, IF THE GUY FROM THE COLLECTION AGENCY SHOWS UP, TELL HIM I'M NOT IN.
YES, SIR, MASTER.
A LITTLE LATER . . .
I'M HERE TO SEE YOUR MASTER.
HE SAYS HE'S NOT IN.
ARE YOU SURE?
WAIT HERE. I'LL CHECK INSIDE.
A MINUTE LATER . . .
HE SAYS HE'S NOT IN. LEAVE A MESSAGE.
BUT YOU JUST SAID YOU'D CHECK WITH HIM.
I DID. I WENT IN AND PLAYED *BACK* HIS *ANSWERING MACHINE*.

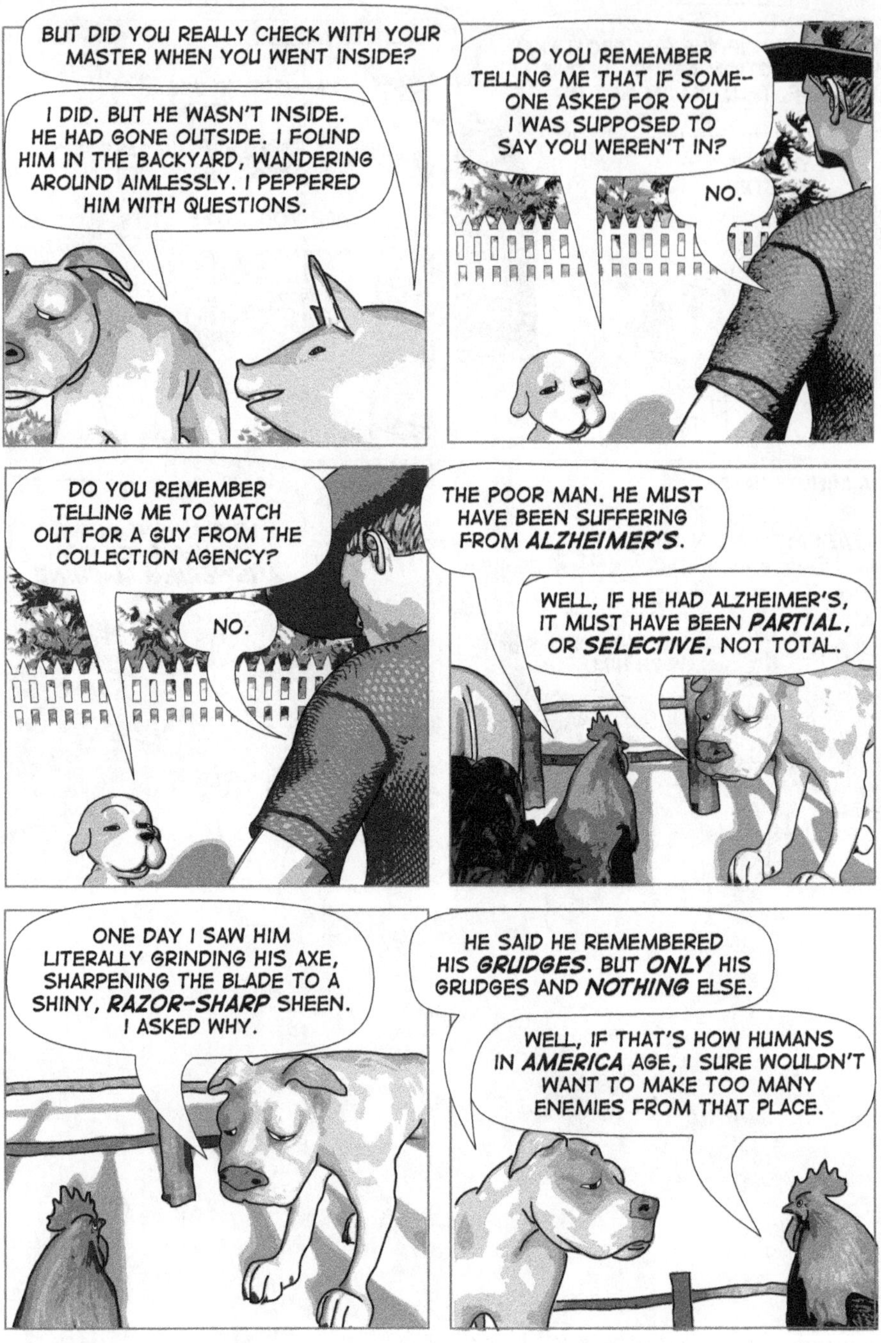
BUT DID YOU REALLY CHECK WITH YOUR MASTER WHEN YOU WENT INSIDE?
I DID. BUT HE WASN'T INSIDE. HE HAD GONE OUTSIDE. I FOUND HIM IN THE BACKYARD, WANDERING AROUND AIMLESSLY. I PEPPERED HIM WITH QUESTIONS.
DO YOU REMEMBER TELLING ME THAT IF SOME-ONE ASKED FOR YOU I WAS SUPPOSED TO SAY YOU WEREN'T IN?
NO.
DO YOU REMEMBER TELLING ME TO WATCH OUT FOR A GUY FROM THE COLLECTION AGENCY?
NO.
THE POOR MAN. HE MUST HAVE BEEN SUFFERING FROM *ALZHEIMER'S*.
WELL, IF HE HAD ALZHEIMER'S, IT MUST HAVE BEEN *PARTIAL*, OR *SELECTIVE*, NOT TOTAL.
ONE DAY I SAW HIM LITERALLY GRINDING HIS AXE, SHARPENING THE BLADE TO A SHINY, *RAZOR-SHARP* SHEEN. I ASKED WHY.
HE SAID HE REMEMBERED HIS *GRUDGES*. BUT *ONLY* HIS GRUDGES AND *NOTHING* ELSE.
WELL, IF THAT'S HOW HUMANS IN *AMERICA* AGE, I SURE WOULDN'T WANT TO MAKE TOO MANY ENEMIES FROM THAT PLACE.

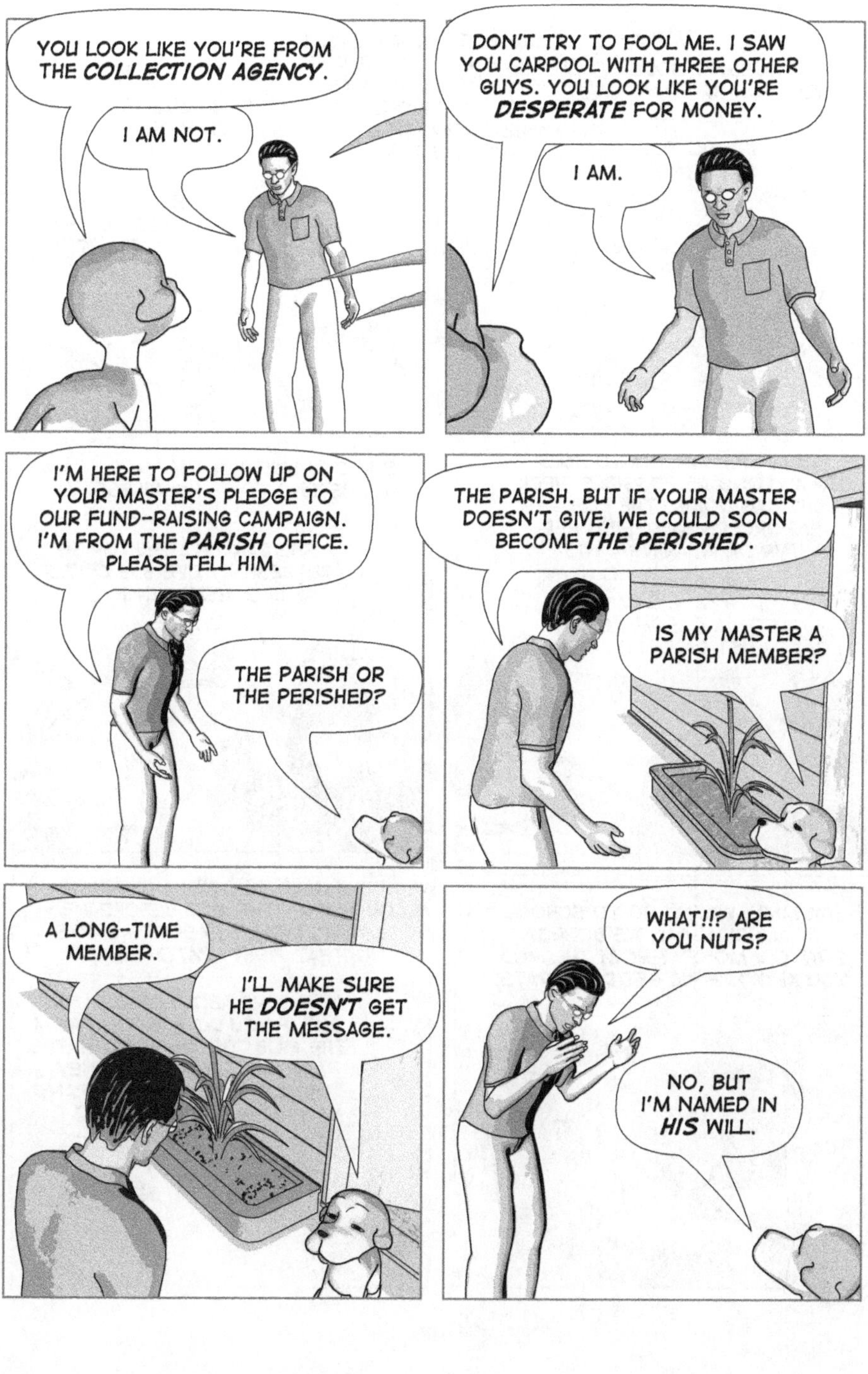
YOU LOOK LIKE YOU'RE FROM THE *COLLECTION AGENCY*.
I AM NOT.
DON'T TRY TO FOOL ME. I SAW YOU CARPOOL WITH THREE OTHER GUYS. YOU LOOK LIKE YOU'RE *DESPERATE* FOR MONEY.
I AM.
I'M HERE TO FOLLOW UP ON YOUR MASTER'S PLEDGE TO OUR FUND-RAISING CAMPAIGN. I'M FROM THE *PARISH* OFFICE. PLEASE TELL HIM.
THE PARISH OR THE PERISHED?
THE PARISH. BUT IF YOUR MASTER DOESN'T GIVE, WE COULD SOON BECOME *THE PERISHED*.
IS MY MASTER A PARISH MEMBER?
A LONG-TIME MEMBER.
I'LL MAKE SURE HE *DOESN'T* GET THE MESSAGE.
WHAT!!? ARE YOU NUTS?
NO, BUT I'M NAMED IN *HIS* WILL.

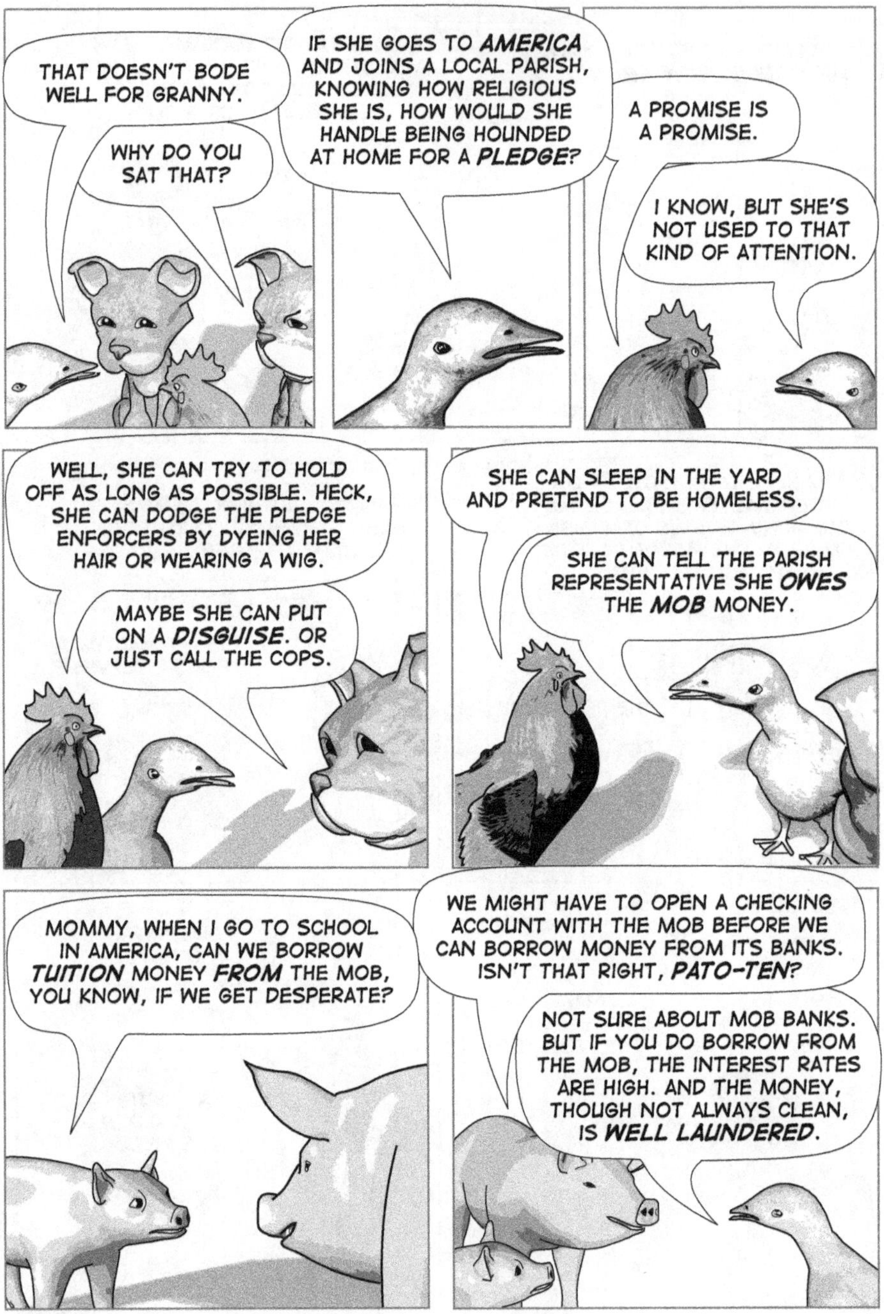
THAT DOESN'T BODE WELL FOR GRANNY.
WHY DO YOU SAT THAT?
IF SHE GOES TO AMERICA AND JOINS A LOCAL PARISH, KNOWING HOW RELIGIOUS SHE IS, HOW WOULD SHE HANDLE BEING HOUNDED AT HOME FOR A PLEDGE?
A PROMISE IS A PROMISE.
I KNOW, BUT SHE'S NOT USED TO THAT KIND OF ATTENTION.
WELL, SHE CAN TRY TO HOLD OFF AS LONG AS POSSIBLE. HECK, SHE CAN DODGE THE PLEDGE ENFORCERS BY DYEING HER HAIR OR WEARING A WIG.
MAYBE SHE CAN PUT ON A DISGUISE. OR JUST CALL THE COPS.
SHE CAN SLEEP IN THE YARD AND PRETEND TO BE HOMELESS.
SHE CAN TELL THE PARISH REPRESENTATIVE SHE OWES THE MOB MONEY.
MOMMY, WHEN I GO TO SCHOOL IN AMERICA, CAN WE BORROW TUITION MONEY FROM THE MOB, YOU KNOW, IF WE GET DESPERATE?
WE MIGHT HAVE TO OPEN A CHECKING ACCOUNT WITH THE MOB BEFORE WE CAN BORROW MONEY FROM ITS BANKS. ISN'T THAT RIGHT, PATO-TEN?
NOT SURE ABOUT MOB BANKS. BUT IF YOU DO BORROW FROM THE MOB, THE INTEREST RATES ARE HIGH. AND THE MONEY, THOUGH NOT ALWAYS CLEAN, IS WELL LAUNDERED.

Extreme Parenting and The Tiger Mom

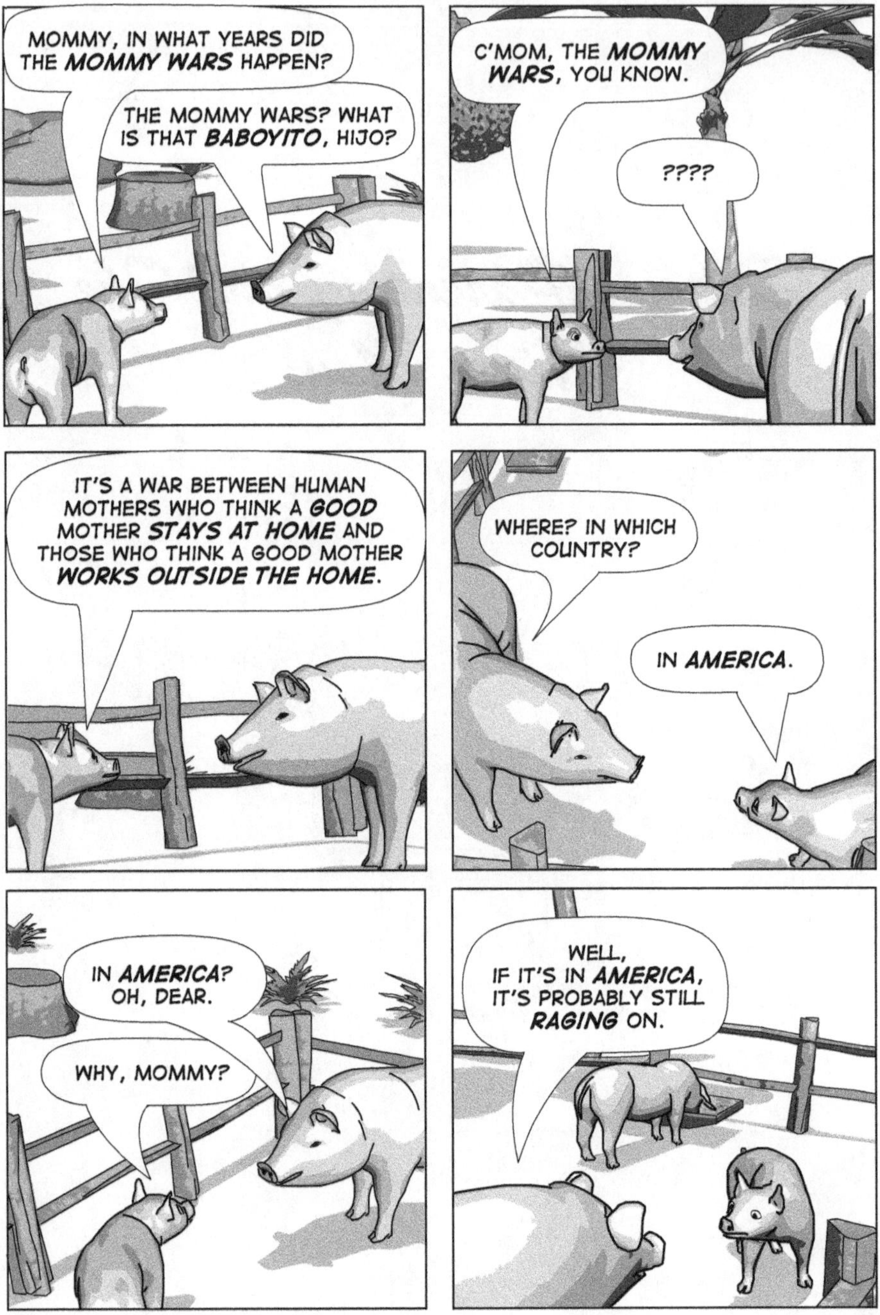
MOMMY, IN WHAT YEARS DID THE MOMMY WARS HAPPEN?
THE MOMMY WARS? WHAT IS THAT BABOYITO, HIJO?
C'MOM, THE MOMMY WARS, YOU KNOW.
????
IT'S A WAR BETWEEN HUMAN MOTHERS WHO THINK A GOOD MOTHER STAYS AT HOME AND THOSE WHO THINK A GOOD MOTHER WORKS OUTSIDE THE HOME.
WHERE? IN WHICH COUNTRY?
IN AMERICA.
IN AMERICA? OH, DEAR.
WHY, MOMMY?
WELL, IF IT'S IN AMERICA, IT'S PROBABLY STILL RAGING ON.

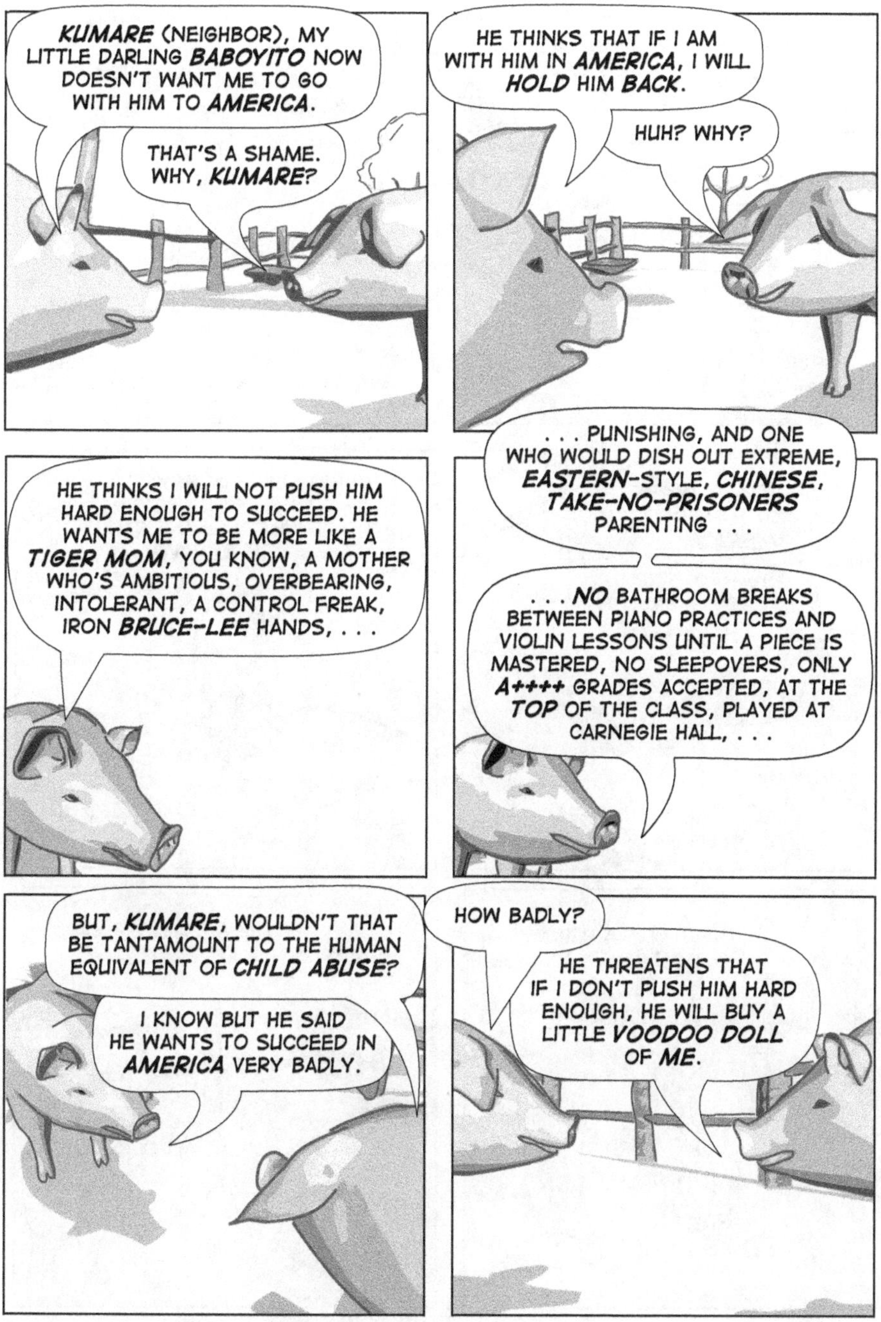
KUMARE (NEIGHBOR), MY LITTLE DARLING BABOYITO NOW DOESN'T WANT ME TO GO WITH HIM TO AMERICA.
THAT'S A SHAME. WHY, KUMARE?
HE THINKS THAT IF I AM WITH HIM IN AMERICA, I WILL HOLD HIM BACK.
HUH? WHY?
HE THINKS I WILL NOT PUSH HIM HARD ENOUGH TO SUCCEED. HE WANTS ME TO BE MORE LIKE A TIGER MOM, YOU KNOW, A MOTHER WHO'S AMBITIOUS, OVERBEARING, INTOLERANT, A CONTROL FREAK, IRON BRUCE-LEE HANDS, . . .
. . . PUNISHING, AND ONE WHO WOULD DISH OUT EXTREME, EASTERN-STYLE, CHINESE, TAKE-NO-PRISONERS PARENTING . . .
. . . NO BATHROOM BREAKS BETWEEN PIANO PRACTICES AND VIOLIN LESSONS UNTIL A PIECE IS MASTERED, NO SLEEPOVERS, ONLY A++++ GRADES ACCEPTED, AT THE TOP OF THE CLASS, PLAYED AT CARNEGIE HALL, . . .
BUT, KUMARE, WOULDN'T THAT BE TANTAMOUNT TO THE HUMAN EQUIVALENT OF CHILD ABUSE?
I KNOW BUT HE SAID HE WANTS TO SUCCEED IN AMERICA VERY BADLY.
HOW BADLY?
HE THREATENS THAT IF I DON'T PUSH HIM HARD ENOUGH, HE WILL BUY A LITTLE VOODOO DOLL OF ME.

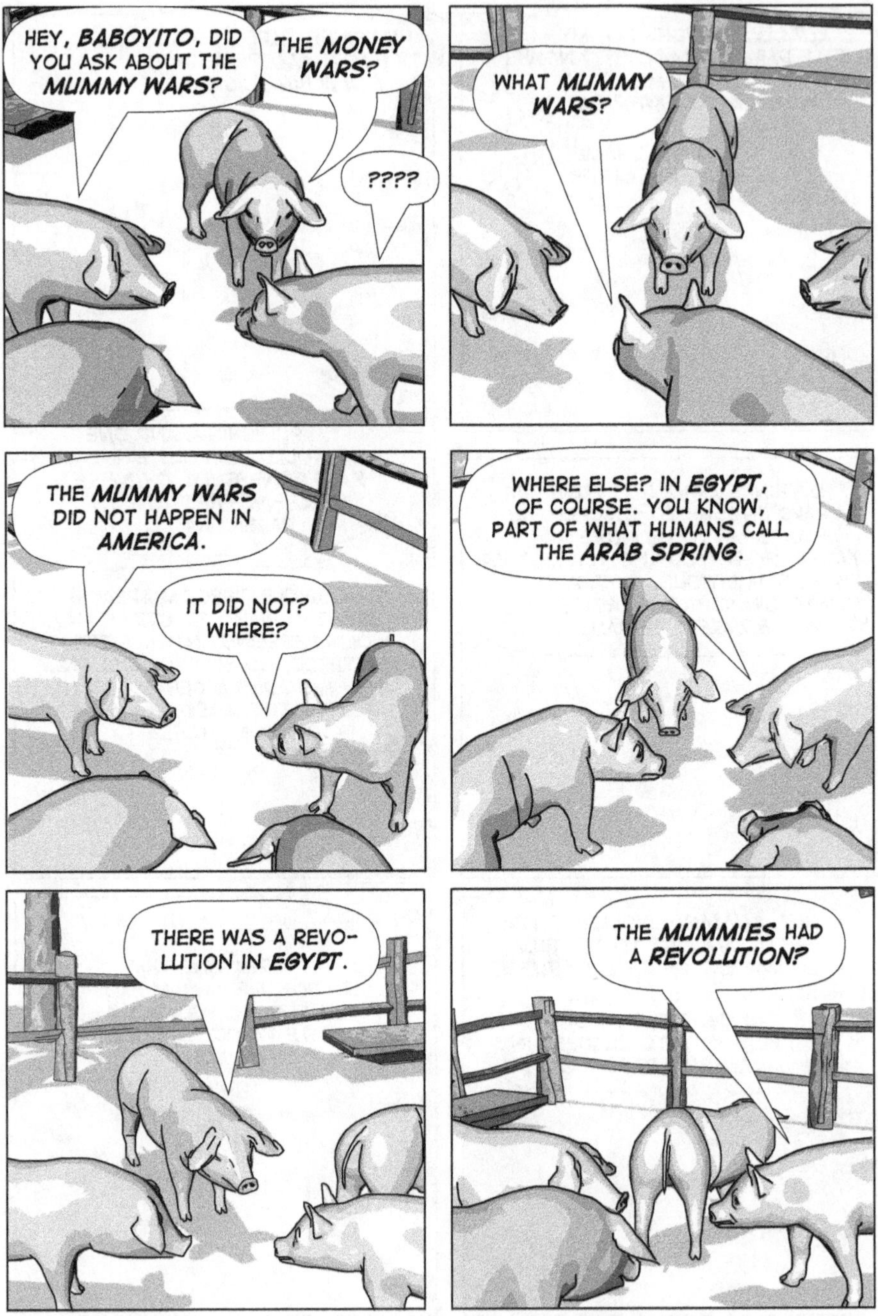
HEY, BABOYITO, DID YOU ASK ABOUT THE MUMMY WARS?
THE MONEY WARS?
????
WHAT MUMMY WARS?
THE MUMMY WARS DID NOT HAPPEN IN AMERICA.
IT DID NOT? WHERE?
WHERE ELSE? IN EGYPT, OF COURSE. YOU KNOW, PART OF WHAT HUMANS CALL THE ARAB SPRING.
THERE WAS A REVO-LUTION IN EGYPT.
THE MUMMIES HAD A REVOLUTION?

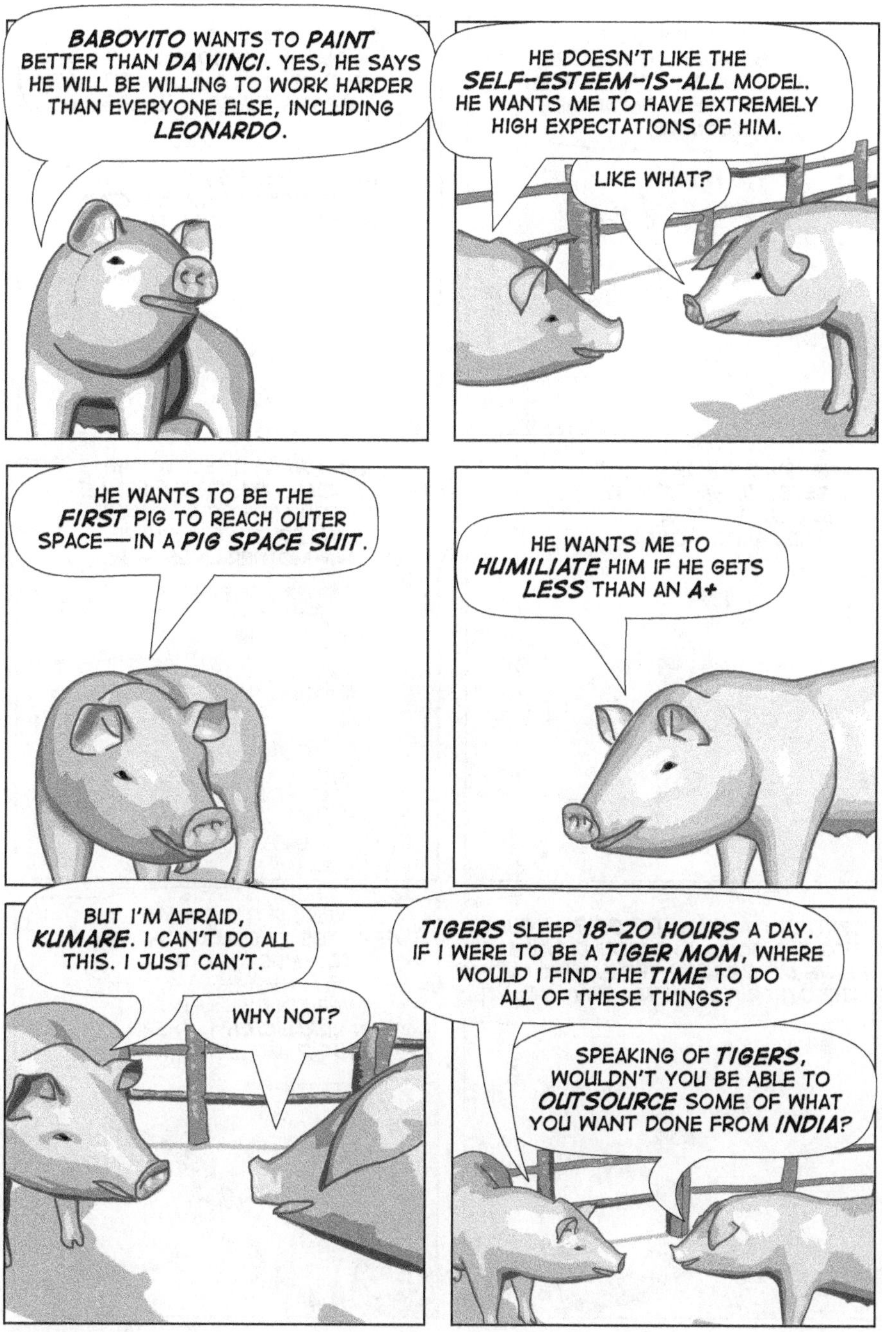
BABOYITO WANTS TO PAINT BETTER THAN DA VINCI. YES, HE SAYS HE WILL BE WILLING TO WORK HARDER THAN EVERYONE ELSE, INCLUDING LEONARDO.
HE DOESN'T LIKE THE SELF-ESTEEM-IS-ALL MODEL. HE WANTS ME TO HAVE EXTREMELY HIGH EXPECTATIONS OF HIM.
LIKE WHAT?
HE WANTS TO BE THE FIRST PIG TO REACH OUTER SPACE—IN A PIG SPACE SUIT.
HE WANTS ME TO HUMILIATE HIM IF HE GETS LESS THAN AN A+
BUT I'M AFRAID, KUMARE. I CAN'T DO ALL THIS. I JUST CAN'T.
WHY NOT?
TIGERS SLEEP 18-20 HOURS A DAY. IF I WERE TO BE A TIGER MOM, WHERE WOULD I FIND THE TIME TO DO ALL OF THESE THINGS?
SPEAKING OF TIGERS, WOULDN'T YOU BE ABLE TO OUTSOURCE SOME OF WHAT YOU WANT DONE FROM INDIA?

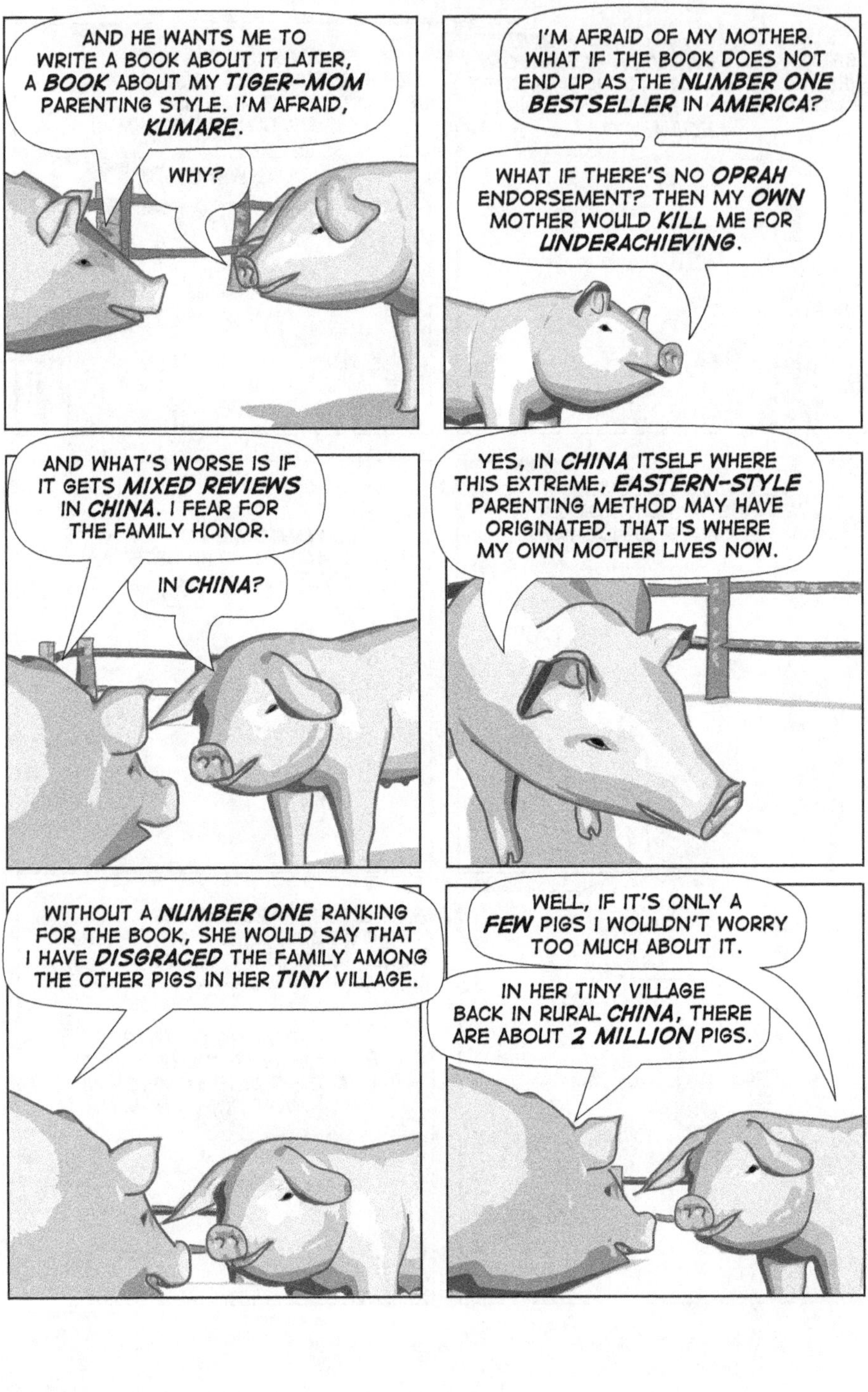
AND HE WANTS ME TO WRITE A BOOK ABOUT IT LATER, A BOOK ABOUT MY TIGER-MOM PARENTING STYLE. I'M AFRAID, KUMARE.
WHY?
I'M AFRAID OF MY MOTHER. WHAT IF THE BOOK DOES NOT END UP AS THE NUMBER ONE BESTSELLER IN AMERICA?
WHAT IF THERE'S NO OPRAH ENDORSEMENT? THEN MY OWN MOTHER WOULD KILL ME FOR UNDERACHIEVING.
AND WHAT'S WORSE IS IF IT GETS MIXED REVIEWS IN CHINA. I FEAR FOR THE FAMILY HONOR.
IN CHINA?
YES, IN CHINA ITSELF WHERE THIS EXTREME, EASTERN-STYLE PARENTING METHOD MAY HAVE ORIGINATED. THAT IS WHERE MY OWN MOTHER LIVES NOW.
WITHOUT A NUMBER ONE RANKING FOR THE BOOK, SHE WOULD SAY THAT I HAVE DISGRACED THE FAMILY AMONG THE OTHER PIGS IN HER TINY VILLAGE.
WELL, IF IT'S ONLY A FEW PIGS I WOULDN'T WORRY TOO MUCH ABOUT IT.
IN HER TINY VILLAGE BACK IN RURAL CHINA, THERE ARE ABOUT 2 MILLION PIGS.

Coming in Volume 3

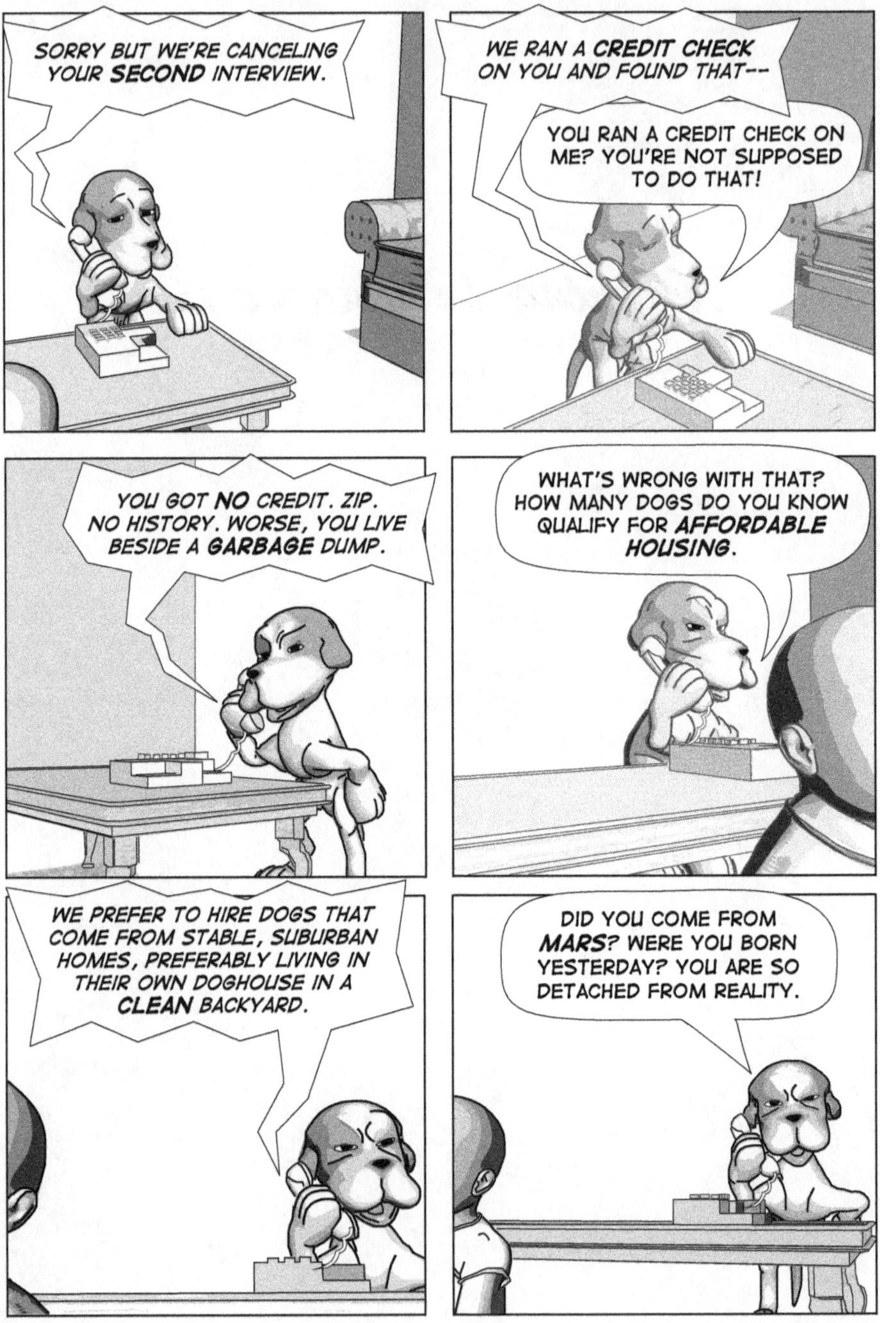
SORRY BUT WE'RE CANCELING YOUR SECOND INTERVIEW.
WE RAN A CREDIT CHECK ON YOU AND FOUND THAT--
YOU RAN A CREDIT CHECK ON ME? YOU'RE NOT SUPPOSED TO DO THAT!
YOU GOT NO CREDIT. ZIP. NO HISTORY. WORSE, YOU LIVE BESIDE A GARBAGE DUMP.
WHAT'S WRONG WITH THAT? HOW MANY DOGS DO YOU KNOW QUALIFY FOR AFFORDABLE HOUSING.
WE PREFER TO HIRE DOGS THAT COME FROM STABLE, SUBURBAN HOMES, PREFERABLY LIVING IN THEIR OWN DOGHOUSE IN A CLEAN BACKYARD.
DID YOU COME FROM MARS? WERE YOU BORN YESTERDAY? YOU ARE SO DETACHED FROM REALITY.

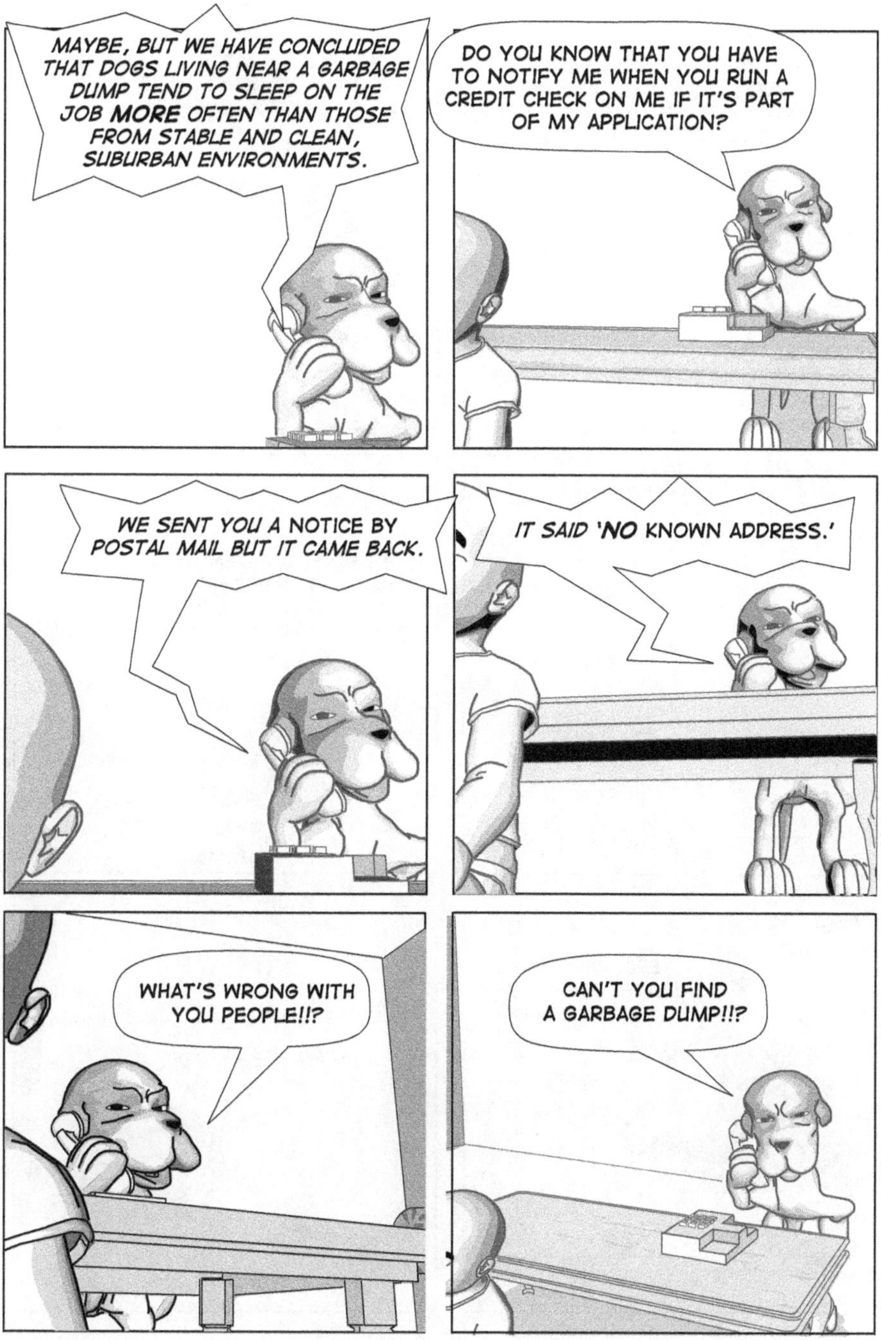
MAYBE, BUT WE HAVE CONCLUDED THAT DOGS LIVING NEAR A GARBAGE DUMP TEND TO SLEEP ON THE JOB MORE OFTEN THAN THOSE FROM STABLE AND CLEAN, SUBURBAN ENVIRONMENTS.
DO YOU KNOW THAT YOU HAVE TO NOTIFY ME WHEN YOU RUN A CREDIT CHECK ON ME IF IT'S PART OF MY APPLICATION?
WE SENT YOU A NOTICE BY POSTAL MAIL BUT IT CAME BACK.
IT SAID 'NO KNOWN ADDRESS.'
WHAT'S WRONG WITH YOU PEOPLE!!?
CAN'T YOU FIND A GARBAGE DUMP!!?

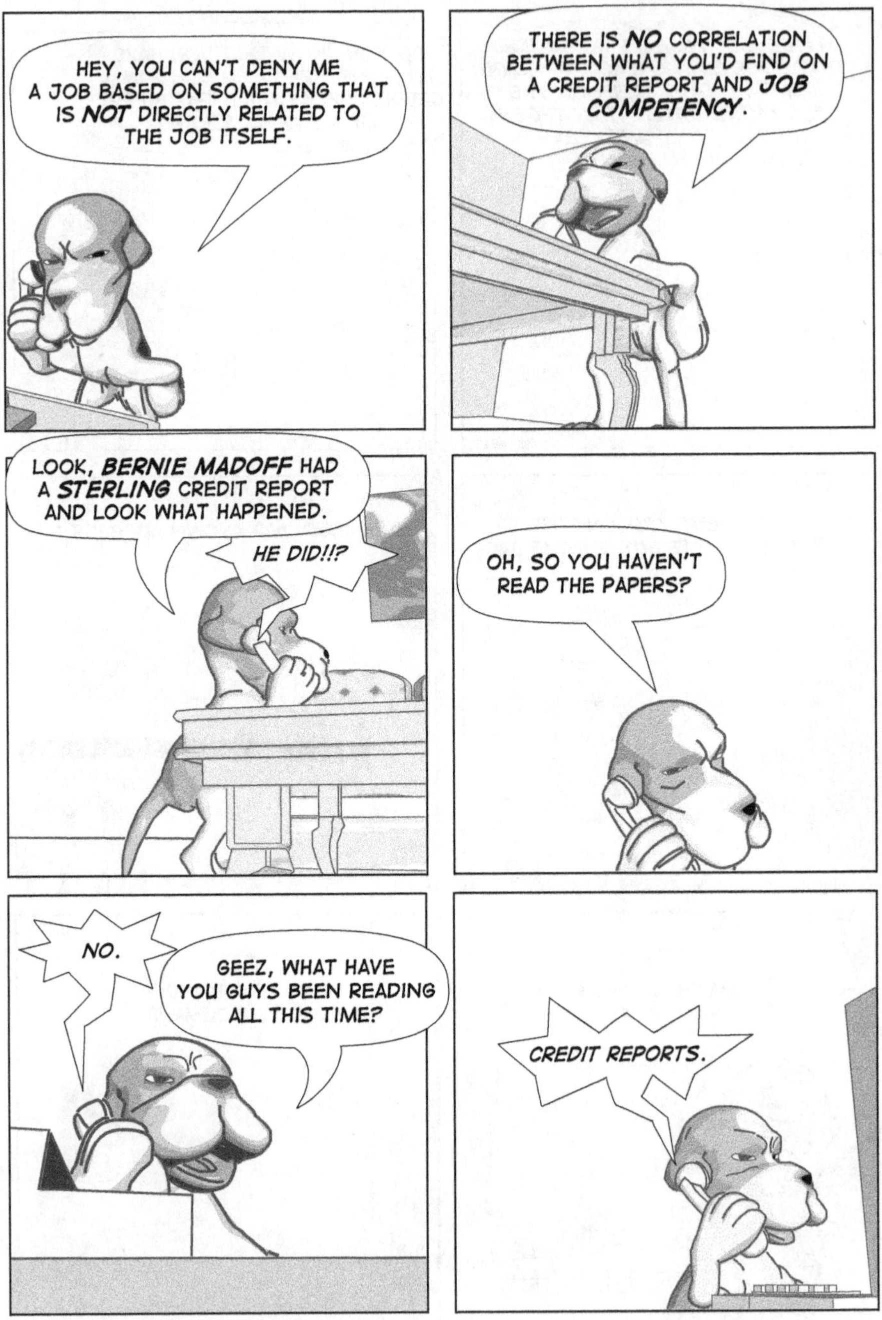
HEY, YOU CAN'T DENY ME A JOB BASED ON SOMETHING THAT IS *NOT* DIRECTLY RELATED TO THE JOB ITSELF.
THERE IS *NO* CORRELATION BETWEEN WHAT YOU'D FIND ON A CREDIT REPORT AND *JOB COMPETENCY*.
LOOK, *BERNIE MADOFF* HAD A *STERLING* CREDIT REPORT AND LOOK WHAT HAPPENED.
HE DID!!?
OH, SO YOU HAVEN'T READ THE PAPERS?
NO.
GEEZ, WHAT HAVE YOU GUYS BEEN READING ALL THIS TIME?
CREDIT REPORTS.

www.ingramcontent.com/pod-product-compliance
Lightning Source LLC
Chambersburg PA
CBHW021156020426
42331CB00003B/82
* 9 7 8 0 9 8 4 8 8 7 4 1 5 *